JOHN IRVING

John Irving. Photograph © Cook Neilson.

JOHN IRVING

A Critical Companion

Josie P. Campbell

CRITICAL COMPANIONS TO POPULAR CONTEMPORARY WRITERS
Kathleen Gregory Klein, Series Editor

Greenwood Press
Westport, Connecticut • London

Library of Congress Cataloging-in-Publication Data

Campbell, Josie P.
    John Irving : a critical companion / Josie P. Campbell.
      p. cm.—(Critical companions to popular contemporary
writers ; ISSN 1082–4979)
    Includes bibliographical references (p.   ) and index.
    ISBN 0–313–30222–7 (alk. paper)
    1. Irving, John, 1942—Criticism and interpretation. I. Title.
II. Series.
    PS3559.R8Z6   1998
    813'.54—DC21   98–9349

British Library Cataloguing in Publication Data is available.

Library of Congress Catalog Card Number: 98–9349
ISBN: 0–313–30222–7
ISSN: 1082–4979

First published in 1998

Greenwood Press, 88 Post Road West, Westport, CT 06881
An imprint of Greenwood Publishing Group, Inc.

Printed in the United States of America

The paper used in this book complies with the
Permanent Paper Standard issued by the National
Information Standards Organization (Z39.48–1984).

10 9 8 7 6 5 4 3 2 1

120-5289

To
Gordon, Isaac, and Samuel

Contents

Series Foreword

The authors who appear in the series Critical Companions to Popular Contemporary Writers are all best-selling writers. They do not simply have one successful novel, but a string of them. Fans, critics, and specialist readers eagerly anticipate their next book. For some, high cash advances and breakthrough sales figures are automatic; movie deals often follow. Some writers become household names, recognized by almost everyone.

But, their novels are read one by one. Each reader chooses to start and, more importantly, to finish a book because of what she or he finds there. The real test of a novel is in the satisfaction its readers experience. This series acknowledges the extraordinary involvement of readers and writers in creating a best-seller.

The authors included in this series were chosen by an Advisory Board composed of high school English teachers and high school and public librarians. They ranked a list of best-selling writers according to their popularity among different groups of readers. For the first series, writers in the top-ranked group who had received no book-length, academic, literary analysis (or none in at least the past ten years) were chosen. Because of this selection method, Critical Companions to Popular Contemporary Writers meets a need that is being addressed nowhere else. The success of these volumes as reported by reviewers, librarians, and teachers led to an expansion of the series mandate to include some writers with wide critical attention—Toni Morrison, John Irving, and Maya Angelou, for example—to extend the usefulness of the series.

The volumes in the series are written by scholars with particular expertise in analyzing popular fiction. These specialists add an academic focus to the popular success that these writers already enjoy.

The series is designed to appeal to a wide range of readers. The general reading public will find explanations for the appeal of these well-known writers. Fans will find biographical and fictional questions answered. Students will find literary analysis, discussions of fictional genres, carefully organized introductions to new ways of reading the novels, and bibliographies for additional research. Whether browsing through the book for pleasure or using it for an assignment, readers will find that the most recent novels of the authors are included.

Each volume begins with a biographical chapter drawing on published information, autobiographies or memoirs, prior interviews, and, in some cases, interviews given especially for this series. A chapter on literary history and genres describes how the author's work fits into a larger literary context. The following chapters analyze the writer's most important, most popular, and most recent novels in detail. Each chapter focuses on one or more novels. This approach, suggested by the Advisory Board as the most useful to student research, allows for an in-depth analysis of the writer's fiction. Close and careful readings with numerous examples show readers exactly how the novels work. These chapters are organized around three central elements: plot development (how the story line moves forward), character development (what the reader knows of the important figures), and theme (the significant ideas of the novel). Chapters may also include sections on generic conventions (how the novel is similar or different from others in its same category of science fiction, fantasy, thriller, etc.), narrative point of view (who tells the story and how), symbols and literary language, and historical or social context. Each chapter ends with an "alternative reading" of the novel. The volume concludes with a primary and secondary bibliography, including reviews.

The alternative readings are a unique feature of this series. By demonstrating a particular way of reading each novel, they provide a clear example of how a specific perspective can reveal important aspects of the book. In the alternative reading sections, one contemporary literary theory—way of reading, such as feminist criticism, Marxism, new historicism, deconstruction, or Jungian psychological critique—is defined in brief, easily comprehensible language. That definition is then applied to the novel to highlight specific features that might go unnoticed or be understood differently in a more general reading. Each volume defines two or three specific theories, making them part of the reader's understanding of how diverse meanings may be constructed from a single novel.

Taken collectively, the volumes in the Critical Companions to Popular Contemporary Writers series provide a wide-ranging investigation of the complexities of current best-selling fiction. By treating these novels seriously as both literary works and publishing successes, the series demonstrates the potential of popular literature in contemporary culture.

Kathleen Gregory Klein
Southern Connecticut State University

Acknowledgments

I have incurred a number of debts in the preparation of this text, and it is both a pleasure and a privilege to acknowledge them here. Professor Kathleen Gregory Klein supervised the edition, and her general editing helped to keep me on track. Dr. Barbara Rader of Greenwood Publishing Group was most supportive of my work and provided encouragement throughout. I also have a debt of gratitude to the University of Rhode Island College of Liberal Arts Faculty Enhancement Fellowship, which allowed a reduced teaching load in the spring of 1997 so that I might finish this book.

I also owe thanks to Barbara A. Murphy, my extraordinary administrative assistant, who helped me through many a computer glitch; to Susan E. Perry, who provided assistance with researching and proofing the manuscript, and whose reading of *The Cider House Rules* lent backbone to my reading; and to Professor Bruce A. Rosenberg, Brown University, who taught me about popular culture.

I wish to thank my husband, Dr. William D. Howden, who read this manuscript in a variety of forms and who thoughtfully offered suggestions, as well as advice on a number of biblical and theological questions. Chapter 9, *A Prayer for Owen Meany*, owes much to his perceptive insights.

Finally, I must claim responsibility for the text on John Irving's novels, although the inspiration is Irving's.

1

The Life of John Irving

Trying to Save Piggy Sneed is the image John Irving uses to describe his novelistic work; it is also the title of Irving's "memoir." The name Piggy Sneed refers to a real-life (possibly) garbage collector whom Irving, when he was growing up in Exeter, New Hampshire, attempted to save from a fire. Piggy died in the fire, only to be rescued and brought to life again by Irving's imagination. This imagination gave life not only to Piggy but also to other unlikely characters such as Garp, Franny Berry, Homer Wells, Owen Meany, and, more recently, Dr. Farrokh Daruwalla. Irving writes: "I realize that a writer's business is setting fire to Piggy Sneed—*and* trying to save him—again and again; forever" (*Piggy Sneed* 21).

John Winslow Irving was born on March 2, 1942, in Exeter, New Hampshire, to Frances Winslow Irving; his biological father was a World War II flyer, shot down over Burma. Until recently, not much has been known about Irving's biological father (Reilly 1), but in conversations at his Vermont home and at Middlebury College, where he read from his novel, *A Widow for One Year* (March 1998), Irving explained that his parents divorced before he was born. Irving's birth name was John Wallace Blunt, Jr., but it was changed when he was six. His mother remarried, and he was adopted by her second husband. Irving claims never to have met his biological father nor to have searched for him. "If I had been unhappy with my mother or my stepfather, I think the quest to find my missing father would have become crucial" (Gussow B1). His biological father, however, was indeed a hero; when he was shot down over Japanese-occupied Burma, he and his flight crew were missing for forty days. They walked to China. Irving used the episode, giving it to the character, Wally Worthington, in *Cider House Rules*. Irving was reared on the campus of Phillips Exeter Academy, where his stepfather, Colin F. N. Irving, taught Russian history. At Exeter, Irving was an indifferent student (he suffered from dyslexia) and a fairly good wrestler—good enough to be awarded a wrestling scholarship to the University of Pittsburgh. He was not good enough, however, to compete with the first-team wrestlers and quit after one year (1961–1962). He never left the sport of wrestling for good; he later became a wrestling coach and a referee, and his two sons became wrestlers who earned the championships Irving could never pin down. Wrestling figures importantly in his writing; it is a central metaphor in *The 158-Pound Marriage* and an important aspect of *The World According to Garp*.

Irving graduated from Exeter in 1961, and in the summer of 1962, he began studying German at Harvard. In 1963 he left for a year of study at the Institute of European Studies and the University of Vienna. Vienna appears in his novels nearly as often as wrestling. The city is the setting for much of Irving's first novel, *Setting Free the Bears*, and is significant in *The Water-Method Man*, *The 158-Pound Marriage*, *Garp*, and *The Hotel New Hampshire*. Vienna, for Irving, frequently represents violence and decadence, the "foreign country" a number of characters come from, grow up in, escape from, and sometimes return to.

In 1964, Irving and Shyla Leary, a Radcliffe student he met while at Harvard, married in Greece. Shortly thereafter they returned to the United States, and Irving completed his undergraduate degree at the University of New Hampshire, graduating cum laude. His first son, Colin, was born in 1965, while Irving was in college and writing under the instruction of John Yount (*Wolf at the Door*) and Thomas Williams (*The Hair of Harold Roux*). During his undergraduate years, Irving wrote two short stories: "A Winter Branch" (*Redbook* 1965) and "Weary Kingdom" (published in 1968 in *The Boston Review*). Both stories are straightforward in development, with none of the comedy and vitality that became Irving's signature.

After graduation, Irving was admitted to the University of Iowa Writers' Workshop, where he worked with Vance Bourjaily and Kurt Vonnegut, whom he says he imitated in *Bears*, which was his master's thesis and which, in 1968, became his first published novel (Random House). The novel received favorable critical reviews and sold slightly under

7,000 copies (Rubin 2). The money earned from this novel allowed him to purchase a house in Putney, Vermont, where he lived while teaching at the now-defunct Windham College. After selling the movie rights to *Bears*, Irving returned to Vienna, where he worked with Irvin Kershner on the novel's movie version. The movie was never made, but the project of filmmaking found its way into his next novel. It was in Austria that Irving's second son, Brendan, was born (1970) and that Irving began work on his second novel, *The Water-Method Man*.

Irving returned to the University of Iowa as writer-in-residence after publication of *The Water-Method Man* in 1972, which was favorably reviewed but by no means a best-seller (6,906 copies). During his three-year residency in Iowa, Irving wrote a number of pieces for popular magazines and published what is arguably his gloomiest novel, *The 158-Pound Marriage* (1973). Although this novel received the best reviews, it was his worst seller—2,560 copies. However gratifying the reviews may have been to Irving, they did not make it possible for him to make a living as a writer, and he took a job as an assistant professor of English at Mount Holyoke College. It was the last academic "day job" of his career.

Irving's fourth and perhaps best-known novel, *The World According to Garp*, was published by E. P. Dutton in 1976. If Irving's critical reputation had been building slowly, *Garp* now ensured financial success. It sold more than 100,000 hardcover copies and more than 3 million paperbacks; it also won the American Book Award for the best paperback novel of 1979. So successful was *Garp*, both critically and popularly, that John Irving became a sort of cultural icon. When *The Hotel New Hampshire* was published by Dutton in 1981, Irving appeared on the cover of *Time* magazine as his novel became the number-one fiction best-seller; "Garpomania," as *Time*'s R. Z. Sheppard called it, hit the country (Harter and Thompson 1).

Time magazine, not only a news magazine but also a production of and about popular culture, helped to promote the Irving personality cult that he himself developed in part. As recently as 1997, Irving appeared on a popular television talk show, where it was clear that none of the other guests—perhaps not even the host—had read any of his books (although they claimed to have seen the movies!). Moreover, the talk-show topics were of little consequence except possibly for "entertainment" value. One might well ask what Irving was doing on such a show—he seemed uncomfortably out of his element, coming across as stiff, awkward, and slightly acid in his comments. Irving's presence on the show suggests his determination to mediate between his art and popular consumption at all costs.

Like Hemingway before him, Irving has always demonstrated the tension between fame and its concomitant financial success, on the one hand, and critical favor, on the other. (Ironically, Irving claims "I was never a Hemingway . . . fan" [*Piggy Sneed* 45]; at one time, he even had vanity plates hyping two of his early novels [Harter and Thompson 1].) For someone who stakes out aloofness, refusing to talk about his private life, Irving has at times seemed to cooperate remarkably well with the image makers. Simultaneously, however, there has always been an edge to his cooperation, a barely veiled hostility, with the mass media.

The commercial success of *The World According to Garp* and *The Hotel New Hampshire* brought Irving to the attention of the media, and the novels' translation into reasonably successful movies ensured the media's continued interest in him. The movie *The World According to Garp* (1982), although given a scathing review by movie critic Pauline Kael (she savaged both the novel and the movie) and a lukewarm review by Roger Ebert, did fairly well at the box office. Directed by George Roy Hill, the movie was more a series of vignettes than a coherently developed whole; Robin Williams played Garp, but John Lithgow, as the transsexual Roberta Muldoon, stole the movie. *The Hotel New Hampshire* (1984), directed by Tony Richardson, is interesting cinematically but loses the magic of the novel.

In 1982, following his divorce from Shyla Leary, Irving moved to New York City, where he wrote *The Cider House Rules*, published in 1985 by William Morrow; it is his, as he called it, most polemic novel. *Cider House* not only sold well (it, too, was a best-seller and was a Book-of-the-Month Club 1985 selection) but was generally praised by reviewers and critics for its "straightforward storytelling" and its "firm focus" (Reilly, *Understanding John Irving* 118). The novel, which has at its center the theme of "rules," personal and societal, is perhaps Irving's most controversial because it takes on the issue of abortion. In 1987, Irving married Janet Turnbull, a Toronto literary agent; they have one son, Everett, born in 1991. They live in Putney, Vermont, and Toronto.

Cider House was followed in 1989 by *A Prayer for Owen Meany*, which was as popular as *Cider House*. In 1998, the movie *Simon Birch*, very loosely based on *Owen Meany* and written and directed by Mark Steven Johnson, was released. Irving by and large dissociated himself from the movie, allowing the credits to read only that the film was "suggested by" *A Prayer for Owen Meany*. Johnson's movie does not include the novel's twin themes of politics and religion; indeed, the movie omits the Vietnam War (one of the main reasons Irving wrote the novel, he has claimed) and presents Simon Birch (the Owen Meany chracter) as heroic, possibly, but in no way miraculous. The novel's complexities are thus reduced to a young boy's (Simon's best friend) search for his father. R. Z. Sheppard, writing for *Time*, noted that Johnny Wheelwright's "challenge to faith" was "vintage Irving"—"simultaneously horrifying and absurdly funny" (qtd. in Reilly, *Understanding John Irving* 141). Maybe so. But *Owen Meany* also presents a challenge to our faith, and the novel remains Irving's most profound to date, followed closely by *A Son of the Circus*.

Circus (1994), like most of Irving's novels, is a sprawling affair. It is his longest book thus far, with numerous intersecting plots (one loses count of them) and innumerable characters. It is one of the few Irving novels to be set outside the United States, though several of its characters are in America. *Circus* is about the despair at the center of modern life, about our loss of innocence, but like *Owen Meany*, it is also about hope.

Irving's most recent novel is *A Widow for One Year* (1998). *A Widow* is the first of Irving's novels to have a female protagonist. Although Irving has shown great sympathy for women—in *Garp*, *The Hotel New Hampshire*, and *Cider House Rules*, for example—*A Widow* is arguably his most feminist novel. His memoir, *Trying to Save Piggy Sneed*, appeared in 1993.

Throughout his career, Irving has been remarkably consistent in his views on the way he writes: like wrestling, writing requires control, discipline, and balance (*Piggy Sneed* 53). Those qualities, in turn, allow Irving to improvise and manipulate his enormously flexible and graceful prose. Regarding his approach to writing, he claims not to be an intellectual (though one should not be misled here; Irving is remarkably well read, well educated, and literate). In a 1996 talk at Boston's Arlington Street Church, he explained his perception of himself as a writer: "I'm a vehicle, not a thinker. I have no intellectual credentials. I attend to storytelling as a carpenter attends to making a good table." Irving attends to both the details of storytelling and the craft of putting them together. The intricacies of plot and the development of character are of extreme importance to him.

The writers he most admires are, primarily, of the nineteenth century. Dickens heads the list. Like many of us, Irving read *Great Expectations* sometime during his teens, but unlike most of us, he was impelled to become a writer by it. "*Great Expectations* is the first novel I read that made me wish I had written it; it is the novel that made me want to be a novelist—specifically, to move a reader as I was moved then" (*Piggy Sneed* 349). Even more unusual for a young man in the 1950s, Irving wished to become a writer of long, intricate, sad/funny novels in the nineteenth-century tradition not only of Dickens but also of Hardy, Melville, and Hawthorne. Influenced by his father, a Russian scholar, he also read Dostoyevsky, Turgenev, and Tolstoy. Many of the contemporary writers Irving admires write novels in, more or less, the nineteenth-century tradition: Gabriel García-Márquez, Salman Rushdie, Robertson Davies, and Günter Grass. Their novels are generally fast-moving, are driven by plot and character, have comedic elements, and follow a character (or characters) through his or her life.

Although not necessarily an admirer of William Faulkner's writing, Irving reveals in his own writing similar characteristics, not in prose style but in the use of certain devices and techniques, as well as in purpose. He has noted that his initial experience with Faulkner was not especially positive: "I struggled with [an unnamed Faulkner novel]; I was either too young or my dyslexia rebelled at the length of those sentences, or both" (*Piggy Sneed* 44–45).

Yet Irving grew to like Faulkner, and in fact they share a number of traits as writers. Both use irony, especially in regard to America and its drive toward acquisition and power, and in its disregard for individuals. Both engage in the tradition of broad American humor: jokes, farce, and the absurd (for example, Faulkner's description of the gangster's funeral in *Sanctuary* and Irving's Homer Wells in *Cider House* mistaking a corpse for Dr. Larch as he confesses his love for the doctor). Both writers view sexual relations as significant, frequently comic, and sometimes frightening. Both see comedy and tragedy as intermixed. Both interlace plots and juxtapose time frames. And both are profoundly moral writers in a modern world given over to violence, fragmentation, and hopelessness. At the same time, both writers are life-affirming; at the end of Faulkner's *The Sound and the Fury*, he writes of Dilsey and her family, "They endured." At the end of *Garp*, the protagonist's "energy" has quickened the lives of those he loved and touched.

John Irving is one of America's most productive and popular writers; like Dickens—and Faulkner—he is also one of the most serious of purpose and sure of artistry. With the body of work he has given us—and, thankfully, he shows no sign of stopping—we can only be grateful that he continues, like a good "carpenter," to attend to his craft, to the making of a "good table."

2

John Irving's Novels:
An Overview

John Irving's novels are all, with the possible exception of two, grand comedies. The term "comedy" here includes the furthest extremes of human experiences: hatred/love; rebellion/defense; attack/escape; sympathy/persecution. Irving's comedy skates precariously on the surface but is not superficial. It is serious business.

When Irving writes in his memoirs that the task of the writer is both to destroy and to save Piggy Sneed—forever and ever—he reflects on a rich comic scene of disaster and triumph: a "sacrifice and a feast," as Francis M. Cornford put it about comedy a great many years ago. Piggy Sneed, the retarded, grotesque garbage collector of Irving's youth, dies with all of his pigs in a ghastly fire. But Irving resurrects him, imagining Piggy is still alive, transforming the grotesque figure into an altogether different man beyond the grave. Indeed, Piggy's imagined afterlife is far superior to his real life in Exeter, New Hampshire.

In *The World According to Garp*, Garp, the writer, also wants to rescue or save the dead. As Garp says, beginning a novel is "like trying to make the dead come alive. . . . No, no, that's not right—it's more like trying to keep everyone alive, forever" (409). To Irving, comedy can be transformative; it is also about loss and restoration. One might go so far as to say that for Irving, comedy is redemptive.

For example, no one thought much of Piggy Sneed when he was alive. He blundered laughably, inarticulately, and even stinkingly through life.

Only Irving's grandmother treats him with any sort of dignity and kindness, never failing to speak to him, calling him always *Mr.* Sneed. When Irving tries to impress her with his imagined—and "better"—story of Piggy's life, she admonishes him by saying it would have been "better" to treat Piggy with greater decency during his lifetime.

As Irving's grandmother attempts to teach him about the potential grace of human relations, so Irving includes the anecdote in his Piggy Sneed story, if not to teach us, at least to suggest that comedy has potentially "corrective" powers. The comic contradictions that permeate this tale are profoundly social, another way of saying they are profoundly human.

Irving is one of America's great writers of comedy. He writes comedy that is both social and life-affirming; thus he is part of a long literary tradition going back at least as far as Dante's *Divine Comedy* and Chaucer's *Canterbury Tales*. If we understand comedy as the "Carrying Away of Death"—not the *doing away* with death but the triumph over it—then we begin to understand the larger than life/death character of Shakespeare's Sir John Falstaff, the hairbreadth escape of Dickens's Pip, the triumph of Austen's women protagonists who win out—or win over—the crushing death of male malevolence, and the bizarre salvation of Melville's Ishmael atop Queequeg's coffin in *Moby Dick*. We may even begin to understand the endurance of Dilsey in Faulkner's *The Sound and the Fury* and the transcendent victory of Irving's Garp. Comedies are not always "happy."

PLOT

Irving's plots are for the most part straightforward. Nearly always they deal with the journey of a young man from innocence to awareness of himself and his world. As others (Harter and Thompson) have pointed out, Irving uses the form of the Bildungsroman, a coming-of-age novel that deals with the growth of the major—and sometimes secondary—characters. Often these characters are young and innocent, for example, T. S. Garp (*The World According to Garp*) and the Berry children (*The Hotel New Hampshire*). At times the characters, though chronologically beyond youth, are emotionally immature (e.g., Fred "Bogus" Trumper in *The Water-Method Man*).

The plot is driven by these characters' fall from innocence into experiences that push them into knowledge of themselves in relation to others. Indeed, for Irving, plot arises out of character and situation. Most of his major characters are first of all concerned with the discovery of their origins; making sense of those origins and perceiving the intelligibility of actions in relation to origins provide the energy of Irving's plots. If this seems perilously close to Freud's "plot" or narrative of human development, it is. Freud's plot begins with the infant, untamed, who ends up tamed—at least in large part—by frustration in the course of "growing up" in a world seemingly hostile to its central being. Irving uses a similar plot over and over, infusing it with suffering, defeat, and sometimes triumph.

Irving's concern with origins (and thus with beginnings and endings) has been noted by himself and others (Harter and Thompson; Miller; see also Irving's "The Narrative Voice"). Many of Irving's critics have seen the search for origins in his novels as a search for the lost father; in his most recent novel, *A Widow for One Year*, the protagonist, Ruth Cole, seeks the return of her lost mother. Critics have also pointed to the predominance of orphans (literal and metaphoric) who seek knowledge of their missing fathers, linking evidence in the novels to the loss of Irving's biological father. Irving's response has been to say that he has always had a (step)father, and he points out that having orphans for characters allows him great freedom in imagining plot possibilities. One does not have to read very far in Irving's body of work to discover that plot possibilities, and probabilities, provide the enormous energy and life of his novels.

In discussing his work, Irving has written that what move a story forward are situations "in which the possibilities for good stories are rich" and characters "to whom good stories can happen." Such characters, he adds, are people "who seem vulnerable enough to have big things happen to them, yet sturdy enough to withstand the bad news ahead" ("The Narrative Voice" 89). What Irving listens for in these stories is the "sound of a potential myth, a possible legend." The great mythic story of our lives is, of course, our own search for origins, our discovery of the individual self. It is an old story, forever new.

Put simply, then, the paradigmatic plot in an Irving novel revolves around the major character's quest to discover the self; there is an account not only of origins but also of the totality of the character's life and its interrelation with those around him. Such a plot is grounded in the here and now even as it looks backward to the past and forward to the future. It is a plot of *becoming*.

Although in one sense Irving's plots are simple, at the same time they are filled with complications, often bizarre complications. In addition, Irving saturates his novels with repetitions that may seem unrelated: Garp's lack of a father; Helen Holm's lack of a mother. Garp's run-in with Mrs. Ralph; his run-in with O. Fecteau, both of which prove dangerous. Garp's fake drowning in his bathtub; Walt's death and Duncan's loss of sight "underwater." The fictions within fictions that Irving is so fond of are also saturated with repetitions of plot and themes. Irving's use of repetitions, seeming digressions or unrelated threads of the story, is similar to that found in the nineteenth-century novels for which he has such respect. Closer to Irving's own time, such use of repetitions can be seen in Faulkner's work. What may seem to be disorderly, even disruptive, in Irving's novels are really loops in the narrative that wind back on themselves, lending a (complex, at times) circularity to the plot. Irving is like a jazz pianist: he plays a relatively simple melodic line with extraordinarily extended riffs. He is the grand master of improvisation.

CHARACTERS

Characters in a John Irving novel generally fall into three categories. The simplest, perhaps, is the grotesque, the kind of character well known in medieval drama's Herod, with his self-absorption; in Shakespeare's Malvolio in *Twelfth Night*; in Dickens's Uriah Heep in *David Copperfield*; in Sherwood Anderson's Wing Biddlebaum in *Winesburg, Ohio*. Such characters, as Anderson tells us, are automatons; they hold fast to one idea. They are often characterized by physical gestures, as Wing is, or by impulses with psychological gestures. Some characters have both physical and psychological "tics." Iowa Bob in *The Hotel New Hampshire*, for example, is obsessed with building up his body—he spends a lot of time lifting weights—and his ruling passion is that no matter how hard the wind blows, in life we are all nailed fast, just like the furniture in the hotel.

The second type of character is intelligent, perceptive, more flexible than Iowa Bob, but still limited in his or her capacity for growth. At times these characters see more than the protagonists of the novel, and often they seem to have more than a goodly share of compassion. Helen Holm in *Garp* belongs to this category, and so does John Berry in *Hotel*. However, John's father, Win Berry, belongs to the same category as his father, Iowa Bob, although Win repeats the "tics" of his surrogate father, Freud (known as "our" Freud). Freud and Win are both blind, physically and psychologically; both have a fixation with bears—and hotels. John Berry, though not blind, has the same fixation. To some extent, then, like father, like son.

Irving's major characters fall into the third category: the comic hero. With the possible exceptions of *Setting Free the Bears* and *The 158-Pound Marriage*, the protagonists of Irving's novels demonstrate growth. They are, to be sure, characters who bumble and fumble their way through life, but they are much more than a bundle of mechanical gestures. They are always in a state of "becoming" even when they find themselves in the most absurd and bizarre situations. In this regard, Shakespeare's Hamlet suggests that he *could* be a comic hero; he is closest to profound meaning when he acts the fool. His counterpart is Falstaff; who cheats death and wears motley; but his poignant line to Master Shallow when he loses his prince, his boy, his Hal, suggests Falstaff *could* be a tragic hero. Garp moves between these two poles; out of his wildest, often most comical, situations come his unsettling questions, his disturbing lusts, his unintentional and most important discoveries about the relations of human beings (on comic character, see Sypher 193–258).

SETTING

John Irving's world is, for the most part, made up of places he is familiar with: the New England landscape, New Hampshire and Maine, and particularly the Steering School (*Garp*) and Gravesend Academy (*Owen Meany*), both of which refer to Exeter Academy, Irving's prep school. In *Owen Meany*, Irving provides a history of Gravesend that comes directly from the history of Exeter Academy. In *The Water-Method Man*, Irving writes of the flat land of Iowa and the University of Iowa, where he earned his MFA and later taught; he also writes of New York City, where he lived for a while. In *A Son of the Circus*, he uses India, where he visited briefly, and Toronto, where he lives part of each year. *A Widow for One Year* is set primarily in the Hamptons, Long Island, and in Amsterdam, especially in de Wallen, the city's center of prostitution.

Vienna is a recurring geographic location in a number of novels, from *Setting Free the Bears* to *The Hotel New Hampshire*. The significance of Vienna, its history, decadence, and corruption—even its beauty—has not been overlooked by critics. Irving himself has responded to the question "Why Vienna?" with "being in a foreign country with another language forced you to notice all commonplace things . . . it made me remember what butter was like when I was fifteen on the coast of Maine" (Miller 179). More recently he has stated that Vienna is not as important to him as to the critics (Boston Center 1996). But Irving also acknowledges that Vienna is used metaphorically; for example, in *Hotel*, it stands for the foreign country, the psychic space "those children *really* go to . . . the place we all go when we're forced to grow up too soon" (Miller 180). Moreover, Vienna provides Irving with an objective correlative for the historical upheavals in the world, those of the past as well as those in the present and future.

For Irving, setting is frequently related to the issues of our time. For example, Vienna, in *Setting Free the Bears*, is directly linked to the *Anschluss*, that period of time when Austria acquiesced to an alliance with Nazi Germany—and to the implementation of the "final solution" that led to the Holocaust. Nor is it coincidental that Gravesend, in *Owen Meany*, is literally the end for so many of the town's young men—boys, really—who go to Vietnam and return in body bags. The major issues of our time, from abortion (*The Cider House Rules*) to feminism (*The World According to Garp*) to racism and AIDS (*A Son of the Circus*), are embedded in the settings of Irving's novels.

In addition to specific geographic locations, buildings and architectural space are important as setting in an Irving novel. There is the Steering School with its infirmary and gymnasium. The young Garp attempts to fly from the school's ledges. In the various houses where Irving's characters live, basements, kitchens, bathrooms, bedrooms are described in detail that both materializes and grounds the fiction. Hotels figure prominently in several of the novels and are crucial, of course, in *The Hotel New Hampshire*, which has five of them. In *The Cider House Rules*, the orphanage is a gray, depressing building, though not frightening. Its gray stones match the oppressively gray climate and landscape of St. Cloud's, which in turn underscore the weary, depressed women who go to the orphanage/abortion clinic to be "delivered" in one way or another. Irving's buildings are not merely physical structures but structures of varying consciousness. The family refrain in *Hotel*, "Keep passing the open windows," takes on psychological resonance as the novel progresses.

Like Dickens and Brontë, Irving uses houses, buildings—and nature— as loose equivalents to politics, to historic events, to character, family, and human relations. Only one other American writer I know of, Sherwood Anderson, uses the architectural space of rooms and buildings (hotels, especially) in the same way.

Space, of course, is where time is. Dwellings are temporary; windows, doors, and certainly ledges all suggest, among other things, the contingencies of the world. One is not protected in the home—or even in the womblike wrestling room of the Steering School gym.

Nature also is an important aspect of Irving's novels. It is usually neither benign nor malevolent but simply "there." Most often it is used metaphorically, linked to historic and human forces. Nature enlarges our (house of) consciousness. In an Irving novel, we often find it linked with the "gale of the world," powers outside of the characters that threaten to, and sometimes do, overwhelm them. In *Bears*, bees are let loose in the wind and kill Siggy. In *The Water-Method Man*, water reclaims Merrill Overturf as he attempts to open a German tank sunk in the Danube during World War II; the waters of the Atlantic swallow Mother and Egg in *Hotel*. In that same novel, out of the mist, a white boat appears, carrying an unknown man in a white dinner jacket to the Hotel Arbuthnot. Perhaps he represents the mystery of death—and life. The Berry children go into the dark woods at the Dairy School and are forever changed. In *A Son of the Circus*, nature has supposedly been "civilized." The lawns of the Duckworth Club spread before us, neatly manicured, but something is killing the bougainvillea. In the midst of the dying flowers lies a man's corpse, the result of murder.

Landscape for Irving represents both the "inscape" of the self and its escape. Irving would probably agree with Gerard Manley Hopkins's view of nature as the "womb-of-all, home-of-all, hearse-of-all night." Irving seems to agree with Proust that setting helps us to understand characters and their situations spatially, as moments in time, yet interrelated. We can read them forward and backward. Finally, Irving's novels are not *about* geographic or architectural locations at all; they are about life and the experience of being alive.

IRVING'S BODY OF WORK

John Irving's early novels—*Setting Free the Bears, The Water-Method Man,* and *The 158-Pound Marriage*—all demonstrate his ability with narrative and his willingness to tackle important issues. In all of these novels, as well as subsequent ones, writing about fiction, as opposed to writing about writing, is an important element. In all of his works, settings are generally familiar ones, to Irving as well as to us; only in *Bears* and *Circus* do we have a setting in a country other than the United States.

The plot of *Bears* is one Irving uses again and again; it recounts the journey of one or more characters seeking to discover the world and his or her place in it. In *Bears*, the journey fails. *Bears* is also a novel in which Irving raises significant questions about history, about the violence of war and its aftermath, and about what constitutes origins and family.

The Water-Method Man, which Irving calls his only novel with a "happy ending," makes use of similar issues, though the protagonist is older than the relatively young men in *Bears*. In terms of narrative, *The 158-Pound Marriage* is arguably Irving's most experimental novel, especially in terms of point of view. In it, issues of family deterioration, of wife-swapping, of betrayal are crucial, but so are issues about various forms of fiction and art.

The World According to Garp, Irving's blockbuster novel, made him a household name. In this novel, Irving demonstrates his ability to juggle a number of issues simultaneously in a plot both simple and complex at the same time. The plot echoes the journey of growing up that had appeared in *Bears*, but this time the journey is more successful. Along the way, Irving tackles fictional forms, audience response, and publishing practices. In addition, he explores issues of rape, feminism, transsexualism, random violence, and, of course, family. In this novel, we recognize the tremendous narrative skills of Irving: his ability to cast wide narrative loops, to play extended riffs, to use improvisation. His use of language makes vivid not only comic situations but poignant ones as well, and creates memorable characters.

The skills demonstrated in *Garp* are repeated in the fairy-tale romance of *The Hotel New Hampshire*, in which Irving makes even the bears talk. In this novel, Irving reveals his talents as a mythmaker, a fabulist. At the same time, he weaves into the fabulous world the crassness of the American Dream and the ugliness of anti-Semitism, racism, and terrorism. In this interweaving, Irving is akin to Shakespeare, who did not leave ugliness out of the forest of Arden or Illyria.

Irving's sixth novel, *The Cider House Rules*, is his most polemic. It contains two intertwined narratives of Dr. Wilbur Larch and the orphan Homer Wells. Larch runs the orphanage at St. Cloud's, Maine: as an obstetrician, he delivers babies; as an abortionist, he delivers mothers. Homer Wells, who is one of Larch's orphans, in a number of ways repeats Larch's own narrative. This novel, which faces the controversial issue of abortion, is also about stories and their power, especially stories of Dickens and Brontë.

Following *Cider House* was *A Prayer for Owen Meany*, a novel that looks at origins, Vietnam, and the Iran-contra affair. In this novel about an amazing individual, the tiny Owen with his huge VOICE, Irving again displays how adept he is with the intricacies of plot, as well as with comedy and irony. *Owen Meany* is also Irving's exploration of faith, as well as its loss. It remains one of his most powerful novels.

A Son of the Circus (1994) pays homage to Graham Greene, especially to his novels *The Heart of the Matter* and *The Power and the Glory*. In *Circus*, Irving adapts the conventions of the crime detection novel and the thriller, Greene's "entertainments," to suit his own ends. With *Circus*, he uses landscape itself as a character in much the way Greene used it in *This Gun for Hire*, for example. *Circus* looks at motiveless killing, poverty, disease, racism, and sexism.

Irving's ninth novel, *A Widow for One Year*, is one of his most experimental works. It has a female protagonist and makes use of two significant women's stories: the Biblical *Book of Ruth* and the Homeric Demeter and Persephone myth. Both of these stories deal with the intense bond between mother and daughter. Although *A Widow* is a coming-of-age narrative, it is also a narrative about love over the passage of more than three decades and even beyond death.

MAJOR THEMES

As readers of John Irving's work, we need to be careful to distinguish themes from social issues. The social issues, which I perhaps overemphasize above, often change from novel to novel. Themes recur from novel to novel.

The range of social issues in Irving's work is large; it includes, but is not limited to, war, rape, incest, abortion, adoption, religion, racism, gender, feminism. In his attention to societal issues, Irving follows his mentor, Dickens, who wrote about materialism, the poor laws, workhouses, and orphanages. Irving is also similar in social consciousness to such contemporary writers as Joseph Heller, Kurt Vonnegut, Joyce Carol Oates, and, outside of America, Margaret Atwood and Günter Grass.

Despite Irving's interest in sexuality, scatology, body parts, and bawdy jokes, he is not only one of our most serious writers but also one of our most moral. His themes generally are associated with shared human experiences. They frequently have to do with growing up, maturity, romance, and initiation. For example, in *The Hotel New Hampshire*, Fraulein Fehlgeburt reads Fitzgerald's *The Great Gatsby* to the children; Lilly catches on immediately that Gatsby is hooked on one version of the American Dream, its romance of material success, its seduction of wealth. Lilly cries out that "our Father" *is* the Great Gatsby; "our Father" will go on looking for the dream forever. *The Hotel New Hampshire* is not *The Great Gatsby*, but it is another version of that romance; one of its themes is the dream of success, of acquisition, of power. There are, however, other themes in this novel: the initiation into adulthood, the contingency that is the world, the blindness of human beings, and the triumph of the human spirit. Most important is the theme of love.

Irving has written that "Graham Greene showed me that exquisitely developed characters and heartbreaking stories were the obligations of any novel worth remembering" (*Piggy Sneed* 48–49). From *Setting Free the Bears* to *A Widow for One Year*, the central theme is initiation. Irving is interested in the journey one is required to make from innocence to awareness, and the search for one's origins is a crucial part of that journey. With the possible exceptions of *Setting Free the Bears* and *The 158-Pound Marriage*, all of Irving's major characters succeed in arriving at a sense of the self, for better or for worse, by the end of the novel. In short, they achieve growth. The sheer energy of John Irving's novels delights us, but it is finally the journey we share with his characters that touches and enriches us.

3

Setting Free the Bears
(1968)

John Irving's first novel, *Setting Free the Bears*, was written as a thesis for his MFA at the University of Iowa's Writers' Workshop; his professor was Kurt Vonnegut. One can readily see Irving's homage to Vonnegut, especially to his novel *Slaughterhouse Five*, published in 1969 but likely known to Irving before its publication date. Irving's novel, set in Austria and with no American characters, was published in 1968, the year of massive demonstrations in this country against the Vietnam War. It was the year Martin Luther King, Jr., who had argued for civil rights and fought against poverty in the United States, condemned the Vietnam War. It was five years after King's "I Have a Dream" speech at the Lincoln Memorial in Washington, D.C., and the year of his assassination. In 1968 would come the Tet offensive, which would undermine even further any support for the war in the United States. Although Irving does not mention Vietnam and makes only a passing reference to the Civil Rights movement, he does emphasize war, ethnic hatreds, sexism, and violence.

Critics generally agree that *Bears*, written by a college-age author, is not a "bad" first novel, a backhanded way of saying it is also not very good. Although the novel has certain weaknesses, it is much better than many critics allow. A number of themes and symbols that recur in Irving's later novels first appear in *Bears*: a concern with origins, Vienna, bears, journeys, violence, war, and death.

PLOT DEVELOPMENT

The plot in *Bears* is structurally simple: the novel is divided into three parts. Parts One and Three provide the "frame" of the novel and occur in present time. Part Two, the center of the novel, contains both present and past time.

Part One introduces Hannes Graff, a student in Vienna, who has just failed his history exam; each day in the park at noon, he sees Siegfried (Siggy) Javotnik, a young man he assumes is also a student, eating radishes with salt. Javotnik convinces Graff to go in with him to buy a British Royal Enfield motorcycle so that they can take a trip to the Riviera, living off the land as they go. In essence, this is a "buddy" or "on the road" novel. Even though the novel is not set in the United States and has no American characters, it is a very American story: two young men who are twenty-one, though adolescent in behavior, seek freedom, take to the open road, and have a series of adventures. A young girl, Gallen, soon enters the picture and threatens to break up the male friendship. The plot of Part One sets up what is to come and is straightforwardly linear.

Before leaving Vienna, Graff and Siggy stop at the Heitzinger Zoo. Here they meet two young girls and with them visit the various animals: the great Asiatic bear, famous for his ferocity; the spectacled bears, loving and gentle; and the mythic oryx, with his enormous testicles. This visit prepares us for Siggy's obsession to free the zoo animals, which is to be "the rarest of fun" (32), and for the culmination of the obsession in Part Three of the novel. At the zoo, the boys also have a brief and somewhat confusing dalliance with the two girls, who prepare us in some ways for the entrance of Gallen, the innocent and very young girl to whom Graff is attracted.

Once Graff and Siggy visit the zoo, it seems a matter of moments before they are off on the motorcycle, away from the city and into the countryside. Time is compressed so that their journey moves at a lightning-like pace. Interruptions occur when the motorcycle comes to an abrupt stop: for picking up Gallen, for fishing, sleeping, eating. These stops, arrests of movement, allow Irving to construct sometimes farcical or bizarre scenes; the stops paradoxically provide short bursts of intensified energy and are usually filled with a great deal of action. In one of these scenes, Siggy must run for his life, and goes back to Vienna to plan the zoo break. When he returns to the country to get Graff, Siggy and his motorcycle collide with a truck filled with beehives, and Siggy is killed. Graff feels responsible for his friend's death because he had loaded the truck, and the hives are not "balanced." Graff himself is stung and must make a rather long recovery from the toxin in his body.

Part Two of the novel, "The Notebook," Siggy's autobiography or history, contains what he calls his "pre-history" in three parts, leading up to and including his conception, and his "real history"—his birth and life. As Graff recovers from his beestings, he reads not only the Notebook but also Siggy's daily journal, kept while he spied on the zoo, laying plans for the breakout. Graff also takes it upon himself to bring some order to Siggy's writing and interleaves the Notebook with the journal entries. As Siggy says, "it's the pre-history that made us and mattered to what we'd become."

The "Notebook" is the center of the novel and takes up the most space. It connects Siggy's family with the Austrian *Anschluss*, the annexation of Austria by Germany in 1938 (Brook-Shepherd xiii and passim), as well as with the internecine warfare in Yugoslavia during the same period. Although the Notebook is Siggy's autobiography, he is not even conceived until three-quarters of the way through it, perhaps Irving's sly nod to Laurence Sterne's *Tristram Shandy*. Eventually Siggy's prehistory turns into "Real History," bringing him into the present day and up to his death.

This section of the novel, with its different tone (after all, it *is* Siggy's "voice" we hear in this part, not Graff's, as in parts One and Three), raises significant questions concerning the state, with all of its power, and the individual. "The Notebook" also explores historical forces and their repercussions for family and society. It asks questions of history itself.

Part Three of the novel winds down the quest for individual freedom. Hannes Graff completes the mission of his "romantic" alter ego, Siggy, and the "liberation" of the animals leads to violence and bloody death. Graff and Gallen consummate their relationship, and that, too, ends in disaster, with hurled recriminations and an acrimonious separation. The novel ends with Graff leaving for Kaprun to find Ernst Watzek-Trummer, the "real" historian, "the keeper of details," who had been Siggy's mentor. Although Graff has matured somewhat, exactly how much is unclear.

SETTING

In this novel, Irving makes use of particular and detailed settings. This is especially true of Vienna; its streets and alleys are described, its parks and many famous buildings. We get this detailed description of Vienna as it existed not only in 1967 but also in 1938. There has been little change, and of course that is one of the points Irving attempts to make. As Siggy writes in his Notebook, Vienna in 1967 "is all pre-history—smug and secretive" (105).

A great deal of attention is paid to the Heitzinger Zoo; the boys literally map it at one time or another, as each crawls about the zoo, evading O. Schrutt, the night watchman, who is believed to be a former Nazi. The mapping takes on ominous meaning as first Siggy, then Graff, makes his way through the labyrinthine zoo, avoiding the infrared lights set up at checkpoints. The description of the zoo at the end of the novel horrifies and repels. The destruction of the Biergarten is complete; there are the "crunchy dust of littered ashtrays" and chunks of the fun-house mirror all over the terrace. This destruction mirrors Graff's near falling apart: "I kept looking down at my puzzlework reflection, looming over myself" (325).

The idea of impending violence permeates even the countryside when Siggy and Graff leave Vienna and ride through Austria's towns and villages. Siggy remarks on the darkness of all the towns they ride through, how they must have been like that during the blackout in the war. Which war? Charlemagne's, alluded to in Siggy's comment about an old helmet with a spike and visor he once found? Or World War I—or II? Siggy and Graff hear the river, and Graff asks, "Is that ahead of us?" (24). Is he asking about this river, or about the helmet, with all of its violent associations? Or is he asking about the river he will learn of later in Siggy's journal, the river that snags the raft "neatly piled with heads"? Time—and space—collapse here; all wars, all violence, all rivers become one and the same.

Occasionally Irving uses setting for humor. The natural landscape symbolically reflects the consummation of Graff and Gallen's affair. Again the river storms by, but this time with a deer, looking suspiciously like the oryx, on an ice floe, as numerous does stand on the shore, "wanting" him to come ashore. The sexual passages are purposefully overwritten and humorously expose Graff's adolescent fantasies.

In *Setting Free the Bears*, however, Irving uses setting primarily to convey the decadence and corruption of power—of the past, of the present, and, one suspects, of the future. Betrayals and failures of nerve take place in the countryside as well as in the city. Even the most bucolic landscape has its surreal underlayer. The Vienna depicted in this novel recurs in a number of Irving's other novels; it often turns out to be our worst dream.

CHARACTER DEVELOPMENT

There is little character development in *Setting Free the Bears*. Siggy, although Austrian, acts like the classic adolescent in much of American literature, ready for sex and adventure. It is his plan to free the animals in the zoo, his plan to buy the motorcycle, to head south to the Riviera, to live off the land. Siggy initiates nearly all of the major scenes and pushes them to the edge of disaster; indeed, he pushes once too often and too far. As a result, he dies. His eccentricities characterize—and perhaps caricature—him; when Graff first notices him, Siggy is sitting on a bench in the park, eating radishes, salting them with shakers that he proceeds to throw away. If clothes make the man, or boy, Siggy's outfit is telling: he "always" wore "the corduroy duckhunter's jacket with its side slash-pockets, and the great vent pocket at the back" (3). We recognize, of course, at least a cousin of J. D. Salinger's Holden Caulfield (with slight modifications) in *Catcher in the Rye*; just as Caulfield's favorite word is "fuck," so Siggy's is the Austrian equivalent, "frotting."

Occasionally, particularly in the excursions into nature to go fishing, we recognize Twain's Tom Sawyer and Huck Finn. To a certain extent, Irving seems to be having some fun with critic Leslie Fiedler's notion of the good–bad boy who is also sensitive, like Salinger's Holden. Siggy carries a notebook in which he writes aphorisms, proverbs, poetry, and his autobiography. He keeps a daily journal. Although attracted to women, as Holden is, Siggy is incapable of having any kind of relationship with them. Siggy also is the one more interested in origins and the one who raises the most significant questions about life.

Hannes Graff's major characteristic is that he is a young man at "loose ends." He is Siggy's alter ego, following passively in his footsteps almost every step of the way. There are three possible exceptions to his passivity: (1) his relationship with Gallen, although it eventually fails; (2) his editing of Siggy's journal; and (3) his setting out to find Ernst Watzek-Trummer. Still, all three situations are tightly tied to Siggy.

It is Graff who first sees Gallen, who has long, thick, auburn braids. And it is Graff who suggests to her that she come along with him and Siggy on the motorcycle. Siggy objects to Gallen right from the beginning, for she intrudes on his relationship with Graff. Graff's desire for Gallen manifests itself immediately, and he pursues her relentlessly throughout the first and third parts, the frame, of the novel. As he approaches her, she dances away each time, until almost the end of the novel. The portrayal of their courtship, if one can call it that, borders on the titillating. The consummation of their affair comes late in the novel, just before she accompanies Graff on the zoo bust. Sickened by the resulting violence and chaos, she leaves him, intending to find work in Vienna.

Graff's second independent act is to edit Siggy's notebook and journal. His editing job is an attempt to bring order out of the chaos of Siggy's entries, both those of his journal, detailing his infiltration of the zoo, and those of his autobiography. Also included are Graff's critical comments on Siggy's use of maxims, poems, and the like. Irving has been criticized for his characters' tendency to write sophomoric drivel, but Irving knows what he is doing here: Siggy *is* often sophomoric, never more so than when he falls back on cliché or on the hackneyed phrase. Even Graff, who is not especially brilliant, recognizes when this happens, and his criticizing Siggy takes the onus off our compulsion to do so.

The final assertion of independence is Graff's leave-taking of Vienna and its environs after the Heitzinger Zoo is "liberated." His decision to "rise up out of this road ditch" and ride his motorcycle "out of this deceptively ordered countryside" suggests at least some growth in character, no matter how minimal. Graff takes responsibility for his actions at the zoo and intends to turn himself over to Ernst Watzek-Trummer, Siggy's mentor, the historian without equal, and the "keeper of details" (340). Graff is no longer at "loose ends."

If Siggy and Graff are little more than sketched in this novel, with Siggy being killed off by the end of Part One, Gallen, the third major character in *Bears*, is given short shrift indeed. She is described physically as childlike, thin, awkward. Only her hair remains vivid to us, and she sells it so that she and Graff will have some money to live on until they can get jobs. The physical description of this girl/child reminds us of Wanga, one of the girls at the zoo early on in the novel. Graff's sexual desire for Gallen is extraordinarily straightforward and urgent, unpleasantly so. But she has no particular role to play, except to intrude on the obvious literary flirtation with homosexuality in the male-buddy relationship. It is clear that Graff's real "love" in the novel is Siggy. Another way of putting this is to say that Graff is in love with himself; he cannot break out of his narcissism until he goes to Watzek-Trummer, until the grass has had time to grow on Siggy's grave.

Although Gallen is merely sketched, she has certain traits that point up the deficiencies of Graff and Siggy. Gallen may be young and innocent of the world, but she demonstrates compassion, especially toward

Graff, throughout much of the novel. When Graff is threatened with arrest for being "deviant" and disturbing the peace, Gallen protects him. When his legs are burned by the motorcycle engine, she nurses him. And when Graff is made ill by bee toxin, she nurses him once again. In addition, she sells her hair to raise money for them to move to Vienna, and even though she is opposed to the zoo bust, she goes along with Graff on this venture, believing his story that it is the right thing to do. Gallen ultimately leaves Graff, asking for her hair money (she plans to stay in Vienna on her own), because he lied to her about the animals he would release; moreover, she is sickened by the violence of the zoo bust. Although Graff claims he will see Gallen again, she—and the reader— knows better.

Other characters in the novel are, by and large, one-dimensional. Some of them, however, are memorable. Ernst Watzek-Trummer, who constructs a bizarre eagle suit from chicken feathers, remains with us when we finish the novel because of his heroic, although futile, action. Zahn Glanz, who takes Watzek-Trummer as his role model, is another of these characters; Zahn is Siggy's "spiritual" father, a man who pushes heroic action further than Trummer, but who disappears in the war. Siggy's biological father, Vratno Javotnik, mesmerizes us in his desire to survive. A sort of Everyman, Vratno resembles us all, perhaps too closely. Irving shows his ability to sketch these characters with such shorthand precision that they come alive and linger in the memory of the reader. They are much more than shadow figures; they come close to being allegorical figures whose actions demonstrate moral ideas.

THEMATIC ISSUES

There are two major thematic issues, tightly linked, in *Setting Free the Bears*: issues of history and of individual freedom. Indeed, Gabriel Miller has called this novel Irving's "meditation on history," in which he portrays "two heroes 'at loose ends,' bent on reforming a static world in 'an interim time' " (48). In this novel questions of history are significant: Who "makes" history? Who sets historical forces in motion? And must the individual submit to those forces? To a certain extent, historical forces seem like fate or at least are associated with what Irving calls the "gale of the world." Is history Kurt von Schuschnigg's version, or Goebbels's? Or even Gordon Brook-Shepherd's? Is it Dr. Ficht's (Ficht was Graff's history professor) footnotes or Ernst Watzek-Trummer's details? Perhaps history is, finally, Siggy's account of his prehistory and selective auto-biography, as well as the "real" history he lives. Siggy's history is personal, subjective, about ordinary men and women. This novel also questions whether history is transmissible, and if it is, whether we learn anything from it. Greil Marcus writes that an "insistence on remembering all that takes place" (71) allows for individual resistance or intervention in Irving's world, but we must at least examine the means and the results of such intervention.

The title of Irving's novel, *Setting Free the Bears*, informs readers that its subject, in some way, has to do with liberation. Thus, it comes as no surprise that the novel's major characters, the youthful Gallen, Siggy, and Graff, stand for individual freedom against what they see as entrenched authority. In 1967, when Irving wrote this novel, such a theme is not surprising, although it is not new, as Irving makes clear. Siggy accuses Graff of being at "loose ends," but the phrase also applies to himself and to Gallen. All three have broken family ties, all three are on the road, all three attempt to live off the land. The boys have rejected the authority of the university; Siggy's plan for the zoo bust is meant to be liberating. In this, Siggy follows in the footsteps of his spiritual father, Zahn Glanz, who was also on the side of freedom.

A large part of the theme of individual freedom has to do with sexual freedom. The novel opens in spring, and Siggy and Graff go to the zoo: "We shouldn't leave Vienna," says Graff, "without seeing how spring has struck the zoo" (12).

On Graff and Siggy's excursion to the zoo, they meet two girls: Karlotta, apparently older, more cynical, and experienced, and Wanga, younger, prepubescent, and innocent. The boys have—or at least Siggy has—obligatory sex because it is spring. The great oryx, the mythical beast with mythically huge testicles, reinforces the fertility of springtime. The many references to the oryx and its "balloon-like" testicles seem also to be part of the sexual fantasies of these boys. Still, the sexual freedom of the young people is forced, and the bawdiness of these scenes lacks humor and joy.

For Graff, Siggy, and Gallen, sex is desired and feared at the same time. The idea of homosexuality is flirted with as part of the search for individual freedom, and at the same time homosexuality seems to be inevitably linked with violence. Siggy tells Gallen's Aunt Tratt that he and Graff are "queer" because he believes she will tell Gallen, who will then leave Graff; boys will be boys, apparently, by sticking together.

Siggy, however, is curiously ambivalent about "queerness," and later in the novel, he bashes a "queer" for no reason.

Aunt Tratt and the townspeople see the boys' "apparent" homosexuality as "sexual deviancy" and as violently disruptive; thus, they combat it with violence of their own. In one of Irving's more frenetic and wild scenes, a milkman arrives at Aunt Tratt's inn and proceeds to beat his horse for not moving fast enough. Siggy, who sees this cruelty from his window, rushes naked into the courtyard and attacks the driver by jumping on his back and beating him. Graff, who by this time has also run into the courtyard, along with numerous other people, beats Siggy's bare backside with a switch. The general melee confirms Aunt Tratt's suspicions about "queerness" and arouses the townspeople to anger. Siggy's attempt to "save" the horse merely drives it into a frenzy, and the milkman is nearly killed. Siggy must flee, and Graff must stay behind to "pay" for the "crime" by working with the bees that will eventually kill Siggy. This extended "riff" by Irving prefigures similar attempts at intervention related in Siggy's Notebook, as well as the zoo bust. It also repeats a number of significant thematic concerns, among which is sexuality.

In much of the youthful groping and panting, joking and winking, we see an underlying sexism that is not attractive and is often disturbing. Women are depicted as old and ugly (Aunt Tratt), cruel even when nurturing (Frau Gippel), fearful and Amazon-like (Karlotta), or boyish, pale, innocent, *too* childlike (Wanga and Gallen). After Gallen has sex with Graff and shows that she cares about him, he fears being trapped by domesticity. When she shows her independence by demonstrating that she can ride the motorcycle, when she sells her hair, when she speaks of getting a job, Graff wants to be rid of her and calls her a "bitch."

The pursuit of Gallen by Graff initially echoes the pursuit of Hilke Marter, Siggy's mother, by Zahn Glanz. But Hilke and Zahn are romantically tender and shy, whereas Graff's courtship of Gallen is darker and more greedy. Zahn and Hilke never consummate their relationship because the war intervenes; Graff and Gallen consummate their affair in a scene that is consciously manipulated by Irving. Although the scene purports to be "romantic," taking place in the woods on a spring night, with Graff in a dreamlike state, envisioning bucks and does and rushing water, it is all undercut by references to "hangies" and "huggies." The positions taken in their zipped-together sleeping bags defy geometry. (One suspects that Irving, in part, may be mocking Hemingway's romantic love scene in *For Whom the Bell Tolls*; in Irving's novel, "the earth" doesn't move, but the "gale" quiets down.) The scene is also meant to be contrasted with Hilke's compassionate and tender lovemaking with Vratno; it is Hilke who "saves" Vratno from total disintegration from the war. Even if one were to read Gallen and Graff's consummation scene as idealistic, it quickly ends in violent outbursts and a cold leave-taking as Gallen moves into a life in Vienna, and Graff goes to Kaprun.

The clash between Graff and Gallen is more subdued, however, than the violence depicted elsewhere in the novel. Hitler's takeover of Austria and the acquiescence not only of Austria, but also of England and the United States, unleashes forces that nearly destroy Europe. The brutality of the Nazis and others, the too-willing collusion of so-called freedom and resistance fighters, the shock waves of the Holocaust and of Hiroshima and Nagasaki have remained in our world—in Southeast Asia, in the Middle East, in Bosnia, in neo-Nazi groups, and in terrorism throughout the world.

In fact, the cultural objects (such as war artifacts), the interventions (especially the zoo bust), and the structural crosscutting in time and space in *Setting Free the Bears* have particular resonance to American readers, since in 1967 the United States was engaged in interventions both at home and abroad: the Civil Rights movement, the war in Vietnam, and opposition to it. Irving alludes to the Civil Rights movement but does not directly mention the war. There are, however, numerous oblique references to Vietnam: for example, the night infiltration of the Heitzinger Zoo, with its chutes and mazes, with its animal noises that could not be distinguished. Neither Siggy nor Graff can tell what to expect on these night forays, just as soldiers in Vietnam could not tell who their enemies were or where they were. The "infrared night" at the zoo is also a link to Vietnam, where FLIR (forward-looking infrared) technologies were first used. Siggy and Graff think they can selectively release animals while containing others, just as the military believed that target acquisition sensors, heat-seeking missiles, and lasers, used for the first time in Vietnam, would selectively destroy only the enemy—or at least "contain" them. But more important are parallels in Irving's novel to government policy in the Vietnam War and to opposition to it. Just as his novel seems full of ambivalences, so was this country ambivalent about Vietnam.

The overall failure of Europe and the allies to respond to Germany's aggression until it was too late—for example, its "reunification" with Austria, its incursion into Czechoslovakia, and so on—had repercussions in Korea in the 1950s and in Vietnam in the 1960s. The lesson of history for policy makers in the United States seemed to be the lesson of Munich, teaching that if aggression by a great power is not stopped early, then it will have to be stopped later, with perhaps horrendous consequences. The parallel for a whole generation of government leaders was that communism filled the role of Nazi Germany. North Vietnam's Ho Chi Minh was supported by the Soviet Union, which had proclaimed often enough that the world would be dominated in the future by communism. What was the difference between this claim and Hitler's that Germany would rule the world? This question was linked to the political idea driving military intervention in Vietnam: the "domino theory." As Vietnam went, so would go all of Southeast Asia.

In 1965, when President Lyndon Johnson met with his advisers concerning Vietnam, the analogy between Munich and Southeast Asia had increasing urgency. The main theme of the discussion on strategic planning had to do with nuclear weapons; as Ambassador Henry Cabot Lodge put it: "I feel there is a greater threat to start World War III if we don't go in. . . . Can't we see the similarity with Munich?" (Schell, *The Real War* 26). If, of course, World War III were possible, nuclear weapons would most likely be used, and if they were used, the outcome of the war would be totally unlike that of World War II. At the end of the domino theory, then, were two possibilities, neither attractive: defeat and annihilation. Such a war could not be won by anyone.

Opposed to the Munich analogy was the theory that Vietnam was engaged in a movement for independence and that it might be a local movement even though it might have strength borrowed from a foreign power. The debate between the two positions mingled in the fighting in Vietnam, reaping bitterness there and at home.

Even though *Setting Free the Bears* includes no overt mention of the Vietnam War, one of its powerful themes, history as "repetitive remembering," suggests that this "interim" war is very much a part of the text. Irving would have had to be blind and deaf not to have known what was happening in the United States during the 1960s; the "crusade for Europe" may have been over but, as Siggy knew, there were "crusades" every day in America.

It is not surprising that the ambivalences of the Vietnam War period permeate Irving's *Setting Free the Bears*. Siggy writes: "I'm not in America. I'm in the Old World, and what makes it old is that it's had a head start" (104–105). In this distancing of his characters (and himself), Irving can focus clearly on the debate over Vietnam that not only raged during the war but continues to this day. Irving, in an interview, has said that being in a foreign country allows him to *"notice"* things, "to see things freshly," about his own country (Miller 178). In this sense, Irving is similar to Hemingway, who found in Europe a way to shift his view of his own country; in *A Moveable Feast*, Hemingway writes: "Maybe away from Paris I could write about Paris as in Paris I could write about Michigan" (7). Perhaps by setting the novel in Vienna in the 1960s, Irving could write about America, both past and present.

In his Notebook, Siggy writes about how Hitler's sweep across Europe disrupts, dislocates, and destroys the lives of millions. Specifically, in his own history, Hilke Marter and Zahn Glanz's romance comes to an abrupt end; no one knows what happens to Zahn—he simply disappears. Siggy's father betrays Gottlob Wut, his only friend, who ends up suffocated, head down in a latrine. Grandfather Marter, in despair, rides to his death in Kaprun. The horrific raft with its pyramid of neatly stacked heads, swaying in the breeze, becomes emblematic of the horror of war and fascism. Even the postwar world is not free of violence. The day of Siggy's birth is the day of the death of Grandmother Marter, who shouts joyfully out of her apartment window, only to be shot by a nervous Soviet soldier of Austria's postwar Allied occupation. The zoo bust simply reiterates the confusion, blood, and chaos of animals and people alike.

A CULTURAL MATERIALIST READING OF *SETTING FREE THE BEARS*

Setting Free the Bears is a novel concerned with individual freedom and its costs, as well as a novel about histories: the prehistory of Siegfried Javotnik and the interim, but nonetheless real, history of 1967 that Graff, Siggy, and Gallen live. Even though the novel is set in Austria with no American characters, it is also a story of United States histories, of the past and the 1960s.

The crosscutting of time and place in Irving's novel may be illuminated by the critical methods used by cultural materialists. The term "cultural materialism" did not become current until 1985, when it was used as a methodology by Jonathan Dollimore and Alan Sinfield in their edition of collected essays, *Political Shakespeare*. Put simply, cultural materialism is "politicized historiography." It pays attention to historical content, political commitment, and textual analysis. Cultural materialism is concerned with how ordinary people intervene in history in order to redefine its shape as prescribed by powerful political and military leaders. The two words in cultural materialism help provide its meaning: "culture" includes *all* forms of culture, including fiction, music, television, as well as things or objects; "materialism"—having to do with specific objects or substances, that is, physical matter—is the opposite of transcendent idealism. Although culture is not merely a reflection of the economic and political system, it cannot be totally independent of it (Barry 183).

For the cultural materialist, relevant history is not simply that of the past, but of our present time as well. We do not read Dickens merely to understand the Victorian age. Rather, we use the past to "read" the present and to reveal the politics of our own society by what we choose to emphasize or suppress of the past. Cultural materialists would agree with Siggy in *Bears*: "[I]t's the pre-history [past] that made us and mattered to what we'd become."

John Irving uses the past—the *Anschluss* in Austria, the tribal warfare in Yugoslavia, the Second World War, and the subsequent Allied occupation of Austria—in an attempt to make us understand what is happening in 1966–1967, not so much in Austria as in the United States. In an interview with Gabriel Miller, Irving talks about these events as related to the "idea of occupation" in *Setting Free the Bears*. This idea of not being "free," of being dominated by authoritative structures, arouses in part a feeling of helplessness and simultaneously an eagerness to do something, to effect change (Miller 183).

It is not coincidental that the centerpiece of the novel focuses on one of the most crucial eras in Europe, an era dominated by a fascist attempt to control the world. The central portion of *Bears* is framed by the adventures of two young men (and a young woman, largely peripheral) who are children born at the end of that era. The Notebook is Siggy's "highly selective" autobiography or history: his "pre-history" in three parts, which leads up to and includes his conception, and his "real" history, which includes his birth and life, what there is of it. As if Siggy's selectivity were not enough, Hannes Graff further edits the Notebook after his friend's death. Graff interleaves another journal, a present-day historical account of Siggy's zoo watch, into the Notebook because Siggy makes "connections" between his own history and his plan to free the zoo animals (263). Irving structures his novel with crosscuts of time and space. We cannot read today's journal entry, nor any future entries, without having read The Notebook of the past.

Even before we read the Notebook, however, we are aware of cultural objects from the past. The motorcycle Siggy and Graff buy is a "veritable beast": "It was an old, cruel-looking motorcycle, . . . lovely like a gun is sometimes lovely—for the obvious, ugly function showing in its most prominent parts" (7). It is a British Royal Enfield motorcycle, which was famous before World War I. During World War II, the factory supplied the Allied forces with 346 cc SV and OHV models in large numbers; the company continued to make these motorcycles through 1971. The boys' motorcycle, a war relic, has been rebuilt and is "like new." On this "beast" the boys wear goggles: "A World War One pilot's goggles—frog eyes, with yellow lenses. They're terrifying!" Siggy also has boots: "I've got real trompers for you" (11).

When they start on their trip, Siggy and Graff ride (ironically enough) through an arch into the Plaza of Heroes, another reminder of wars past. The morning seems "more golden than it was" to Siggy, the present-day "hero," because of his tinted pilot's goggles. Even the Heitzinger Zoo, which is relatively new, is read by the past of its buildings: "as old as Schönbrunn; a part of the palace grounds, the buildings were all rubbled now . . ." (13). The links between the present and the past could not be made clearer right from the beginning of the novel.

But the Notebook itself provides the key to what Irving is up to. Siggy writes that if you are twenty-one in 1967 and in Austria, you have no history . . . and "no immediate future that you can see" (104). If you are twenty-one in 1967, you are "at an interim age in an interim time . . ." (104). Unlike Vienna, which is all prehistory, Siggy and Graff are "alive between two times of monstrous decisions—one past, the other coming" (104). The past monstrous decisions, of course, included the *Anschluss*, Yugoslavia's civil wars, and Hitler's sweep across Europe, which unleashed the Holocaust and Hiroshima; the future holds possible nuclear annihilation.

In the interim, one "waits" for the future and plays "waiting" games, which turn out to be serious and dangerous. As Siggy "waits" for the zoo to open, he asks his waiter why he has no index finger; the waiter explains that he was run over by a tram in the Balkans. Siggy says if he asked a fingerless American man how he lost his index finger, "he'd tell you how a red-hot trigger burned it off while he was shooting the enemy in Manchuria" (105). Irving refers here to Korea, but it is also very possible that he uses "Manchuria" as a code word for Vietnam, thus predating by three years Robert Altman's *M*A*S*H*, followed by the popular television show of the same name. Although Altman's movie (and the subsequent television spinoff) was ostensibly about the Korean War, the film was clearly a critique of America's intervention in Vietnam. At any rate, Manchuria is the closest Irving comes in his novel—geographically, that is—to Vietnam.

But Siggy is not in America, where, he notes, "there are crusades every day" (105). In the United States, he continues, racism is expressed with fire hoses and police clubs and police dogs. Although Siggy speaks of America as a country very different from his own, we know better—America's racism is akin to that of Austria in the 1930s and 1940s.

In the United States in 1955, the Montgomery, Alabama, bus boycott took place after Rosa Parks was arrested for refusing to give up her seat to a white passenger. In 1960 and 1961, there were lunch counter sit-ins and Freedom Rides; federal troops were sent to the University of Mississippi in 1962. As late as 1965, the "Riders" to the South were greeted by a wave of terrorism as Southern segregationists retaliated. Martin Luther King, Jr., was arrested and jailed repeatedly. Black children were murdered, and churches were burned by racists.

We read and understand racism and violence in the United States by the anti-Semitism depicted in Siggy's Notebook: the squirrel in the park, crazy with fear and fright, with a shaved swastika on its head; the old Jewish man, "caught in a gale," who was shoved under a tram by Nazi youth; Mara Madoff, found raped and hanging in her coat on a coathook in the closet of the Vienna State Opera. The performance was *Lohengrin* that evening, and Fraulein Madoff suffered star-shaped stab wounds in her heart. The state apparently subsidized more than Wagner's opera.

In Irving's novel there are three major interventions where men and women attempt to make their own history against such a backdrop of racism and murderousness. The first intervention in *Bears* is initially undertaken by Ernst Watzek-Trummer, the chicken farmer who becomes the archetypal historian, keeper of details. The second intervention is by Vratno Javotnik, Siggy's biological father, in thuggish intrigue in Yugoslavia. But it is the third intervention, the zoo bust planned by Siggy, that concerns us here. The zoo bust for Siggy, if not for Graff, represents political commitment in a specific and material way: to free the zoo from what he believes are "atrocities."

The night watchman at the Heitzinger Zoo, O. Schrutt, pits the animals against each other and inflicts pain upon them for his perverse pleasure; although Siggy never witnesses any evidence of atrocities, there are, he writes, "unhappy arrangements" orchestrated by O. Schrutt. The watchman is linked with the O. Schrutt who had been a member of Vienna's

Nazi youth, the same youth who terrorized old men and killed Mara Madoff (143). Although Siggy may have created O. Schrutt in "one fiction or another, . . . this O. Schrutt is real" (152). As Siggy says, "Vienna is full of Schrutt families."

The proposed zoo bust, then, is not merely to free the animals but to make Schrutt pay for crimes present and past. In Part One, Siggy's plan for the zoo bust may seem "the rarest of fun" (32), but it takes on greater seriousness in the Notebook, which comes to light after Siggy's death. Although freeing the bears may still appear to be folly, there is a measure of heroism and justness to it as Schrutt becomes more and more sinister. Nevertheless, there is always the question of whether this Schrutt is the same one who strutted around Vienna with the Nazi youth; nevertheless, he is linked with them.

Hannes Graff ambivalently takes over the zoo bust after Siggy's sudden death by bees. In part he pursues the plan because he feels guilty over Siggy's death, and he wishes to make amends. In part he also feels guilty because his family lived out the war in Salzburg, which escaped much of its horror, and where the American occupation was more benign than the Soviet. Graff's family suffered little and lost little, he says; when the American forces leave, all that Graff's mother loses is their music. Graff also gets caught up in the zoo bust because he comes to believe in Siggy's mission to free the animals and to make O. Schrutt pay for his "war crimes." Furthermore, when Siggy dies, it is as if Graff loses himself. Hannes seems to believe that the zoo bust will in some way help him to regain his lost self.

The zoo bust succeeds in only one respect; it reduces O. Schrutt to babbling Jewish names from his past. The animals are freed, but the result is destruction and chaos. Gallen leaves Graff, and Graff's very self nearly disintegrates. The animals eat each other; the primates engage in destruction that is "a vandalism of a shocking, human type" (325). Even the great oryx, symbol of fertility and life, is killed.

And in the shrubs hide "anonymous men with ancient weapons . . . an army of diehard meat eaters," waiting to participate in the killing. The blood, the brutality, the sheer senseless violence repeat the horror of a much earlier zoo bust when people broke into the zoo to eat the animals. The carnage also echoes that of the war (one might say, *any* war) and its aftermath. Graff leaves the destruction behind him, escaping on his British Royal Enfield motorcycle, and heads for Kaprun to turn himself over to Ernst Watzek-Trummer: "Historian without equal, and the keeper of details. He should make a fine confessor, for sure" (340).

Those critics (Harter and Thompson 32) who see the ending as ambivalent at best have some justification. Although there is hope at the end—Graff sees the peace-loving rare spectacled bears going "hand-in-hand" into the forest—we are left with horrifying images of the zoo. Gabriel Miller, however, sees optimism at the end of the novel: Graff has grown up enough to admit responsibility for those "casualties" at the zoo. He rides into the country and into the "full-force wind." "But I didn't panic. . . . I truly outdrove the wind. For sure—for the moment, at least—there was no gale hurrying me out of this world" (340). But of course, this is only for the "moment." We are too aware that no one has been able to escape the "gale of the world," from the old Jewish man shoved under a tram, to Mara Madoff, to Zahn Glanz, to Vratno, and to Siggy. Indeed, the "gale" is the only thing "for sure" in Irving's world.

Setting Free the Bears is Irving's most chilling book. The center of the novel, the Notebook, with its deadly seriousness, is surrounded by a frame of foolishness—quixotic adventures, juvenile jokes, and adolescent lusts—that turns deadly. The quest to "free" the bears is a "lark," but it contains echoes and repetitions of horrors from the Notebook, from Siggy's prehistory. At the end of the novel, Graff rides the British Royal Enfield motorcycle out of the frame but back into the Notebook, into the past that is now his present. He returns to Kaprun, never completely a safe haven: Grandfather Marter's brother, the postmaster, was burned to death there by Nazis; Grandfather Marter later rode the mail sled to his death out of despair. To be sure, Ernst Watzek-Trummer—the "genuine survivor," as Harter and Thompson (31) note—the "true" historian, the "keeper of details," will be Graff's "confessor," and perhaps comforter, but he is also the "keeper" of graves: his family's, Grandfather Marter's, and now Siggy's. For all Graff's use of the future tense at the end of the novel, as well as his positive insistence on stability and balance ("for sure" is repeated four times), he rides into the center of the novel, to death and to Siggy's grave.

4

The Water-Method Man
(1972)

John Irving's second novel, *The Water-Method Man*, appears to have little or nothing to say about the incredible flux the United States was in during 1969–1970, the time frame of the novel. Yet the social upheaval of the late 1960s, mirroring the chaos in Vietnam that followed the failed Tet offensive in 1968, is reflected in the novel: by the movies Ralph Packer makes; by the topic Fred Trumper chooses for his Ph.D. dissertation, a translation of the Old Low Norse epic "Akthelt and Gunnel"; and by the dislocations in the basic social unit, the family itself. Questions concerning family life were being answered, some thought, by young people forming communes as divorce rates increased. In Irving's novel, such questions as Does father really know best? Are Ozzie and Harriet really our parents? drive characters and plot.

Irving said of *The Water-Method Man* that he wanted to write a book with a happy ending, a book "absolutely comic" (Marcus 72), and to a large degree he succeeded. On a structural level, Irving tells the story of Fred "Bogus" Trumper, who grows from an irresponsible bumbler, incapable of making decisions or commitments, to a man who settles down to work and family.

The novel is one of Irving's most complicated in terms of its narrative, which cuts backward and forward in time and moves between first-and third-person points of view. In addition, Irving includes bits and pieces of a variety of "writerly" modes: several movie scripts (one of them about Trumper's life); the epistle (wonderful letters to Humble Oil, to Trumper's father, and others); a chapter from Helmbart's postmodern novel, *Vital Telegrams*; an epic ("Akthelt and Gunnel"); and Trumper's diary. In addition, there are a number of extended comic "riffs," situations with an energy that gives them a narrative life of their own.

The form of Irving's comedy is farce. Events are speeded up even as time elapses. For example, we are as unaware as Trumper that six months pass while he is looking for his best friend, Merrill Overturf, in Austria. Farce concentrates on the human body with such intensity that we are conscious of every quiver, every movement, every cerebral twitch.

Irving's use of farce, particularly in the extended comic riffs, is nothing short of brilliant. For example, Trumper's impotence with Lydia Kindle leads to double exposure: of his "prick" and of himself as a "prick." Similarly, the two duck hunters who pick up Trumper after his fiasco with Lydia act like his kin in their mad chase of the young woman and in their voyeurism. In addition, they are linked to Trumper's father and a duck-hunting excursion his son hated. When Trumper arrives home and exposes himself, literally, to Biggie, his wife, their son, Colm, ends up playing with the dead duck, a gift to Trumper from the hunters. What starts out to be a sexual dalliance for Trumper runs amok in hilarious fashion. But at the same time, and more significantly, the situation points to connections between sex and death, as well as connections between fathers and sons.

PLOT DEVELOPMENT

For all the narrative strategies of the novel, the plot of *The Water-Method Man* is itself simple. Fred "Bogus" Trumper, the protagonist, goes to a urologist, Dr. Jean Claude Vigneron, for a "cure" of his long-term problem of a blocked urinary tract, which has caused him a great deal of difficulty and pain in two important areas of his life: urination and sexual climax. Vigneron offers Trumper essentially two choices: a simple operation or the "water-method" treatment: drinking large quantities of water, especially before and after sex. Trumper chooses the latter treatment and hopes for the best.

At the time he sees Vigneron, Trumper is living in New York City with Tulpen, having left his wife, Sue "Biggie" Kunft, and his son, Colm. Trumper had been at the University of Iowa as a Ph.D. student in English, working on his dissertation. He left that, as well as his family, behind.

In New York City, Trumper works as a sound engineer for Ralph Packer, who makes avant-garde "art" films (that are often murky and downright unintelligible) about social issues, such as youth communes, and personal conflicts. Tulpen also works for Packer and for a brief time had been his lover. One of Packer's films, *Fucking Up*, stars Trumper, with Tulpen, in a cinematic documentary of his life.

For some mysterious reason (to the reader, at any rate), Tulpen loves Trumper and wants to share her life with him; in addition, she wants to have their child. Despite his repeated assertions that he does not want another child—Colm is "enough," he says—Tulpen "loses" her intra-uterine device and becomes pregnant. Overwhelmed by the thought of commitment, Trumper leaves her and everything behind, setting off for Austria to find his best friend, Merrill Overturf, from his old student days.

Overturf was Trumper's boyish, romantic sidekick, full of bravado and drink, and—like Hannes Graff of *Setting Free the Bears*—at "loose ends." In a number of ways, Irving recasts the Graff/Javotnik symbiotic relationship in this, his second novel. Overturf, like Trumper, has a physical problem, diabetes, which he usually ignores until he goes into near insulin shock.

In Vienna, Trumper searches for Overturf, has a nervous breakdown, gets involved in a convoluted drug-smuggling plot, and eventually learns that his friend has been dead for two years—drowned in the Danube while searching for a World War II tank supposedly submerged in the river. Overturf's drowning occurs when he attempts to impress a young American girl he has picked up; his death is as senseless as his life has been.

Forced to return to the United States by narcotics agents, who buy his airline ticket home, and give him money and a limousine ride into New York City, Trumper convinces the limo driver, Dante Calicchio, to drive him to Maine. There he hopes to see one of his other boyhood friends, Cuthbert "Couth" Bennett, the caretaker of the Pillsbury estate. Couth is, of course, the caretaker of more than the estate: he cares for Trumper and sends him money when he needs it. He also cares for Biggie and Colm, so much so that when Trumper leaves his wife and child, they go to live with Couth. When Trumper finds them at the estate, his response is to get raving drunk and return to New York City, at least momentarily.

Seeing Biggie and Colm with Couth seems to be what prompts Trumper to change his life and to grow up. Aware that he has never finished anything in his life, he returns to the University of Iowa and completes his dissertation. When Trumper began his translation of "Akthelt and Gunnel," he fabricated large portions of it; no one would know, he rationalized, because no one knew the language, Old Low Norse. The second time around, Trumper eliminates his "creative" work and sticks to the more literal meanings of the words; he even writes the required "graduate school" introduction and footnotes. The completion of his Ph.D. is only one of a number of "loose ends" tied up in the novel.

Trumper reconciles with his father, who, throughout much of the novel, plays an ogre. Rather than continue with the water-method treatment, which never really worked, Trumper has a successful urinary tract operation; in response to Tulpen's "How's the new prick?" he answers, "Perfectly normal." He returns to Tulpen, who by now has had their child, named Merrill. Trumper even has the good possibility of a teaching position. The movie, *Fucking Up*, is finished and released to rave reviews.

In addition, Couth and Biggie have married and have a child, Anna; even Ralph Packer marries—Matje, who is soon to have a child. The novel ends with all of the families, including various children and dogs, in Maine at the Pillsbury estate, with the model caretaker, Couth. Irving achieves his "happy ending" in a celebration of the flesh, marriage, fertility, and family. There is much feasting, drinking, singing, and storytelling in the festival of Throgshafen, truly a time of giving thanks.

SETTING

There are four important locations in *The Water-Method Man*: the University of Iowa, Iowa City; New York City; Vienna; and Georgetown, Maine. Within these locations, with the exception of the Pillsbury estate, houses and rooms are extremely important, as befits a novel with a strong family theme.

In Iowa, the house Trumper shares with Biggie and Colm is in a state of disrepair. Screens fall out of the windows or crumble at the touch of a hand. The electricity fails; the plumbing doesn't work; there are mice. Trumper seems totally incapable of making repairs or of maintaining the home. Biggie is the one who must "cope" with the deterioration of their house—and their marriage. Within the house, the bedroom, bathroom, and basement provide the focus for a family that cannot hold itself together.

In the bedroom, Biggie and Trumper talk at cross purposes; often Trumper's comments are disjoined from Biggie's. Indeed, he talks more to his tape recorder than to his wife, thinking all the while of his marriage to a former Olympic-class skier "who can do more sit-ups than he can" (71). He is afraid to "wrestle" with her for fear of being "pinned." The machine records his thoughts and feelings. When Biggie calls out to him, "Bogus?" he responds, "Nothing, Big." Their profoundest recurring conversation has to do with how "sorry" he is and whether he has paid the electricity bill. The tension, tiredness, and even hostility are palpable in their bedroom.

The bathroom is a reminder, as is the bedroom, of Trumper's urinary and sexual problems. It is in the bathroom that one of the funniest scenes takes place, when Trumper urinates in a condom he has forgotten to take off after a failed attempt to have sex with Lydia Kindle, an undergraduate at the university. When Trumper sees the condom, he frantically tells Biggie to "get the scissors," which she refuses to do. The scene is absolute farce with the focus on Trumper's body parts and their functions; the situation rapidly spins out of control, spilling out of the bathroom and into the hallway, with Trumper and Biggie screaming, Colm humming and playing on the floor, and the mailman at the door. For all the knockabout comedy of the scene, however, it also spells the end of their marriage.

Trumper enters this bathroom scene after coming through the basement, a place he visits every day, theoretically to set the mousetrap for the mouse he never wants to catch. The trap symbolizes Trumper's feeling of being trapped in his marriage, and so each day he unsets the trap, wishing the mouse a good life. Ironically, the day of the Lydia Kindle fiasco, Trumper is himself snared by the mousetrap, which sends him howling up the basement stairs and to the bathroom. Not coincidentally, when Trumper finally returns to Iowa to complete his Ph.D., he lives in the basement of his dissertation adviser's house.

In New York City, Trumper and Tulpen's apartment seems even less a home than the one he left with Biggie. Again the focus is appropriately on the bedroom and bathroom. In Tulpen's bedroom, Trumper does not communicate any better than he did in Iowa; he still has his tape recorder. Tulpen urges him to have the operation on his urethra, but he insists on the water method. Although Trumper seems fond of Tulpen, she is more an "object" to him, and when his son comes to visit, Trumper even forgets to introduce her.

In this bedroom, Trumper sits on the bed "like a cigar-store Indian" (245). When Tulpen tells him that he does not make love to her "nearly enough" (247), Trumper fails to respond. Later, he confuses her with Biggie and even calls her by his wife's name. Tulpen's bed is surrounded by fish tanks, with the gurgling sounds of the water pumps, the dim lights, and the movement of the fish within the water. The room to Trumper is "fishy dark," like "turtle murk." The fish tanks reinforce the importance of water as a symbol in the novel: just as Merrill Overturf drowns in the water of the Danube, so Trumper feels he is drowning in his life. And as Merrill will be "resurrected" through Tulpen's amniotic waters in the birth of her son, so will Fred Trumper be reborn.

Trumper's six-month stay in Vienna is an attempt not only to locate Merrill Overturf but also to recapture their earlier life together. During Trumper's student romance with Biggie, the focus is also on bedrooms, theirs as well as Overturf's. These bedrooms are "way-stations," disaster areas. Merrill's is filled with insulin, needles, and other paraphernalia to test his urine and to control his diabetes. Trumper's room has a chaos all its own; although it is here that he loves Biggie for the first time, the room remains too "full of" Merrill.

Trumper's return to Vienna finds the city more sinister: the coffee-house he frequents appears surreal to him. Mysterious characters speak unintelligibly, and hashish is passed to him. Not only pastry and coffee are served in the restaurant.

But the most significant house in Vienna is the hotel/brothel where Trumper rents a room and works at his typewriter, trying to write order into his life. The brothel, with its constant flux, represents his life; the transient male customers reflect Trumper's own transiency, his lack of commitment to the women in his life and to his child. A darkly humorous scene in the brothel revolves around the supposed sexual death of a customer at the moment of climax, a reflection of Trumper's own fear and pain during sexual orgasm. In contrast to the customer, who is not dead, Trumper remains stone cold in his emotional detachment. His nervous breakdown in Vienna leads to the eventual death of his old self and to a rebirth.

Only the Pillsbury estate, at Mad Indian Point, Georgetown, Maine, offers sanctuary from the turmoil of the world. It is not so much the house that is important here, but the natural setting. The estate is an "island," though still connected to the mainland, similar to Shakespeare's Forest of Arden, Illyria, or Titania and Oberon's magical forest world; as on Prospero's island in *The Tempest*, the magic of Couth's island restores broken relationships, minds, and hearts.

The natural landscape of the estate is far different from the stubbled, flat Iowa cornfields through which a naked Trumper runs in his escape from Lydia Kindle. Although, as in Shakespeare's comedies and romances, there are threats of wild tempests, in Shakespeare and in Irving nature is regenerative.

On the island, Trumper communicates with Biggie and recognizes her value in ways that he could not when married to her. He also talks *with* his son, Colm, instead of at him. Father and son's favorite story is *Moby Dick*, with the whale as the hero. They share poignant moments at the end of the dock, looking at the ever-changing ocean. The water may recede, but it always returns. No matter the scars, Moby Dick always lives.

CHARACTER DEVELOPMENT

The Water-Method Man is more a novel of theme and situation than of character. It is easy to agree with Michael Priestley that the characters in the novel are "sometimes vapid" (88). Even Irving felt that "Bogus Trumper wasn't enough of a character" (Miller 192); certainly this is true of some of the lesser characters such as Ralph Packer, perhaps even Couth. Yet the very multiplicity of names for Trumper make him interesting, if not especially complex.

As Fred Trumper says, names are "facts," and perhaps more. His parents, Dr. Edmund and Mrs. Trumper, name him Fred, but no one, except for them, calls him by that name. Biggie calls him "Bogus," as does Couth "when he first caught him lying" (16). Merrill Overturf called him "Boggle" for "vague reasons," according to Trumper. Merrill apparently recognized the fear and doubt in "Boggle" and the evasiveness of him. Ralph Packer calls him "Thump-Thump," a name Trumper despises because it points to his childishness. Tulpen calls him Trumper, a name he understands as "closest to a fact. . . . Male surnames don't often change" (16–17), and Tulpen is quite sure Trumper will not change either his name or himself.

All of Trumper's names fit him. Bogus is a liar who tries to convince his wife he has done nothing wrong in being with Lydia Kindle. Technically, he has not been unfaithful to Biggie, but he "boggles" here: his dalliance with Lydia is surely a betrayal. Thump-Thump's own son, Colm, is more grown-up than his father. Colm, for example, recognizes death for what it is: a part of life.

It takes Trumper a long time to change, to shed these names. He must first of all suffer loss—of his family and of his other self, Merrill Over-turf—and recognize the meaning of such loss. Perhaps Merrill Overturf's name for Trumper, "Boggle," is the most accurate: Trumper boggles or evades life because he fears his own emotions. As Tulpen perceptively notes, he is all "surface," operating only on the level of sentimentality. Trumper is maudlin but lacks real emotion.

Gabriel Miller writes that Trumper is a "bungler," a *"schlemiel*, yet a humane and rather nice guy" (48). A bungler and schlemiel, yes, but perhaps not so nice. In many ways Trumper remains throughout much of the novel a whining adolescent, still longing for the old days when he was "free" and roaming the bars with Merrill Overturf and his "boob loop," a lasso contrived from the wrist thong of a ski pole. When he lost Merrill, Trumper says, he lost "god" (127). Trumper's longest dreams of heroes are about Merrill.

Trumper is more than a schlemiel in his relationship with Biggie. He despises her when they are in Iowa, calling her "Lady Burden" and "The Mistress of Cope." He cheats on Biggie and lies to her, then cries in her lap when he loses his job selling football pennants by trying to impress Lydia Kindle. He deserts Biggie and their son, just as he later deserts Tulpen and their unborn child. It is only when Trumper grows up that he stands a chance of becoming a "rather nice guy."

Other male characters in the novel are not as complex or as fully de-veloped as Trumper. They are meant to be compared and contrasted with him. Merrill is Trumper's reckless and daring, "romantic," other self, who defies death. Merrill is also the perennial adolescent, who de-spises women and uses them only to "score." As Trumper says after Merrill's death, he was no hero, he was an "illusion."

Trumper's father is significant both as a contrast to his son and as a model for him. Whereas Trumper seems to have no opinions and to make no decisions, Dr. Trumper is full of opinions and tries to make decisions for everyone. He is puritanical and demanding. When Trumper disappoints his father by marrying Biggie without permission, the doctor "cuts off" his son; disapproval and disinheritance go hand in hand. At the same time, much of Trumper's lack of emotional commitment, his detachment, can be traced directly to his father. In addition, Trumper's desire to keep his son "safe" is not much different from Dr. Trumper's desire to rule his son's life.

Cuthbert "Couth" Bennett is the most sympathetic male character in the novel. He is the "caretaker" of Biggie, Colm, and even Trumper. He opens his house and himself to all. Of all the men in the novel, he is without pretension, without malice, and the most secure in his sense of self. He works magic in his gentle, civil—"Couth"—way. It may not be coincidence that Couth was fatherless from the time he is fifteen.

With the exception of Couth, the women in *The Water-Method Man* are far more sympathetic than the men. Biggie and Tulpen are committed to their families. Both are intelligent and to a large degree independent. Both are adult in ways the men are not.

Biggie's name is directly linked to and reflective of her physicality and character. She is big of both body and heart. She is shabbily treated by almost everyone in the novel except for Couth. When Biggie and Bogus meet, she is a giant slalom racer, and a good one at that. She gives up her place on the American Olympic team because of her affair with Trumper, which results in her pregnancy. Merrill sees her merely as an "athletic" lay with big "boobs"; indeed, he uses his "boob loop" on her, which seizes her breast and pulls it up into her armpit. But Biggie, more than a match for Merrill, pins him to the floor and jabs him with the ski pole. Both Merrill *and* Trumper are afraid of Biggie, with her "catlike coordination and wonder-mother strength"; both treat her as a sexual object. And Biggie is intelligent enough to recognize Merrill and Bogus's perception of her.

When Sue "Biggie" Kunft is skiing in Austria, she is interviewed by a reporter who mangles her name: "Zu 'Biggie' Kunft," he says, even after she corrects him. "*Zu-kunft*" in German means the future, that which is to come; there is a sexual pun here as well—to "be-coming" forever. Sexually, Biggie is threatening to Bogus; as the future, she apparently is horrifying.

Yet, Biggie is the one who holds the family together for Bogus while he attends school. She works at a menial job, emptying bedpans at the local hospital for low pay. She nurtures both Colm and Bogus; she cleans the house and maintains it physically as well. Biggie is independent with a streak of bravery: she writes to Bogus's father, calling him a "prick" for refusing to help his son through school. To be sure, Biggie accuses Bogus of infidelities he has not committed—technically. Life overwhelms her as much as it does Bogus. She, too, is humiliated in public (when her check is "no good" at the grocery store, for example) and at home.

With Couth she finally finds the "peacefulness" and the gentle commitment and love she both desires and deserves.

Tulpen's character is not as well-developed as Biggie's. It is difficult to understand why Tulpen loves Trumper, since we have no courtship scenes between the two. Still, Tulpen, whose name means tulip (the flower signifies "admiration") is "practical"; the live-in arrangement between the two is one of Tulpen's "facts."

Although Tulpen's body is not quite as large as Biggie's, her breasts are equally fascinating to Trumper. (Lydia Kindle is the only slender, boyish female in this novel; she has hard, little "pointy" breasts; Packer's fiance, Matje, is also slender, but she is hardly sketched as a character.) Breasts seem to be an obsession for Trumper; for the reader, they are a not-too-subtle symbol of his desire for the nurturer–mother, for life itself.

Like Biggie, Tulpen is accused of not having a sense of humor, until near the end of the novel. And like Biggie, Tulpen is committed to having a family that includes children. Indeed, Trumper leaves her because she wants a child and he does not.

There are, however, some differences between Tulpen and Biggie. Tulpen leaves Trumper to grow up on his own; although she loves him, she refuses to "mother" him. She forces him to make his own decisions, to be responsible for them, and to suffer their consequences. She seems to be more independent than Biggie; when Trumper leaves, she does not try to track him down as Biggie does. When he returns to her and their baby, Merrill, he wants to marry her, but she refuses. She will "see" how the relationship works out. Trumper reminds her that with a baby, she "must" not be able to work, but she declares that she can, and does work. In short, she does not "need" him, though she may desire him.

It is incorrect to say, as Trumper does, that Tulpen cares only for facts and lacks emotion. As she says, Trumper broke her heart. She may be committed to having a family that includes Trumper, but not at any price. She has one child and does not want Trumper as a second. Trumper must be an adult in an adult relationship for it to work.

With the exception of Couth, Biggie and Tulpen are by far more attractive than any of the men in the novel. In contrast to Biggie, Tulpen, and Couth, all of the male characters are insecure and fail to accept life.

THEMATIC ISSUES

The fundamental theme of *The Water-Method Man* revolves around the family, its generational and sexual conflicts, and its connection to both the individual and the larger community. Fred Trumper grows up in a family of highly regulated order. His mother is simply "there" in the background, well-meaning but a ditherer who plays no decisive role. His father, a urologist—and thus a "professional man"—sets rules, makes decisions for everyone, and controls the family.

When Trumper is fifteen, he and Couth get the "clap" from Elsbeth Malkas; Dr. Trumper responds with puritanical rage and penicillin. When Trumper is twenty-eight, married to Sue "Biggie" Kunft, and himself a father, Dr. Trumper is equally outraged and responds with the same puritanical coldness, but without the penicillin (although Trumper does write and ask him to send some for his urinary tract problems). In both instances, Trumper's liaison with Elsbeth and his marriage to Biggie, the results of his sexual activities are somehow dirty, and certainly irresponsible, to Dr. Trumper.

What Dr. Trumper desires, of course, is to possess his family and rule it completely and forever. As the father, Dr. Trumper knows best. Biggie sees through him for not helping his son financially while he completes his Ph.D. Certainly, as a physician, he has the money to help his son, but his moral rigidity prevents his doing so. Dr. Trumper's smug self-righteousness and his failure to give assistance to his son go far in creating tensions between Biggie and Trumper. In short, Dr. Trumper deserts his son, just as Bogus deserts his.

Compared with Trumper's family, Biggie's appears generous and loving. At least the Kunfts accept both Biggie's pregnancy and Trumper. There is even humor in the Kunft household, something unthinkable in Trumper's family. Aunt Blackstone, who is quite deaf, asks Biggie's mother if Sue has put on weight. Biggie's mother responds by staring ahead "stonily," as Biggie replies, "I'm pregnant!" and adds, "But it's all right!" Trumper cries out, "Yes! It's all right!" Aunt Blackstone is right on target when she reminds the family, "Of course it is." She chides Biggie's "dumbstruck" mother with "*Gracious*, Hilda, is that any way to greet your daughter? I can remember *you* always put the old weight on and off, any time you pleased" (244).

To be sure, Hilda (somewhat like Trumper's mother) can be vapid, yet the Kunfts can find "graciousness" in a new family and a yet unborn child, just as Aunt Blackstone advises. Biggie later points out that her family helps her and Trumper with what little money they have. Dr. Edmund Trumper, who has plenty of money, does nothing.

Against this rather unpromising familial background, Trumper, Biggie, and Colm must make their own way. That they fail to do so as a family is not surprising. Biggie must work as an aide in the local hospital; Trumper must also work, in the University of Iowa language lab, where he meets Lydia Kindle, and at the football games, where he sells pennants and pins—with disastrous consequences. He loses the second job, and the first does not pay enough to sustain the family. He owes money; his electricity is cut off periodically. Occasionally he borrows money from Couth, with little or no hope of paying it back, but essentially Biggie is responsible for paying the bills.

Trumper is not much better at being a father than Dr. Trumper was. Trumper wants to control his son's every move as well, "to bring [Colm] up in some sort of simulated natural habitat—some kind of pasture or corral—rather than the gruesome real natural habitat itself, which seemed too unsafe" (157). When Couth asks, "You mean, sort of graze him, like a cow?" Trumper replies, "Cattle are *safe*, Couth, and they're *content*" (157). Couth reminds Trumper that "Cattle are cattle," a point on which Biggie agrees.

Both Trumper and Biggie are disappointed in the way their lives have turned out. Biggie misses skiing and the life of an athlete, and Trumper misses Merrill Overturf and a life of no responsibility. Trumper's response to disappointment is to cut and run; Biggie, in much more adult fashion, moves into the future.

Given the fact that Trumper evades his problems (his father among them), it is no wonder he cannot commit himself to having a family with Tulpen. As a result, she, like Biggie, must single-handedly create a life for herself and her child. It is only after Trumper "grows up" that he can have any kind of life with Tulpen and their baby, Merrill. Tulpen, the wiser of the two, says he owes her "nothing more than [his] straight, honest feelings. . . . If [he has] any" (365). For the first time, Trumper realizes that those feelings "were a long way down in a bog he'd been skirting for so long that now it seemed impossible to dive in and grope" (365). But this time he is willing to try.

Couth—and the young women—seem to know not only the importance of family but also what it requires: love, care, nurturance, and, perhaps above all, perseverance. Couth seems to manage all of these mostly by being there when needed, and by not obstructing the flow and rhythm of life itself. Indeed, he accepts life as it is, both welcoming and embracing it.

The theme of family may seem a "small matter," as a number of critics (even Irving himself) and Trumper point out, but Irving has not interwoven the Old Low Norse epic, "Akthelt and Gunnel," in his novel for nothing. In that dark, murderous, and grim poem, kingdoms rise and fall to rise again, all because of family matters. Cold fathers, unloving husbands, sexist men who treat women as objects literally lose their heads, to have them served on a platter, stuffed with eels!

At the end of Irving's novel, the young families, newly sorted out, meet in communal celebration on the old Norse holiday of Throgshafen. By merging "Akthelt and Gunnel" with the story of *The Water-Method Man*, Irving shows us how profoundly family is linked to the larger community and to life itself.

A PSYCHOANALYTICAL READING OF *THE WATER-METHOD MAN*

Irving wanted to write an "absolute" comedy, with a happy ending, and this he does with *The Water-Method Man*. The essence of the comedy is Oedipal, as it so often is in comedy, in which the father, the *senex iratus* (the old, raging man), is the blocking agent to the young man's desires.

A psychoanalytical reading of Trumper's character and situation can help to illuminate the meanings of the novel as a whole, including its comic structure. In 1905, Freud published his *Jokes and Their Relation to the Unconscious*. Simply put, Freud states that laughter occurs when energy is freed from keeping something forbidden under repression and away from consciousness. The two key terms here are "unconscious" and "repression." Freud's notion of the unconscious, that part of the mind beyond our consciousness that influences our actions, permeates his work. Repression is the "forgetting" or ignoring of unresolved conflicts, traumatic past events, or desires. Almost everything connected with the unconscious and repression, according to Freud, has to do in some way with our sexuality (Mitchell 5–74, passim).

In Trumper's case, it is easy to see that repression follows, at least to a certain extent, what Freud called the classic Oedipal situation (based on the Greek drama *Oedipus*): the infatuation with the mother figure, the rebellion of the son against the ogre-like father, the fear of punishment by castration for the crime—in thought or action, whether conscious or unconscious—of desiring the mother's favors and the father's death (Grotjahn 272–273).

In comedy, however, the Oedipal triangle of mother, father, and son is often played out in a slightly different way: "The son plays the role of the victorious father with sexual freedom and achievement, while the father is cast in the role of the frustrated onlooker" (Grotjahn 273). The rivalry between father and son often suggests the rivalry for the same girl, perhaps not literally but certainly psychologically. Indeed, the psychological alliance between the young protagonist's bride and the mother is either explicit or implicit.

Although Dr. Trumper does not seem to be a major character, his relationship with his son dominates the novel. Trumper's memories of his childhood and his father's disapproval of him are related to Trumper's doubts of himself. Moreover, Dr. Trumper's peremptory treatment of his wife and his dismissal of Biggie color Trumper's treatment of women. When Biggie gives her opinion to Trumper of their financial problems, she says: "It's your father, the prick" (67). But she could as easily be speaking of the reason for Bogus's failure to grow up.

Indeed, one might go so far as to say that the only bond between father and son *is* the penis. One of Trumper's strongest memories from his youth is of the time he and Couth "share" both Elsbeth Malkas and the clap. When Fred urinates "what felt like razor blades, bent bobby pins and ground glass," he screams so that his father, who is shaving, cuts his face. "Let me see that!" Dr. Trumper shouts (145). Fred's penis is always referred to by his father as "that" or "it"; sex is referred to as "being into it." The great irony, of course, rests in the fact that Trumper's difficulties, urinary and sexual, are in the area of his father's medical specialty. Dr. Trumper, as urologist or father, is hardly sympathetic.

Nor is he sympathetic when Fred returns from Austria to marry Biggie, who is pregnant. Biggie writes to Dr. Trumper: "What exactly is it you don't approve of? That I was pregnant? That Fred didn't wait to do things in the order *you* did them in?" (147). Although there is no evidence in the text that Biggie looks like Mrs. Trumper, it is clear that Biggie fills the role of the mother figure, perhaps even more so than Bogus's own mother, who seems to be no more than a submissive wife. And it is equally clear that Biggie is far more independent and threatening than Mrs. Trumper; Dr. Trumper keeps his wife in her "place" and never responds to Biggie.

Dr. Trumper wants his son to be a "professional man"; the implications here are extraordinary. Just how does one become a man—professionally? Dr. Trumper seems caught in a Freudian slip of his own. That is, he betrays unconsciously his own fears about what it means to be a man. At any rate, for Fred to please his father, he must unquestioningly follow Dr. Trumper's rules, which cover every aspect of life, including "that," "it," "what you're holding." A smug, self-righteous, and cold man, Dr. Trumper attempts to infantilize his son.

For Fred, what "that" gets into causes no end of pain. No wonder he is afraid of Sue "Biggie" Kunft, whose coming (*Zu-kunft*) threatens to dominate his life. When he sees her cleaning their house, he gapes at her "as if she were some animal, ugly and scary and able to eat me whole" (81). This image of the devouring (castrating) mother, with her "breasts flopping," is both ugly and horrific. Trumper exhibits similar fears of castration with Tulpen. In her apartment, the bed is surrounded by fish tanks, in which fish face the prospect of being eaten or drowning in the murky water; for Trumper, being with Tulpen is also like drowning.

Both Biggie and Tulpen are big-breasted women. Late in the novel, when Tulpen nurses Merrill, Trumper watches with erotic fascination. These mother figures are contrasted with Lydia Kindle, the overly slender, boyish figure, with sharp, "pointy" breasts, from whom he runs. She reminds him of young girls raped in the war. Trumper's fantasies of women, then, are linked to those of rape or of physical harm. His fear of women results in evasion and running from them. Eventually, the only woman he can have sex with is a prostitute; for money, Trumper can dominate her with neither responsibility nor consequence.

As Freud pointed out, the unresolved Oedipal conflict can also lead to latent or overt homosexuality. And in Trumper's case, he is most at ease with men his own age: Couth, Merrill (whose penis he handles as if it were Trumper's own!), Dante (his limo driver), the "faggot" he rescues in the bar, Ralph Packer, even the narcotics agents he becomes involved with. Merrill, the daredevil Trumper desires to be, seems to represent the "escape" from the tyrannical father with all his rules. Merrill is the "god"–father Trumper desires because Overturf expects nothing from him. Merrill seems to represent not only perfect freedom from rules and order but also escape from death at the last minute. The shock of Merrill's death forces Trumper to recognize that Merrill is an illusion, not a god at all. The irony that Merrill dies a watery death may escape the water-method man, Trumper, but it does not escape the reader.

Water figures in Trumper's two recurring dreams. One group of dreams is of heroes who always turn out to be Merrill; in those dreams, Merrill always escapes from a watery grave. He can swim. His second dream is equally, if not more, significant: "I'm in a duck blind in the New Hampshire salt marshes with my father. I am wondering how old I am; I don't have a gun, and when I stand on tiptoe, I can just reach my father's throat" (162). (We recall the dead duck that Trumper brings home to Biggie after his failed tryst with Lydia Kindle.) This dream of killing his father is juxtaposed with Trumper's waking "horror" of looking for a "real job," of "earning a living"—in short, of growing up to *be* his father, a professional man. The phrase "earning a living" is, to Trumper, "like those other obscene propositions offered on a men's room wall" (162).

Yet Trumper does "grow up." He has his operation and can give up being the water-method man. He finishes his Ph.D. and reconciles with his father; Trumper becomes "a professional man." The ending of Irving's novel is similar to that of a Shakespearean comedy: the young man replaces his father (or is reconciled with him), as the father nears the end of his life in failing health. Trumper establishes his own family, discarding, one hopes, many of the entrenched rules of his father. (Somehow, we feel that Tulpen will make sure of this.) Irving, like Shakespeare, includes as many people as possible in the final scene. It is a great social and festive ending, with all of the couples flinging open the windows of the house and greeting the morning of a new day with "Happy Throgshafen."

Irving is aware that the stuff of his comedy may be considered "small" matter. In fact, Irving does not believe this any more than we do. The struggle between the sexes and the generations is an old, yet continuing, story, with profound psychological and mythic import. Furthermore, Irving's comedy is played out against the iconography of modern wars: World Wars I (with reference to the zoo bust in which the animals are eaten) and II (the tank at the bottom of the Danube). In the background is a war not quite over, the Vietnam War, with all its social upheaval. In addition, Irving weaves the Old Low Norse epic "Akthelt and Gunnel" throughout his comedy. This epic explores precisely the same themes as *The Water-Method Man*, though using a different literary formula. The epic is also a watery tale in which fathers (two generations of them) attempt to control their sons and to have them grow up as "professional men." To do this, each father attempts to keep his wife in her place; he never trusts her. The epic is a story of family warfare, of sexual lusts, of castration, and of murder, on which the fate of nations hinges.

By including "Akthelt and Gunnel" in *The Water-Method Man*, Irving shows what happens when the same story is pushed to different extremes. Both are epic struggles; both, watery tales of transition and rebirth. In "Akthelt and Gunnel," we get a happy ending that we know is momentary. In *The Water-Method Man*, we can only hope the happy ending will last.

5

The 158-Pound Marriage
(1973)

Critics refer to *The 158-Pound Marriage*, John Irving's third novel, as his most bitter, with little of the humor found in his other works. Gabriel Miller finds at least some affirmation at the end of the novel when Severin Winter's "darker self is sublimated and he renews his connection with the more responsible part of his nature" (82), but most readers find the ending filled with ambiguities at best. *Marriage* remains one of Irving's quirkiest novels, with its trenchant look at society during a time of upheaval and flux in this country. In *Marriage*, Irving comments on John F. Kennedy's assassination, the first in a series of assassinations (180). The narrator in the novel attempts to explain to his wife how extraordinary such an act is, but his wife is only bewildered by it. Looking at the image of Jacqueline Kennedy in her naked grief makes "voyeurs" of us all, as the narrator points out; we suddenly "see" not only the violent power struggles underlying society but the very fragmentation of society itself. Irving writes his novel with that image in the background: the vacancy of her face represents the lack of any moral center in our century.

PLOT DEVELOPMENT

Irving begins *The 158-Pound Marriage* with two epigraphs, one from Ford Madox Ford's *The Good Soldier: A Tale of Passion* (1915), the other from John Hawkes's *The Blood Oranges* (1971). Both novels deal with the same topic as Irving's: spouse-swapping. Ford's novel deals with the moral collapse of Europe and America during World War I, whereas Hawkes's work concerns itself with imagination and art; Irving attempts to interweave both themes in *Marriage*. The quotations Irving uses as epigraphs are telling in their undertones of hostility, anger, and violence.

Irving's novel does not follow Ford's or Hawkes's work exactly, but there are certain similarities worthy of note. Each of the three novelists wrote in a time of near social collapse (Ford, for example, wrote his novel within the shadow of war). The corrosion of moral values, of the social fabric itself, is felt in all three. Ford's novel, like Irving's, uses a first-person narrator (the American, John Dowell—his name is a pun) who is also an ambiguous, "unreliable narrator."

Yet, even as Irving acknowledges his literary indebtedness, his novel remains singularly his own. The plot in *Marriage* is both simple and straightforwardly linear. To be sure, there are several flashbacks delineating the lives of the four major characters, but *Marriage* lacks the narrative loops and extended comic riffs to be found in Irving's other works. *The 158-Pound Marriage* is the story of two couples, the narrator (who is never named) and his wife Utchka (called Utch), and Severin Winter and his wife, Edith, who decide to swap spouses in order, ostensibly, to regain sexual excitement and romance in their lives. Both the narrator and Severin teach at a New England university: the narrator, a history professor and a writer of historical novels; Severin, a professor of German and the wrestling coach. Their wives stay at home and care for their children.

Edith, however, attempts to be a writer. Indeed, writing is what draws the narrator and Edith together. Severin and Utch share their pasts. Both Austrians, they were undoubtedly saved from death in World War II by their mothers; they also fell in love with and married Americans and came to the United States. Each couple has two children: the Winters, two girls; the narrator and Utch, two boys. The couples agree to swap spouses under certain rules and conditions, of which the most important is that no one gets hurt, especially the children.

As usually happens in such situations, of course, someone—or more—does get hurt, in this case the Winters' two children, who are injured in a freak accident while bathing. Utch, too, gets hurt because she has the misfortune of falling in love with Severin. In both cases, the "injuries" are caused by neglect. When the Winter children are hurt by a sliding glass shower door that falls and shatters upon them, the two sets of parents are dining together, basically ignoring everything outside of themselves. The Winters had known for some time that the glass door could break at any moment, as did the narrator, who had used the shower with Edith.

The children's injuries highlight the irresponsibility and selfishness of the adults over the fragility and vulnerability of the children. Although the children are not fatally or even seriously injured, the bathroom and their bodies are covered in blood; the room looks like a "war zone." This event brings to an end the "quaternion" and brings to the surface Utch's deep hurt in her loss of Severin. Like the children, Utch and her feelings have been neglected; no one has paid any attention to her, as Severin points out.

Because Utch cannot find any comfort in her marriage, she leaves her husband and takes their children with her to Vienna, the scene of her growing up. The narrator, who has been blind to his wife's and children's needs all along, finally recognizes the depth of his loss and at the end of the novel sets out for Vienna, hoping to reconcile with his family.

Severin, who has had doubts all along concerning the spouse-swapping, must reconcile with Edith. As she says, he has tried to force his life upon her while denying her any life of her own. They, too, return to Vienna, in an attempt to recapture the love they had for each other when they first met.

Although on the surface the plot seems to suggest a fall from grace, or at least from good sense, and a regaining of romance, the novel's tone is dark. The hoped-for eroticism and sensuality of the spouse-swapping are undermined at every turn by furtiveness, smugness, and often downright nastiness. A good bit of the tonal discordance comes from the first-person narration. The narrator remains ambivalent, ambiguous. Certainly he is shallow, always thinking only of himself. Utch cries out at one point, "How could you have let this happen to me? . . . You weren't looking out for me! You weren't even thinking about me!" (215).

The narrator misreads others. He wasn't "thinking" about Utch because he saw her as self-sufficient. He calls Utch a "carnival" figure, which is clearly not borne out by the evidence. He cannot see her suffering because he believes only Edith suffers terribly at the end of the spouse-swapping, that is, at the end of her trysts with him. He is wrong about Edith (as well as about Utch), for Edith makes it clear that she never loved him. In addition, Edith catches the narrator unaware when she has a novel published. The narrator is also blind to his own failings, even as he speaks of them: "I knew once again that I knew nothing"

(254). His blindness and his lack of knowledge make him a highly unreliable narrator.

The narrator's unreliability proves problematic. Because everything is
seen through the narrator's eye/I, we are forced to rely on him. As Gabriel Miller notes, "Although his [the narrator's] narrative continually
implies that all essential information has been included, the faultiness of
his perceptions makes of his tale-telling a complex and possibly decep-
tive business" (72). A further problem has to do with the character of
the narrator: not only is he opaque to us, but he is also unlikable and
often despicable. Further, his telling of the tale keeps us at a distance;
the present-time story of the spouse-swapping is told in a self-
consciously "literary" fashion. The novel comes to life only in the narrator's recounting of the past, the history of the characters. Perhaps this
befits the narrator's profession as a historical novelist. Although he
comes close to breathing life into the history of the characters, he fails
to learn much from their history or to carry over their past lives into the
present.

The forward action of the plot is complicated by flashbacks to the
couples' pasts. Indeed, the flashbacks threaten at times to take over the
central plot. Severin and Utch were born at the time of the Austrian
Anschluss, and both were saved from the war. Perhaps the horrors they
faced cause them to perceive the dangers and risks of the spouse-
swapping. Although it is largely Severin who doubts the quaternion will
"work," Utch also is aware of the "terrible trouble" they are in (215).
Edith and the narrator have no such fears, possibly because their early
lives were privileged and protected.

Severin's father had been an artist; his mother, Katrina, a struggling
and mediocre actress who often modeled in erotic poses for her husband.
When she discovers she is pregnant, her husband sends her to England,
along with a number of paintings of her. Thus, Severin, ensconced in his
mother's womb, is saved from the horrors of the war; his father disappears as the result of war. Katrina Winter finds work as a model on the
basis of the paintings, which turn out to be her economic salvation. When
the war is over, mother and son return to Vienna and take up residence
with a motley, bohemian group that includes an older woman, possibly
a friend of Katrina and surely Severin's one-time lover. There are also
two so-called bodyguards, former Olympic wrestlers and Severin's wrestling coaches, who act as his surrogate fathers.

Edith, who comes from a well-to-do patrician family, meets Severin
when her mother, who works for the Museum of Modern Art, sends her

to him to buy some of his father's paintings. Severin and Edith have a passionate affair, marry, and return to the United States. They bring with them the erotic paintings of Severin's mother, to whom he obviously is still attached.

Similarly, Utch is a child of World War II, and her story is even more horrifying than Severin's. Her parents own a farm in Austria, and her father is killed by the Nazis as a suspected munitions saboteur. Her mother hopes to save Utch by hiding her in the womb of a dead cow. Village men come to the farm and rape and kill her mother; Utch patiently remains in the belly of the cow until she is "delivered" into the hands of a Russian captain named Kudashvili. He takes her to Vienna, educates her (she becomes a Russian translator), and protects her by hiring one of the Benno Blum gang as a bodyguard (the Blum gang appeared as thugs in Irving's first novel, *Setting Free the Bears*).

Utch is a university student who meets the narrator when he goes to Vienna to study and write on Pieter Brueghel's *The Battle Between Carnival and Lent*. Utch, who becomes his tour guide, just as Severin was Edith's guide, falls in love with the narrator; they have a tempestuous affair, marry, and return to the United States.

During the time Utch and the narrator are in Vienna, the narrator shares the men's room with two students, former lovers of Utch. The scenes in the men's room are the few truly comic ones in the novel, but they also serve an important purpose. They are displays of male competition, vanity, and sexual power. The metaphoric wrestling for position, the smugness of sexual success, reiterate major themes in the novel. It is also in the men's room that Utch's bodyguard, the sinister and mysterious man with a hole in his cheek, leaves the narrator with a warning that he will always be watching him to see that he looks after Utch. Although the narrator promises to care for her, he fails to do so.

The histories of Severin and Utch help us to understand the characters' motivations, perhaps, but more to the point, they reflect the collapse of moral and social values both during the war and in the postwar years. The spouse-swapping does nothing to restore those values. The best we can say at the end of the novel is that the Winters remain together, although what sort of marriage they have is questionable. The narrator is set to leave for Vienna to reconcile with Utch; the question is whether she will have him. When Utch left him, she took his passport so that he could not follow her; later she sends it back to him. The narrator reads this as a sign that they will get back together, but readers cannot be so sure. The narrator has been wrong before.

SETTING

There are two main settings for *Marriage*: a university campus and
town in New England, and Vienna, where each of the characters met his
or her spouse in the past, and where all of them will return at the close
of the novel. There is also one brief interlude on Cape Cod. In the New
England and Vienna settings, space is claustrophobic, reinforcing the
self-centeredness of the couples. In both settings, the bedroom is often
the focus, appropriate to a novel that makes voyeurs of its readers. If we
reach back to the beginning of the pasts of Severin and Utch, of course,
space is confined to the womb; we wait for their birth into the world.

In the New England setting, occasional moves into the kitchen or dining area, as well as the bathroom, underscore potential changes in character and/or plot direction. In addition to these rooms, of utmost
importance is the university wrestling room with a long, dark tunnel
leading into it and to the adjacent pool room. The wrestling space functions metaphorically to help delineate character and to emphasize thematic issues. Although the space of the wrestling room is akin to that of
the womb, rebirth never seems to occur there.

The houses—they are not homes—of the couples are interchangeable,
as are the spouses. Interestingly, but perhaps not surprisingly, the men
are the ones who swap not only their wives but also their bedrooms.
That is, the women wait in their houses; the men circulate between them
(the proximity of the houses affords convenience to this spouse-
swapping). Within the rooms, the emphasis is on touch, taste, sight, and
smell. Scenes in the bedroom and bathroom titillate; we see bits and
pieces of the room and of the bodies in them.

When Edith and the narrator meet for sex at the Winters' house, they
shower first and then have sex in the shower, before going into the bedroom for more sex. The bed is surrounded by candles, apparently to
evoke romance. They litter the house with ashtrays and wineglasses,
leaving a trail to the bed. Their bodies suggest a literary romanticization;
both Edith and the narrator are tall, thin, ascetic-looking. One gets the
feeling that their sexual relations are also literary encounters.

On one of the evenings the narrator spends with Edith, the Winters'
daughter Dorabella, who has had a bad dream, comes into the bedroom.
The narrator must hide under the covers to prevent the child from seeing
that it is not her father in bed. Edith mistakenly calls the child Fiordiligi,
the name of the other daughter, an error she consistently makes. Dora-

bella corrects her mother and notices that a shirt in the bedroom is "not Daddy's shirt, is it?" (128). When told that "Daddy traded something for it," Dorabella asks, "What did he trade?" (128). Her question to her mother goes unanswered, but the narrator remembers the "silence." This little scene poignantly marks not only the adults' failure to face the truth about their spouse-swapping but also the failure to think of their children. As the narrator says, "My own children I hardly remember at all, and I used to know them quite well. . . . I forgot the children, but I remember the silence" (128).

At the narrator's house, Utch and Severin leave the bedroom in total disarray. The pillows end up on the floor, the mattress is askew, clothes are flung about. Crumbs and apple cores litter the bed and room, something the narrator hates, just as Severin despises the ashtrays left about his house. Severin's and Utch's bodies seem to match the physical mischief caused in the bedroom. Their bodies are short, compact, powerful. Severin works out with the "boys" he coaches; Utch, also physically strong, can lift adults, even her husband.

The significance of bedrooms is reiterated in the house owned by Edith's mother; this house, on the Cape, is where the couples spend a "holiday," leaving the children behind with sitters. Severin had renamed all of the rooms, changing the names from colors (Green, Master Red, Lady Yellow) to the "Wet Dream Room," the "Hot and Cold Flashes Room," the "Come If You Can Room," the "Great Green Wrenching Orgasm Room," the most private of the rooms. Severin notes that the highest number of orgasms takes place in this room despite the fact that a daughter finds it difficult to have orgasms under her mother's roof. This room also has a brass bed that tends to fall apart under the least activity.

As a matter of fact, it does fall apart with the narrator and Edith in it, as they pretend (for Severin's benefit) to be having wild and multiple orgasms. The result is that the couples end up sleeping with their mates that night: Utch and the narrator in the "Come If You Can Room" (she is sick from too much wine), and Edith and Severin in the "Hot and Cold Flashes Room."

Of equal importance is the wrestling room at the university. At least three crucial scenes—two with Severin and one with the narrator—take place here. The "old cage" of a wrestling room, all that remains of the old gym, is in a new building of "slick concrete and glass." Severin Winter "love[s] the building" (74) and feels at home in it. To the narrator, the wrestling room looks "like a crematorium for athletes" (74) and smells "like a greenhouse." It matches Severin's "machine-steady gaze

... as lifeless as the building'' (211). The cage is womblike, heated to "over 100 degrees" by the sun shining through its ivy-laced skylight. The mats become "liquid ... [a] kind of liquid plastic" (93). The cage is connected to the rest of the gym by a long, dark tunnel through which Severin guides his "boys," the drugged-looking wrestlers who emerge into the light of the cage in a perverse ritualistic birth before matches.

In this cage, Severin has an affair with the maimed Audrey Cannon, which in turn gives "leverage" to Edith and leads directly to the spouse-swapping in order to "even" things up in the Winters' marriage. In addition, Severin and Utch engage in a sexual wrestling match in the cage that leads, in part, to Edith's attempt to seduce George James Bender, Severin's best wrestler, before a championship match. He loses the match because he lacks "focus," and Severin resigns as wrestling coach. The reconciliation between Severin and Edith also takes place in the cage— or the adjacent pool—an event the narrator and Utch witness, which leads to Utch and the boys leaving for Vienna. The narrator and Utch also have sex in the cage shortly after the halt in the spouse-swapping, which halted Utch's ability to have an orgasm. In the cage, Utch becomes orgasmic with her husband, but the narrator "shrivel[s] and completely los[es] contact" with her (237). As Utch watches her husband jealously shrink from her, she reminds him, "you can spoil anything you've made up your mind to" (237).

Gabriel Miller perceives Irving's reliance on wrestling metaphors, and especially his use of the cage-space of the wrestling room, as a serious weakness in the novel (86). But wrestling as metaphor is, as much as the Brueghel painting *The Battle Between Carnival and Lent*, a key to the meanings and themes of the novel.

CHARACTER DEVELOPMENT

Character development is problematic in *The 158-Pound Marriage* because nearly all events and commentary come from the first-person narrator. Not only is he biased, but he often misses the mark in his judgment of others—even of himself—and in his reading of situations. His most common refrain, "I knew once again that I knew nothing," punctuates the novel at critical points, perhaps nowhere more tellingly than near the end. The narrator, a historian with an eye for details, misses the meanings of events. He lacks "wide-angle" vision and so cannot see the broad picture; his myopic focus is misleading at best, obscuring at worst.

Irving said of the characters: "I felt in *The 158-Pound Marriage* as if I were writing about people I didn't like, especially the narrator" (Reilly, *Understanding John Irving* 50). The narrator is not accepted as a scholar at the university where he teaches; he also is not accepted by his father, a retired Harvard professor. His mother is his greatest fan and, unlike her husband, reads all of her son's work and praises it indiscriminately. Although the narrator feels no close attachment to his father, whom he still calls "Sir," nonetheless they are quite similar; both are quick to make judgments, are detached, and are totally self-absorbed. Even though the narrator may love Utch and his two sons, he has at various times quickly forgotten them. Even before the spouse-swapping, he had numerous affairs, all meaning "nothing," where "no-one" got hurt. He is surprised to learn that Utch knew about these affairs all along.

The narrator's arrogance and vanity color his relationship with Edith. His primary attraction to her stems from the fact that he can "help" her with her writing. He expresses astonishment and chagrin when he discovers that she has published a novel after their breakup. The unspoken question is how she could have done so without his help. Worse, he cannot believe Edith never loved him, even though she states as much and provides evidence of her love for Severin.

By the end of the novel Utch, too, makes it clear that she is at best ambivalent about the narrator. Indeed, the only time the narrator shows the potential to break free of his self-absorption is after Utch and the boys leave him. He begins to feel a sense of loss; he sleeps with Utch's slip clutched to him, then takes to wearing it. He dresses the dining-room chairs in the boys' jackets to create the illusion that the family is still together. Finally, after his father's death, and at the behest of his mother, the narrator leaves for Vienna to reconcile with Utch; he also goes to Vienna to work on his Brueghel book again. He thinks of the history of Vienna, especially of its numerous treaties, "truces" that "run long and deep" (254).

Irving loads these lines with irony. His first novel, *Setting Free the Bears*, attests to the corruption and brokenness of Austrian treaties. Moreover, the narrator has consistently misread the Brueghel painting, viewing it myopically and finding in it a too-neat dichotomy between license and piety. In addition, the narrator's decision to go to Vienna follows directly from his refrain that he "knew nothing." Arrogant as ever, he claims that if he sees Edith and Severin, who are also in Vienna, dining with another couple, he will understand that "other couple" instantly and will warn them, "Watch out." The narrator also remains vindictive and petty.

Utch had written that she saw Edith eating a pastry; the narrator "hope[s] she gets fat" (255). We can imagine the kind of "treaties" to be made in Vienna.

The ambiguities surrounding the narrator go far to cloud our reading of the other characters in the novel as well. Severin Winter's name gives some notion of his character: of his coldness and self-containment, and of his ability to sever his relationships with others. Harter and Thompson, and Miller have made much of his obsession with his children and his "androgynous" character (he cooks; the narrator says he really desires to be a "wife," though only in the most stereotypical ways). Critics also perceive in Winter the capacity to change and to wrestle with hard moral questions.

In fact, however unlike Severin and the narrator are physically, they are very much alike mentally and emotionally. Severin is also a university professor (of German) and is equally an academic nonentity, though it seemingly does not matter to him. His wrestlers fill his classes, and his repeated question to them, "Wie geht's?" is always answered "Gut." As the wrestling coach, Severin seems also to be mediocre at best.

Although Severin claims to be reluctant to engage in spouse-swapping, he is the one who sets it up. Like the narrator, Winter has had an affair, although it meant "something"; he claims to have loved Audrey Cannon. Winter arranges the spouse-swapping to "even" things up in his marriage. When Edith finds out about Audrey, the knowledge gives her "power" over her husband. Severin is out to make things "equal" between them. There are hard moral questions here, but they are posed to the reader and totally ignored by Severin.

Critics (Harter and Thompson 67, for example) like to point out that a saving grace for Severin is his love—obsession—for his children; but here, too, Severin is similar to the narrator. Winter does not think of his children when he is meeting Audrey Cannon in the wrestling room, nor when he is on "holiday" with Edith, Utch, and the narrator. The scene in which the narrator, Edith, and Utch find Severin in a woman's dressing gown, sleeping peacefully with all of the children (132), is often used as evidence of Severin's androgyny and of his great care for the children, but the gap between this "picture" and the actions and the events in the novel is too great for us to bridge. It is important to keep in mind that Severin left "one of the warm women, grabbing the nearest garment handy," and fell among the children "like a benign bomb" that had fallen "through the roof of an elementary school" (132). It is impossible here to transform Severin into a caring, nurturing figure, and Irving deflates the very idea by his combination of *"benign bomb"* and "elementary school." Severin cares for his children only when he hears them crying or when he fears losing them. When he discovers his children in the bathtub filled with blood, when his children are cut by shattering glass—surely a metaphor for the shattering of family—then Severin truly cares for his daughters.

Severin and Edith bring the spouse-swapping to a close, but even their manner of doing this is hardly to be commended. Severin tries to control Edith by forcing her to attend the championship wrestling matches because he is afraid that she might see the narrator if left on her own; Edith "equalizes" matters by attempting to seduce George Bender, Severin's star wrestler. Severin also is unspeakably cruel in his treatment of Utch, from the wrestling scene with her in the cage to the ending of their relationship.

Severin's desire to control relationships, especially those with women, may have something to do with his erotic attachment to his mother. His mother had been a rather unsuccessful actress, but a more successful model, who apparently was quite beautiful. In fact, one can readily see that Severin's love for Audrey Cannon, who also is beautiful, is in some way connected to his love for his mother. Paintings of his mother, naked and in various "near-pornographic" poses, surround Severin and Edith's bed. One of the paintings, graphically described, shows his mother masturbating. This image of isolated and closed sex, which represents his mother as a "model," seems to be associated with her son's own detachment and coldness; Severin's desire to control women may be linked to his belief that women do not need men to be sexually stimulated and satisfied.

Spouse-swapping may not be new to the Winters; they apparently had engaged in such a quaternion with another couple, the Ullmans. Did that "holiday," as Severin likes to call such an arrangement, also end badly, with the women being bruised, as Edith is literally and Utch, metaphorically? The Winters' decision to return to Vienna is as mixed in motivation as the narrator's. They ask for Utch's address: Severin hopes to tell Utch that she should return to her husband, but the narrator does not trust him. The reader does not, either.

Edith is not much more likable than Severin. Because he has had an affair with Audrey, she threatens to have an affair, too. She also threatens not to let him see the children. She is quite willing to enter into a spouse-swapping arrangement, and she also agrees to call it off because of the injuries to the children. She is cruel at times to both the narrator and Utch.

It is clear, however, that Edith loves Severin—or at least desires to possess him—and she remains loyal to him. Although Harter and Thompson believe she is a character who grows throughout the novel, most readers would disagree. To be sure, Edith can play Severin's own game; she does not go into the wrestling room until late in the novel, but she knows how to get there and to Severin: through George Bender. Edith notes that she intended to show Severin that he could not push his life onto her without allowing her the same freedom. Utch sees very clearly what Edith is doing: "She hit him close to home." Her being able to "beat" Severin does not especially serve to show Edith's "growth" as a character.

Although it can be claimed that Edith asserts herself—at last—with Severin, her assertion is minimal. She stays with him, aware that he does not trust her; and she does not leave him after he strikes her with the book she has written. Her willingness to go with Severin to Vienna may reveal a desire to begin again—but to begin what? It is highly unlikely that the Winters wish to see Utch again because of some bond of friendship, and guilt does not seem characteristic of them. Throughout the relationship of the quarternion, even though Edith and Utch "share" conversations over the phone, they remain at a wary distance from each other. The only time we see them in (very) close proximity is when they engage in sex with one another, and that encounter is quickly taken over by the narrator and Severin. When the quaternion ends, Edith and Utch go into the bedroom, shutting out the men; although we do not see this scene, the narrator tells us that the two women end up crying. Presumably they comfort each other: "The language they were speaking was stranger than English or German" (208). Because as readers we do not have access to this scene except through the narrator's eyes, it is impossible to tell how close these women are.

Whereas Edith is intelligent and aware of events, Utch comes across as more perceptive, as one who experiences relationships more deeply. She is certainly the most sympathetic of all the characters. At one time or another, nearly everyone treats Utch cruelly. Gabriel Miller says of her, "Things seem to happen to her—she mostly gets drunk and falls asleep—though she does rouse herself to fall in love with Severin Winter" (83). Her passivity is, of course, consistent with her past, when her mother saved her from rape and death by placing her in the womb of the cow, to be "born" into the hands of Captain Kudashvili. Her history has taught her "patience." Miller, like the narrator, Severin, and even Edith, perceives her as bovine (Severin calls her "a poor cow-like creature" [152]).

Yet Utch is not unintelligent. She sees that her husband is totally self-absorbed. She also understands both Severin and Edith far better than the narrator does. The fact that she is capable of falling in love marks her as different from the other three. (Although Severin claims to have loved Audrey Cannon, he leaves her quickly enough.) Utch genuinely cares for her children, and takes them with her to Vienna. Also, smartly, she takes her husband's passport so that he cannot follow her.

That Utch is unashamedly physical is undeniable; as she says, she likes bodies, all sorts of bodies. She is devastated when Severin breaks off the relationship, and she discovers she cannot have an orgasm. She participates in and seems to enjoy fully the wrestling match with Severin, a match in which she holds her own for a time. Yet she is not "Carnival all the way," as the narrator says. When the narrator tries to use some "pop" psychology on her, she points out that "Psychology is better suited for plants." Also, when the narrator persuades Utch to marry him, telling her she "would always be safe" with him, she answers, "I'm going to live with you, yes! . . . But I'm not going to be guarded by you" (175).

At the end of the novel, Utch recognizes that the couples were never friends; they swapped spouses simply for sex (214). She also understands that the spouse-swapping has led to "terrible trouble" for them. And when her husband takes Utch to the wrestling room to reveal, as he thinks, Severin's betrayal of Utch and a return to Audrey Cannon (or someone like her), she leaves him.

The narrator, when he decides to follow Utch to Vienna, thinks again of the Brueghel painting *The Battle Between Carnival and Lent*; Irving also wants his readers to think of the painting but not to attempt, like the narrator, to locate too precisely the novel's characters in Brueghel's world. Although there are some general associations to be made, they do not always hold true. Severin seems to belong with those on the side of Lent—but not completely, not when on "holiday." Utch may be Carnival, but not "all the way." Where does Edith, who ultimately feels the blow of her husband, belong? In the farce *The Ugly Bride*? The narrator identifies with the burgher, but this is his elitist arrogance talking. Irving is aware that there is little merit in either Carnival or Lent, in and of itself. There is more than enough folly in both camps.

THEMATIC ISSUES

There are at least two major themes in *The 158-Pound Marriage*, and they are intertwined: one has to do with marriage and family; the other, with power or leverage. Both themes raise moral questions as evidenced in Brueghel's painting concerning Carnival and Lent, which hangs in the narrator's kitchen.

Marriage and the family seem to exist within a vacuum in this novel. Utch and Severin were orphaned by the war; though they have had bodyguards looking after them, they have no extended family to sustain them. Edith and the narrator might as well be orphaned for all that their parents seem to care about their marriages. The children of both couples appear to provide little focus in their lives except when there is the threat of their loss. The professions of the men offer an outlet for their energies only in part, and they apparently derive little satisfaction from their jobs. Severin may feel at "home" in the wrestling cage, but he easily gives it up.

Marriage seems tedious, yet comfortable. Severin says his children provide all the danger and excitement he requires, and this proves, ironically, to be so. Nonetheless, these couples enter into spouse-swapping to inject both danger and excitement into their lives. They thrill to something forbidden, as the world of the couples quickly becomes one of the flesh—Carnival—a holiday, apart from ordinary time. Irving, like Ford Madox Ford and John Hawkes before him, not only depicts characters empty and shallow for the most part, but he places them in a world lacking any moral center. Accident—the Winter children escape serious injury—not moral compunction, causes the end of the spouse-swapping. We have little difficulty believing that after a time the Winters, at least, will enter into such an arrangement again. The moral questions the characters need to wrestle with are left unattended. Instead, the couples wrestle with each other, for sexual satisfaction and for "leverage."

As Edith tells Severin after she discovers his affair with Audrey Cannon, "But now I've got this leverage on you" (204). And even though Edith says she will use it, "and then it will be gone," we don't quite believe her. With the possible exception of Utch, all of the characters attempt to get leverage. The narrator wants leverage over Severin, and vice versa, just as Severin hopes to regain his power over Edith—and over everyone else.

Severin tries to convince the narrator that the spouse-swapping never would have occurred if Edith had not found out about Audrey Cannon. Even within the foursome, Severin claims leverage: it was his responsibility, his decision to begin and end the spouse-swapping. As he tells Edith, she will never gain power over him again; they will always be equal from now on. Edith hits the mark when she asks sarcastically whether she is therefore to believe that he will never sleep with anyone other than her again. Severin's answer, "No, never," (206) is no more believed by Edith than by us. To ensure his viewpoint, to maintain "leverage," Severin must hit—and make—the mark: "A mark the color of a plum stretched Edith's skin tight over one cheek and tugged one eye half-closed; her bruise was the size of a good novel" (206–207)—her own, it turns out.

Marriage, in this novel at any rate, is not based on love but on lust for leverage. The narrator enters into the relationship because he hopes to rekindle the lust he once felt for Utch. As he becomes more involved in the spouse-swapping, he identifies more closely with the rich burgher in Brueghel's painting; the burgher, too, believes in leverage, perhaps that his alms to the poor will gain him access to heaven. The burgher is on the "side" of Lent, of piety, but it is a false piety, as false as the narrator's belief that somehow he perceives the "truth" about the Winters and Utch. Until the narrator can perceive his own arrogance and self-deceptions, he remains as blind as some of Brueghel's beggars and "good" burghers.

GAME THEORY: A READING OF *THE 158-POUND MARRIAGE*

The title of Irving's novel, as Edward C. Reilly notes, refers to the 158-pound weight class for Severin and George James Bender (*Understanding John Irving* 56). Reilly also points out that seven of the ten chapters derive their titles from wrestling as a metaphor linked to birth, possible rebirth, and sexuality. For Irving, wrestling represents not only sport but also moral conflict. Irving's driving insistence on wrestling in this novel is matched by his use of Brueghel's *The Battle Between Carnival and Lent*, painted in the sixteenth century. Brueghel's great painting depicts a Flemish village festival filled with "pleye and sporte," as well as with somber reminders of pain and suffering.

The meanings of Irving's use of "pleye and sporte," both in wrestling and in Brueghel's painting, may be better understood through game theory. Irving appears to be highly knowledgeable of the concepts of "pleye" and "game" in medieval and Renaissance terms and represents wrestling as such, at least until the championship wrestling meet in which George Bender is to star. Johan Huizinga, in his landmark *Homo Ludens* (1938), describes play as freedom and separateness from social constrictions, yet paradoxically regulated with certain rules or conditions. For Huizinga, play could be competition for something and/or a representation of something (74). In the Middle Ages, Huizinga notes, play was closely related to the spiritual: the use of ritual space, the motions of grace, the creation of festival time, for example. One sees evidence of these aspects, of course, in Brueghel's painting and in *The 158-Pound Marriage*: in the wrestling cage, in the long, darkened tunnel leading to the light, and in the procession of hooded wrestlers who make their way there.

In one of the most recent and interesting comments on game theory, Jacques Ehrmann argues that we "play" our reality, our work, our religion. We play for excitement and joy, for creativity, for control, out of fear. Play relocates and redistributes "*immediate* satisfaction of needs and desires" (41, 44). There is little doubt that the spouse-swapping in *Marriage* takes place for the excitement the participants hope to generate among themselves. Severin and the narrator, at least, also play for control, which in turn is profoundly linked to male needs and desires.

Wrestling, as a game or sport, has to do with leverage. Its terminology centers on position, focus, throwing down, the riding and the pinning of one's opponent. In short, wrestling is about control, gaining the upper hand; it is a perfect metaphor for power play, for one-upmanship. In wrestling, position is all. The coach must show or demonstrate the control and positions necessary to win. In Irving's novel, if Severin has any reservations about wrestling—or spouse-swapping—they have to do with his coaching ability. When he believes he has failed, as a coach, to control either game, it is over. Both spouse-swapping and wrestling merge, first in Severin's wrestling match with Utch, and finally in Edith's seduction of George James Bender. The game gets away from Severin and, as a result, he quits as wrestling coach and hits Edith with her book.

Just as wrestling is about leverage, at least for Severin and Edith, so, too, are sexual relationships. Severin's affair with Audrey Cannon may have given him some pleasurable leverage over Edith, but when she discovers he has been sleeping with Audrey, she gains leverage, as she points out to him. Although she claims not to "like having it any better than [he does]," Edith's actions—and Severin's—proclaim the opposite.

Leverage is clearly power, and all of the characters, except possibly Utch, attempt to gain it. Edward Reilly's contention that Severin and Edith's "genuine love for each other" stops the (wrestling) match seems wishful thinking. The match for them ends in a "draw" and only for the time being.

In Irving's novel, leverage over one's spouse is not the only power sought, however. Of equal, if not more, importance is "the fancy footwork" between Severin and the narrator, as each looks for the opening to "pin" the other. The narrator, who "despises" Severin's use of wrestling terms, is quick to rush, with Utch, to the wrestling room to expose Severin as a liar and a cheat; to pin him at last. As it turns out, Severin is in the pool with Edith, and the narrator fails to gain leverage over Severin, losing Utch in the bargain.

Irving's novel, in fact, paints a dismal picture of such leverage as a "boy's own" sport. Severin may do the cooking, may wear Edith's dressing gown, may wish to be a "wife," but he is most at home in the gym, leading his "boys" through the dark tunnel to the "light" of the game that counts: power. That he does not consider Edith's learning this game and playing it as well as or better than he, leads to Severin's resigning as coach. If George James Bender loses his "focus" or concentration because of Edith, then so does Severin.

The narrator also seeks leverage over Edith and Severin, as well as Utch. Indeed, the narrator has always believed he has leverage over Edith in terms of his writing. She, after all, is merely a beginning writer, whereas he has a publication record. The narrator's astonishment is genuine when he learns Edith not only does not need him for her writing, she may even be a better writer.

Both the narrator and Severin wrestle for power right from the beginning of the spouse-swapping. Each attempts to gain leverage over the other in petty ways. Severin makes an absolute mess of the narrator's house and takes food into bed, knowing the narrator hates it. The narrator is equally childish; he smokes and leaves full ashtrays in Severin's house. He also overstays his time allotted with Edith. At the end of the novel, both men continue to strive for leverage: Severin asks for Utch's address; the narrator provides the address of a church.

Of all the characters, Utch is the only one who seems not to care about leverage (with the possible exception of her sexual wrestling with Severin, and she is aware she has no hope of pinning him). She knows that her husband has had affairs, but she does nothing to "equalize" the situation. She participates in the spouse-swapping, perhaps out of inertia, perhaps for excitement; we recall that she likes bodies. Everyone dismisses, ignores, or mistreats her, and although she feels these hurts, she does not retaliate except in one telling action, an action that demonstrates her keen perception of what the spouse-swapping is all about. She cuts the crotch out of her husband's underwear. Utch sees the insane competitiveness between the men and their desire for control. She does more than cut up her husband's underwear; she leaves him.

The 158-Pound Marriage might be read as a lightweight, albeit hard-edged, novel if it were not for Utch—and Brueghel's painting *The Battle Between Carnival and Lent*. References to it reinforce the ambiguities and the moral questions of Irving's novel. The narrator has a copy of Brueghel's painting hanging in his kitchen and moves "into" the painter's world to escape his own. He does this particularly when Utch describes in great detail her "wrestling match" with Severin at the gym. The narrator identifies with the rich burgher because he has power, or so the narrator believes, in the medieval town Brueghel depicts. The narrator desires to see himself as both powerful and charitable—the burgher gives alms to a beggar in the shadow of the church—and in a morally superior position.

Brueghel's painting depicts a world seemingly split in two: on one side, Lent, with pious countrymen drinking plain water and eating bread and fish; on the other side, Carnival, a gross, fat man astride a wine barrel. To the right of Lent, one sees penitents coming from church, some of them giving alms to the diseased, the maimed, the poor. On the right, in addition to the church there are numerous Christian symbols, bread (in the wafer form) and fish.

To the left of Carnival are also beggars, totally ignored by the carousers and gamesters. In front of the Inn of the Blue Boat, actors play out a farce called *The Ugly Bride*. In the window of the inn a couple kisses. Also near the inn, gamesters play at dice. The inn lacks the strength and bulk of the church. Yet we see on the left of the painting the same symbols as those on the right, wafers of bread and, whatever we might wish to make of it, wine.

Brueghel does not, apparently, see the world as neatly binary. Almost in the center of the painting are industrious women scrubbing windows, cooking food, tending children. In the upper right, coming out of the church, are folk poorer than the burgher, carrying their own chairs. But in which direction are they headed? Diagonally to these folk, games spill over to the side of Lent: young women "guessing which hand," people "whipping tops" and playing marbles. In short, we see human beings indulging in play of great variety. On the so-called "pious" or "good" and "right" side of the painting, a fishwife engages in her favorite sport: the business of making money. Capitalizing on Lent, she hustles her fish to a throng of customers.

Dividing the halves of the painting are a young bride and groom who march up the painting behind a motley-dressed fool. Brueghel paints not to praise Lent and to condemn Carnival but to satirize the follies, games, and sport of both. Irving writes his novel for similar reasons. Brueghel created his painting in a time of great social and national upheaval; Irving, too, created his novel during such a time. And just as we find barely a hint of Brueghel in his painting, so we find little of Irving in his novel. In Brueghel's painting there are no individuals; even the narrator's burgher lacks any facial character. The people express emotions—fear, greed, horror, lust, indifference—but lack individual features. In Brueghel's great satiric painting, the figures remain totally self-absorbed.

The 158-Pound Marriage is Brueghel's painting written for our century by John Irving. The novel depicts the follies and games people play to gain leverage, power, in a world that has no other meaning for them. The characters, perhaps with the exception of Utch, are totally self-absorbed in their activities, just as Brueghel's nearly faceless figures are. Irving's novel is no easier to take than Brueghel's painting, for all its emphasis on game.

Huizinga stressed that the basis of game is agony or conflict; the goal is to play for self-knowledge. In ancient games or athletics (such as wrestling), the competition (for leverage) was "agonizing," "involving . . . mental and physical hardship" (39, 50–51). In *The 158-Pound Marriage*, Irving depicts characters who do precious little agonizing over anything. The one character who feels deeply, who loves, finds she can only retreat to her past.

6

The World According to Garp
(1976)

John Irving's first three novels have seemed to many critics merely warm-up exercises for his "major" works. Although this is not accurate—the early novels, especially *The Water-Method Man* and *The 158-Pound Marriage*, stand up very well on their individual merits—*The World According to Garp* was in a number of ways Irving's "breakthrough" novel. Garp became a household word; even for those who may not have read the novel, the movie, directed by George Roy Hill in 1982, made T. S. Garp a well-known character. *Garp* allowed Irving the freedom to pursue writing as his only "job." With this one novel, Irving became both rich and famous.

The World According to Garp reiterates many themes from Irving's first three novels: random violence and death; obsessions with family and children; gender and sexuality; love and marriage; art and the artist. In *Garp*, as in the early novels, there are links to Irving's life: his education at Exeter Academy, his wrestling, his writing. Still, while pursuit of biographical details in Irving's work may be fascinating, it does little to illuminate the text; other aspects of his novels ultimately prove more worthy of discovery. In *Garp*, we note especially the richness of its many layers, the extraordinary flexibility and grace of its prose, and the fulfillment of Garp's—and Irving's—criteria for good fiction; the novel makes the reader wonder what will happen next, and what happens is not so much real but "true."

PLOT DEVELOPMENT

The narrative of *The World According to Garp* follows a mythic curve, with moments in the plot marking off significant segments of Garp's life: his conception and birth; his growing up and education; his marriage and children; his death and life thereafter. Garp's story begins in the 1940s, with the impregnation of his mother, Jenny Fields, by Technical Sergeant Garp, a mortally wounded ball-turret gunner who lies near death in Boston's Mercy Hospital. The plot follows Garp's growing-up years and his education at Steering Academy (a thinly disguised Exeter Academy) in New Hampshire, where Jenny is the school nurse. At Steering, Garp has numerous adventures, primarily with the Percy children and their dog, Bonkers; becomes a wrestler; discovers his desire to be a writer; is initiated sexually by Cushie Percy (a fateful event that redounds upon him later in his life); and meets Helen Holm, the wrestling coach's daughter, whom he later marries.

Upon Garp's graduation from Steering, he and his mother go to Vienna so that Garp can "absorb experience" in order to be a writer. He excels mostly in lustful experiences, especially with Charlotte, a prostitute, who, he learns, is dying of cancer. His experiences with sex and death will be repeated throughout Irving's novel; in Vienna, these experiences lead to what is considered one of Garp's better works, *The Pension Grillparzer*, which contains not only recurring patterns in Garp's life and subsequent writings but also a number of themes in Irving's novel. Garp is not the only writer in his family. Jenny Fields also begins to write—in greater quantity and with greater diligence than her son, though, if we are to agree with Garp, not with greater artistry. " 'In this dirty-minded world,' Jenny begins, 'you are either somebody's wife or somebody's whore—or fast on your way to becoming one or the other' " (157). This opening sentence provides the basis of her autobiography, *A Sexual Suspect*, which becomes an international best-seller.

When Garp and his mother return to the United States, they discover that Jenny has become a famous and controversial political figure; she officially retires from nursing and moves to her parents' home at Dog's Head Harbor on the New Hampshire coast. Here she sets up a home for abused and victimized women in need of a safe and healing haven. Although she is considered by many women to be a feminist, Jenny never agrees with this label; she claims to do only what she believes to be the "right" thing. One of the women Jenny takes into her home is Roberta

Muldoon—before her sex change, Robert Muldoon, "old number 90," tight end for the Philadelphia Eagles—who becomes one of Garp's best friends and a devoted, but failed, bodyguard to the Garp family.

Garp marries Helen Holm, who is by now a professor at a nearby university. They have two children, Duncan and Walt. While Helen teaches English, Garp stays at home with the children, does the cooking, and continues to write—more or less. It would be pleasant to say they live happily ever after, but of course this is not possible in Garp's world any more than in life. Garp has a number of infidelities with young baby-sitters and assorted women, but the most traumatic infidelity turns out to be Helen's "lust" for one of her students, Michael Milton. Her affair ends violently and bizarrely, with young Walt dead, Duncan minus one eye, and Helen and Garp maimed both physically and emotionally. Michael Milton has three-fourths of his penis bitten off.

Healing of the Garp family takes place at Dog's Head Harbor, where Helen conceives another child, named Jenny, after Garp's mother. Garp finally writes another novel, *The World According to Bensenhaver*, which, like *The Pension Grillparzer*, is included in *Garp. Bensenhaver* depicts a dark world, in part a corollary to Garp's world, of rape and random, violent death. Garp's mother is assassinated, after which Helen, Garp, and their two children return to the Steering school, where Garp, too, is assassinated—by Pooh Percy, who links Garp's adolescent lust for her sister Cushie to Cushie's death in childbirth.

Irving's novel concludes with an extended epilogue, "Life after Garp," that ties up many of the loose ends in the novel and includes a "warning" for the future, not only for the remaining Garps but for readers as well. The epilogue tells us what happens to Helen, Duncan, Jenny, and a number of other characters in the novel. It also affords Irving an opportunity to reiterate significant themes and issues in his novel.

The plot's mythic curve is marked by various rites of passage, beginning with Garp's extraordinary conception and birth, his naming, puberty, continuing education and adventures, and ending—but not quite—with his death and burial. He is "resurrected" in the memories of those figures in the epilogue, as well as in his biography, *Lunacy and Sorrow: The Life and Art of T. S. Garp*, written by Donald Whitcomb, himself a "resurrection" of Garp's English teacher at Steering, Mr. Tinch. The rites of passage that Garp undergoes are crucial, of course, to him, but they also touch all who know him. Garp's adventures, which make up his life, are part of his life's education; when he has learned what life's experiences can teach him, he dies, but lives on in the memory of friends and family (and, one might add, of readers). Insofar as the narrative follows these rites of passage, it is simple. The complexities arise out of Irving's extraordinary playfulness with the rites themselves and the interconnections he makes among them.

In *The World According to Garp*, we first see Irving's indebtedness to Dickens (as well as to other eighteenth- and nineteenth-century writers); added to the plot is not only a wealth of social and psychological resonance but also complex situations and characters. There are numerous comic riffs, such as Garp running down speeding motorists, including O. Fecteau, Plumber, and Mrs. Ralph, to warn them to drive more slowly through his neighborhood in order to protect the children, especially his own, who live there. Each chapter is a self-contained story in its own right, with beginning, middle, and end (as in Dickens), and yet "hooks" into the following chapter, just as each chapter is charged with its own emotional intensity that spills over into the next sequence. Irving casts these wide and often comedic loops that fly out from the main narrative and then reels them in again, pulling them snugly into that narrative.

In a novel that is so much about memory, Irving's narrative loops are appropriate; they force readers to use their memories as they move through the text. Irving, like Garp, seems terribly aware of the import of Marcus Aurelius' commentary, in which he writes of the brevity of a man's life. All the more reason, then, "to remember everything" (576). If there is no life after death, including the death of fictional characters, there is memory, paradoxically restoring life.

SETTING

The settings in *The World According to Garp* act as spatial markers of the "world" of Garp and of the important moments that make up his life. These fictional settings also remind readers of the spatial markers of a world and life that we all share with Garp, beginning with our conceptions and (not quite) ending with our deaths, which spill over into "epilogues" in which we live on in the memories of our children and of the people we touch.

Boston Mercy, the hospital in which Garp is conceived, is also where Jenny Fields works as a nurse, much to the dismay of her wealthy family. This hospital theoretically provides a place of healing for the injured of World War II—the Externals, the Vital Organs, the Absentees, the Goners, as Jenny classifies them. Jenny Fields's pragmatic approach to the wounded and dying does nothing to mitigate the appalling consequences of war. The hospital is also a setting in which Irving demonstrates the fluidity with which he moves between "comedy and murderousness," life and death, and vice versa. As we witness the death of Technical Sergeant Garp's linguistic abilities and his body, we await the life of his and Jenny's son, T. S. Garp, and his extraordinary articulateness. From the beginning of the novel, which is also the beginning of young Garp's life, whenever we experience the force of death, we also feel it quicken into the energy of life. The hospital is one part of the frame for Irving's novel, which begins with Jenny Fields, the nurse, trying to save lives, and ends with her granddaughter, Jenny Garp, the doctor, still working with the same wonderful energy quickened in Garp, still trying to save lives.

Steering Academy, the private boarding school where Garp is edu-cated and grows up, is formative space; here Garp becomes a wrestler and decides to be a writer. He has initial encounters with danger and sex, he runs into both stupidity and prejudice with the Percy family, and he meets and falls in love with Helen Holm. It is to Steering Academy that Garp returns before he is killed. Ironically, he ends up buying the Percy house, the oldest at Steering; the Garp family puts down roots. Both Garp and his mother have buildings named after them, and both are buried in the Steering graveyard.

At Steering, the wrestling room is the most important space. It is not only where Garp learns how to wrestle and feels at home, but also where he proposes to Helen Holm. It is, further, the space that Pooh Percy enters, in a nurse's uniform (like his mother's), and kills Garp. Pooh had become one of the Ellen Jamesians, women who had their tongues cut out in sympathy with Ellen James, the eleven year-old-girl who had been raped and had her tongue cut out so that she could not testify against her rapists. Pooh is the dark "Under Toad," as Walt called the undertow, the threat of chaos and death that Garp and Helen know so well. The wrestling room is also the space in which Helen feels at home. To Helen, the room is warm and comforting, similar to the comfort of the womb. In this space, Helen, as a girl, spent her time reading while her father coached the wrestling team. In the scene in which Garp is shot, Helen is once more in her "place," reading. In this novel, if the wrestling room is womb-space, it is also tomb-space.

As in a number of Irving novels, Vienna is an important setting. It is where Garp experiences sex with prostitutes, especially Charlotte, and with schoolgirls, Vivian and Flossie. From Vivian or Flossie, Garp contracts venereal disease; from Charlotte, who is dying of cancer, Garp learns about death. Thus, for Garp, sex, disease, and death are inextricably linked. Vienna is not merely the setting for lust, disease, and death, however. It is also a place for writing—Jenny, her autobiography; Garp, *The Pension Grillparzer*, a strange but beautiful work of dreams and death.

The New England university community in which Garp and Helen spend the early years of their marriage could be any college town, since it functions only to mark off the emotional lives of Garp, Helen, and their sons, Duncan and Walt. Garp and Helen's home life is like life in *The Pension*; both are "rich with lu-lu-lunacy and sorrow," as Mr. Tinch had told Garp about his story. Garp and Helen have affairs, but it is Helen's affair with Michael Milton that precipitates Walt's death and Duncan's loss of an eye. Garp and Helen are both scarred by this affair.

It is to Dog's Head Harbor and to Jenny Fields that the Garp family retires to recover from their wounds. Dog's Head Harbor, along with Steering Academy and the wrestling room, is arguably one of the most significant settings in the novel. It is similar to the Pillsbury estate in *The Water-Method Man*, and to the magical hotel at the end of *The Hotel New Hampshire*. Dog's Head Harbor is not only a haven for abused women, including Ellen Jamesians, and the redoubtable Roberta Muldoon; it is also regenerative space for the Garp family.

At Dog's Head, the Garp family can mend their physical and emotional hurt. This place, where earth, sun, air, and water are emphasized, affords them time and space in which to heal. The sound of the ocean is restorative, just as it was in *The Water-Method Man*; at Dog's Head, Garp and Helen console each other over the loss of Walt and conceive their third child, Jenny. Dog's Head Harbor is not forgotten, even after Jenny Fields's death, because she designates Garp to lead the Fields Foundation, which dispenses grants, as well as offering a safe place, to women who need to heal. The novel, marked off structurally by setting, comes full circle when Garp is killed in the wrestling room by Pooh Percy; Helen is still there, reading, when Garp's assassination takes place. The epilogue collapses time and space: we learn that the Steering Academy grounds contain the graves of Jenny Fields and her son, Garp, and that the infirmary and annex are named for them; Duncan and Jenny Garp, in remembrance of grandmother and father, continue to direct the Jenny Fields Foundation at Dog's Head Harbor.

CHARACTER DEVELOPMENT

Irving peoples his novel with a wonderful cast of characters, from Fat Stew and dim-witted Midge Percy, with their many children, including soft Cushie and mad Pooh, to O. Fecteau, Mrs. Ralph, the Fletchers, especially Alice ("O, yeth!"), and Michael Milton. These characters are much more than ciphers or mere background; Irving breathes life and energy into them. For example, John Wolf, Garp's publisher, has a credible personal and professional life. Even Jillsey Sloper, Wolf's cleaning lady and trusted "reader," has these lives, as do Ellen James and, of course, Roberta Muldoon.

Roberta (formerly Robert) Muldoon becomes part of the Garp family and is perhaps more fully developed—certainly larger—than many of the other peripheral characters. Irving uses Roberta to demonstrate not only the blurring of gender "boundaries" but also our sexual prejudices. Roberta encompasses our more stereotypical views of women as seductive, nurturing, compassionate, and our equally stereotypical view of men as aggressively physical.

Jenny Fields, like Roberta, pushes gender boundaries. Jenny's story begins in the 1940s. Fiercely independent and determined to go her own way, the daughter of the Fields fortune, she drops out of Wellesley, which she decides is simply a school to prepare for marriage to the right man, and becomes a nurse. At Boston Mercy, where she works initially on the pediatrics floor, Jenny makes up her mind to have a child but to forgo marriage. When she is transferred to the ward for war-injured servicemen, she finds an opportunity to be impregnated by Technical Sergeant Garp, who is a "Goner." Jenny never changes her name, nor does she pretend she was ever married. Until her son, Garp, marries, Jenny devotes her life to him. Hence her job at Steering Academy so that her son can get a good education. There is little doubt she is domineering; she picks out or advises him on courses to take, since she herself sat in on all the courses at Steering. The only things she leaves for Garp to do for himself are to wrestle, to write, and to marry.

It is in Vienna that Jenny begins to break away from Garp; both Garp's lust (which Jenny cannot forgive) and their individual habits and styles of writing divide mother and son. Jenny starts and completes her autobiography, *A Sexual Suspect*. This work sums up, to a large degree, who Jenny Fields is and how she sees the world. She writes that she wanted both a career and a baby, but that she did not want or need a husband in her life. This makes her a "sexual suspect."

Jenny's autobiography makes her famous and gives her even more money than she already has. Her notoriety makes her both loved and hated by a large public, gives her a credible voice (to women, at least), and ultimately gets her killed. Her money allows her to support Garp and Helen after their marriage so that Garp can continue to write and, after Jenny's death, so that Garp can run Dog's Head Harbor for women. Jenny takes in Roberta Muldoon while she undergoes her sex change, just as she takes in her son and family to nurse them to health. Always a nurse, eminently pragmatic, resourceful, compassionate, and intelligent, she leaves her money and her house to Garp after her death, but with a clear purpose in mind: "I want to leave a place where worthy women can go to collect themselves and *just be themselves, by themselves*" (527). As Roberta tells Garp, Jenny wanted her son to understand women's needs and their problems.

It might have been helpful to Helen Holm if Garp had started this process much earlier. Helen, as much at home in the wrestling room as Garp, is a passive observer in many instances. She sits in the wrestling room, reading, her glasses fogged over. Thus, she often does not see things until too late (Pooh Percy with her gun, for example). Garp expects Helen to marry him (167), and so she does: "she did what he asked" (181). She has babies because Garp wants them and will look after them while she teaches English literature at the local university. In addition, she is Garp's "reader" and "listener" to his work and stories. Freed from the more mundane household tasks, Helen might be considered a "liberated" woman, but one wonders whether that is the case. The one time she steps "out of line" on her own—with Michael Milton—disaster strikes not only her but her whole family.

Yet Helen, like her surrogate mother, Jenny Fields, is pragmatic and down-to-earth. She sees through Garp's evasions and lies. She also recognizes his lusts, but unlike Jenny, Helen is quick to jealousy and anger over them. Though she initiates spouse-swapping with the Fletchers— for reasons unlike those in *The 158-Pound Marriage*—she is also quick to end it, whereas Garp remains infatuated with Alice Fletcher all his life. Helen begins her affair with Michael Milton in large part as a reaction to Garp's failure to recognize her physical and emotional needs for love.

Helen, also like Jenny Fields, believes that things can be "fixed." Even after the disastrous accident that kills Walt and maims the rest of the family, she believes in recovery and reconciliation. Thus, she is the one who proposes to Garp that they have another child; this child is Jenny Garp, "the name Jenny Fields would have had if she had gone about the business of having Garp in a more conventional way" (443).

It is Helen, in many ways, who makes it possible for Garp to write, and it is she who holds the family together. She may hide her feelings, but her love and strength enable the family to continue in times of sorrow and death. When Garp is shot in the wrestling room at Steering, Helen pins Pooh Percy to the mat, preventing her from firing a third shot. And it is Helen who helps keep Garp's memory alive, paradoxically by protecting his letters, journals, and jottings from would-be biographers. She tells them, as Garp would, "Read the work. Forget the life" (580). She goes to live with Roberta at Dog's Head Harbor and leaves instructions not to be buried with Garp and Jenny at Steering Academy, since the school, before it became coeducational, had refused her admission despite her brilliance. Perhaps Helen is a feminist after all.

However we might wish to classify Helen, it is clear that Garp loves her first, last, and deeply. As one of Irving's richest and most complex characters, Garp is difficult to classify at all. Obviously intelligent, imaginative, stubborn, independent, and self-absorbed, he has his prejudices (against the Ellen Jamesians, for example), but he is quick to recognize them and to change.

Like Bogus in *The Water-Method Man* and to some extent like Severin Winter in *The 158-Pound Marriage*, Garp is obsessed with the safety of his children. Although Garp is a househusband, he stays at home not for ideological reasons but because it suits him. He likes to cook and care for children, though his housecleaning is sporadic; perhaps more important, being at home allows him time to write. Further, he seems to be totally unqualified for any job. Garp is certainly no feminist and has little interest in politics. What he despises is the maniacal adherence to a cause or an idea, to the exclusion of everything else. Thus, he sees the Ellen Jamesians, those women who cut off their tongues to identify with the real Ellen James, as horrifying. In fact, he sees them as capitalizing on Ellen's pain for perverse and selfish reasons. He has no problem taking Ellen James herself into his household and seeing her as one of the family. His adamant—and public—opposition to the fanaticism of the Ellen Jamesians is in part what gets him killed by Pooh Percy.

Pooh also is motivated to kill Garp because she connects his youthful lust for her sister, Cushie, with Cushie's death in childbirth. Although Pooh suffers confusion, she is right about Garp's lust for women. In fact, one gets the impression that lust is one of the driving forces in Garp's life, even though its consequences prove disastrous, even deadly. While Irving is an equal opportunity creator of lustful characters—Helen and Roberta also feel lust—Garp seems to feel more than his fair share: for Cushie, for prostitutes, for Flossie and Vivian, for baby-sitters, for Alice Fletcher, and for Mrs. Ralph. Somehow Garp perceives lust as being connected with rape, a connection he graphically expresses in *The World According to Bensenhaver*. Lust as a driving male force also creates tension in Garp's relationship with his mother; she accepts his lust, seeing it as "natural" to all men, but she never forgives it—in her son or in men in general. The insistence on lust, particularly male lust, as an essential, natural drive is one of the more troubling aspects of this novel.

Garp's relationship with his mother is complex. He accepts money from her because it frees him from the drudgery of a job and allows him to write. With his family, he goes to Jenny after Walt's death; in large measure, his mother provides him with the love and space that allow healing. Even after Jenny dies, she does not let go of Garp, nor does he deny her hold on him. As director of the Fields Foundation, Garp is mindful of his mother every day.

What makes Garp so memorable to those around him—and to us, as readers—is his sheer energy. After Garp's death, Roberta runs the Fields Foundation, with such force that Ellen James calls her "*Captain Energy*" (593). Roberta and Garp's children agree, however, that Garp was the "real" Captain Energy; he was the "original." After Roberta's death, Duncan, Jenny, and Ellen James drink to Captain Energy, that is, to Garp. They write, phone, telegraph each other: "How's the energy?" They describe themselves, when full of energy, as being "full of Garp" (606). This is but another way of saying "full of life."

THEMATIC ISSUES

Irving gathers all of the issues in his earlier novels and includes them in *The World According to Garp*. Themes of marriage, family, and children recur from *The Water-Method Man* and *The 158-Pound Marriage*. These thematic concerns are projected into the future in Garp's unfinished manuscript, "*My Father's Illusions*, a portrait of a father who plots ambitiously and impossibly for a world where his children will be safe and happy" (605). This unfinished novel, which sounds suspiciously similar to Irving's fifth novel, *The Hotel New Hampshire*, is put in publishable form by Duncan and young Donald Whitcomb, Garp's official biographer. Duncan illustrates the manuscript with portraits of Garp.

Linked with family themes are issues of sexual roles and gender identities, which no longer exist in easy categories. Women dominate not only Garp's growing-up years but also his later life, from the independent Roberta Muldoon, to the little girl he "saves" after she is raped in the park, to Ellen James, to the Ellen Jamesians, who try to emulate her victimization. Garp's own lust for baby-sitters, Alice Fletcher, and Mrs. Ralph intensifies his anxieties about and compassion for victimized women, even, finally, for the Ellen Jamesians.

Beneath all of these themes is the "Under Toad," as Walt mistakenly called the undertow at Dog's Head Harbor; he is told to be careful of the undertow, or it will snatch him away in an instant. Walt's malapropism becomes a catchphrase that the Garp family uses to refer to imminent danger, violence, and death. The randomness and suddenness of death are brought to our attention at the very beginning of the novel when Garp's father, the ball-turret gunner, becomes a "Goner." Although violence and death abound in Irving's first novel, *Setting Free the Bears*, in *Garp* there is one disaster after another. We have the "lunacy" of Helen's biting off Michael Milton's penis, which leads to the "sorrow" of Walt's death and Duncan's loss of an eye. Ignorance and hatred stalk and assassinate Jenny Fields, just as madness and anger kill Garp. As John Wolf thinks, Garp's "was a death . . . which in its random, stupid, and unnecessary qualities—comic and ugly and bizarre—underlined everything Garp had ever written about how the world works" (576).

Not coincidentally, Duncan makes a hundred paintings "in a series called *Family Album*—the period of his work he was known for" (604)— in which there is a collection of a dozen paintings of a dirty-white Saab. This vehicle had been used by an Ellen Jamesian in a failed attempt to kill Garp by running him down. Duncan calls this collection "The Colors of the World" because, as he says, "all the colors of the world are visible in the twelve versions of the dirty-white Saab" (604).

Although "lunacy" and "sorrow" are linked with specific violent incidents in the novel, they are also linked to Garp's concerns with his art, as Harter and Thompson point out (78). Garp attempts to create art in which "laughter" and "sympathy" (232) are connected. *The Pension Grillparzer*, which comes at the beginning of Garp's career—and in the first quarter of Irving's novel—links "lunacy" and "sorrow" in an almost gentle and dreamlike balance. *The World According to Bensenhaver*, which comes later in Garp's brief career (and after Walt's death)—and in the final quarter of Irving's novel—seems to be all "sorrow." The ability to combine laughter and sympathy in art, as in life, is of concern not only to Garp as a writer but to Irving as well.

AN INTER/INTRA-TEXTUAL READING OF *THE WORLD ACCORDING TO GARP*

Much of the critical analysis of *Garp* has focused on feminism—for example, in Marilyn French's "The 'Garp' Phenomenon"—or on aesthetics, as in Margaret Drabble's "Muck, Memory, and Imagination." The novel is one of Irving's most "literary" works, as Gabriel Miller suggests (ch. 5 passim); Irving's novel includes references to such additional works as Marcus Aurelius' *Meditations*, Laurence Sterne's *Tristram Shandy*, Randall Jarrell's "The Death of the Ball Turret Gunner," Franz Grillparzer's *The Poor Fiddler*, Dostoyevsky's *The Eternal Husband*, and Ovid's *Metamorphoses*. In addition, Irving alludes to his own works—*Setting Free the Bears* and *The 158-Pound Marriage*, for example—and projects into the future—*The Hotel New Hampshire*. Because of the importance of many of Irving's literary references, an intertextual analysis is helpful in enriching our understanding of *Garp*.

Intertextuality is the relation between two or more texts. Further, intertextuality is used "to indicate a more diffuse penetration of the individual text by memories, echoes, transformations, of other texts" (Hawthorn 99), rather than by specific quotation or slavish following of other texts. As if Irving's work were not complex enough through his use of "outside" texts, he complicates *Garp* further by references to "inner" texts, Garp's own writing, including both allusion to and direct quotation of these works. The use of "inner" texts might appropriately be called intratextual.

Of all textual allusions in *Garp*, perhaps none is more important than those to Ovid's *Metamorphoses* and *The World According to Bensenhaver* because of the significance of both rape and transformation to Irving's novel (see Miller, who also notes their importance [113ff.]). Rape occurs right at the beginning of *Garp*, it can be argued, when Jenny Fields takes advantage of Technical Sergeant Garp's near-comatose state in order to impregnate herself. In addition to this rape, Ellen James, at age eleven, is raped and mutilated, and a number of women, out of anger and sympathy, mutilate themselves to become the Ellen Jamesians. Moreover,

Garp "saves" the little girl in the park who has been raped by the "Mustache Kid," who has raped other children. Garp himself is believed by Pooh Percy to have "taken" her sister Cushie, which, Pooh thinks, leads to her death in childbirth. The word "lust" occurs repeatedly in the novel and seems directly, or at least obliquely, connected with rape. Whatever the connection, sex and violence are related throughout the novel, and Garp finds himself confronting them at nearly every turn.

Garp's writing of *The World According to Bensenhaver* follows a sequence of central—and centered—traumatic events in Garp's life: Helen's lust for Michael Milton, Garp's irrational and aggressive jealousy, Walt's death, and Duncan's loss of an eye, concomitant with the emotional and physical maiming of Helen and Garp. *Bensenhaver* is Garp's artistic response to these events and is, in itself, a story of lust, rape, murder, and madness. Just as the events in Garp's life are profoundly disruptive of his marriage and family, so *Bensenhaver* in itself is equally disruptive as a narrative.

The act of rape itself is disruptive; the word itself is not so much written as it is acted. To "rape" is to speak hatred; and the act itself, in Garp's story, is accompanied by offensive verbal and bodily language. Rape is an act against the integrity of the body of another; it is an act of cutting or penetrating the flesh, of destroying its wholeness. It separates or alienates the victim from herself (as Irving so brilliantly shows in *Garp*).

In *Bensenhaver*, the very name of the boy—*Oren Rath*—who enters the house of Hope Standish reiterates the idea of verbal abuse coupled with the hatred that cuts. Rath, who is also a pig farmer (and who not only is animal-like but also bears the name of pig products), carries, of all things, a fisherman's blade, with which he makes a quick cut on the face of Hope's baby, Nicky, to show her that he means "business."

Thus begins Hope's horrifying abduction by Oren and their pursuit by Arden Bensenhaver, a policeman whose wife had been gang-raped in a laundromat and who suffocated in the sheets inside the drier into which they stuffed her. Garp presents the rape of Hope (whose name is as symbolic as Rath's) in a matter-of-fact, yet horrific, way. Oren's voice is flat, nearly monosyllabic, in its repetitive "I got to find a good place to *have* you," "I just want to *have* you," and "After we do it, I'll *have* to [kill you]" (408–409). He warns her not to speak, "Don't talk!" (415); the body that speaks is forbidden.

The disruption between the body and its ability to speak takes place *because* of the rape, with its cutting, penetrating, dividing. Oren effectively silences Hope's mouth, the usual weapon of negotiation, and thereby deprives her of any power—almost—against him. Deprived of herself as a speaking person, deprived of "Hope," she takes Oren's weapon, his fisherman's blade, and turns it on him by cutting, penetrating, and separating him from his body. In short, she does to Oren what he has been doing to her.

Rath and his brothers—who contrive to protect him until Bensenhaver threatens them with castration—represent "benign corruption" (421), Arden thinks, a corruption these Rath men cannot even comprehend. As Bensenhaver pursues Oren and Hope in an attempt to save her, Hope performs her surgery, her own cutting. She saves herself; all that is left to do for Bensenhaver is to comfort her.

The ending of *Bensenhaver* has to do with guilt. Hope's husband, Dorsey, who feels he neglected to protect his wife, desires now to keep Hope (and their children) safe always. (Hope and her husband, like Garp and Helen, have another child.) Of course, this proves impossible, "[and] Standish seems destined to create one monster of paranoia after another" (445). He begins to think Hope may be having an affair and wants Bensenhaver, who has become the family bodyguard, to spy on her. Because Bensenhaver refuses, Dorsey becomes his own spy, and while he is gone from the house, trailing Hope, his younger child chokes to death. The story ends with Bensenhaver accidentally killing Dorsey, thinking he is an intruder in his own house—which he has indeed become—and with the old policeman paralyzed and insane. As it turns out, Hope does have a lover, and eventually another child; she is seen "as a strong survivor of a weak man's world" (447).

This brutal story, which in many ways mirrors Garp's own life, is meant to provide him with financial security, which it does, so that he can protect his own family from hurt and misfortune—the "Under Toad" of life—which, of course, it does not. Garp learns that his mother is assassinated; so much for life "protection."

Not only is *Bensenhaver* related to Garp's life, but the story is linked to other rapes in Irving's novel, especially to that of Ellen James. The rape of Ellen James is also about cutting, about alienating the victim from her self. The Ellen Jamesians, who are obsessed—mad—with rape, choose a horrifying method of protest: they cut their own tongues out. Garp fails to understand their self-mutilation, that by cutting their tongues out, these women point correctly to the essence of rape. As Bensenhaver shows, rape is an act of violating the body of another; rape cuts into, penetrates, the flesh. It destroys the body's wholeness. Garp, as a writer, is understandably disgusted with the Ellen Jamesians' action; he believes they deprive themselves of words, of the ability to tell a story. What Garp fails to understand is that their self-mutilation "speaks" the very subject of rape. The Ellen Jamesians' cut flesh becomes the word for rape—but it does not make for a pretty story.

As Gabriel Miller points out (113–114), the Ellen Jamesians correspond directly to the mythical story of Philomela in Ovid's *Metamorphoses*. Philomela is raped by her sister Procne's husband, Tereus, who cuts her tongue out so that she cannot speak of the deed. She creates from this act a weaving that "tells" her story and sends it to her sister. Tereus, who has told Procne that her sister is "dead" (to him, dead women can not speak), pays for his act: Procne kills their son, Itys, with a dagger, cuts him up, cooks him, and serves him to Tereus for dinner. When she tells him what he has eaten, Tereus attempts to kill both Procne and Philomela, but before he does so, all three are turned into birds: Tereus into an ugly bird with a huge beak, Procne into a sparrow, and Philomela into a nightingale (in the Latin version).

This mythical story is a tale not only of rape and mutilation, of rupture and revenge, and of family hatred and abuse, but also of devoted sisterhood, of voice and artistry, and of transformation. *Bensenhaver* seems bleak by comparison; the best that can be said of Garp's tale is that Hope survives and endures in a world apparently dominated by aggressively violent, yet weak, men.

The story about Garp is more problematic. The Ellen Jamesians display a sisterhood that is as terrifying—and as strong—as Procne and Philomela's, and Garp is disgusted by it. Perhaps Irving is as well. Ovid, in the *Metamorphoses*, saves the sisters, but he can do so only by the magic of transformation. To be sure, Tereus also lives on, though his brute ugliness does not change, and the innocent Itys is sacrificed because of and to that ugliness. Irving, too, must rely on the magic of transformations at the end of his novel. Irving's use of transformation is not new here; he uses transformation in *The Water-Method Man* and will use it again in *The Hotel New Hampshire*, for example. Garp comes to terms with the Ellen Jamesians, and he takes Ellen James herself into his family. He becomes the director of the Jenny Fields Foundation, that is, he becomes more like his mother, Jenny (who "*always did what was right*"). And he is not unfaithful to Helen anymore. One senses he will write more and better work—*My Father's Illusions*, for example. At the end of Garp's life, there is plenty of transformative power to go around, for others are transformed as well: Ellen James writes poetry; Helen loves Garp as she once did; even Pooh Percy is rehabilitated and has a child! And Garp transfers "energy," even after his death, to his children and those lives he touched.

Out of one of the most terrible of events—"Rape was an outrage even God couldn't understand"—come transformative power, reconciliation, and reintegration. Like Philomela and Procne, Garp learns to sing. One wants to believe that transformations can arise out of this most terrible crime, and yet there is the sense that *only* "magic" can bring such change. Still, there is enough affirmation at the end of Irving's novel so that readers perhaps do not worry too much about *how* the creative magic works. And if we have read Ovid's *Metamorphoses*, we are alerted to the hope and possibility of transformation (in *Bensenhaver*, only Hope Standish's name points in that direction). The ending of *Garp* gives us reconciliation and reintegration, as well as a wonderful epilogue. The last line in the novel, "But in the world according to Garp, we are all terminal cases," suggests finiteness, yet we recall that Garp himself was born out of a union between Jenny Fields and the terminal "Goner," Technical Sergeant Garp. And the line occurs, after all, in the epilogue, a magical literary device in itself, at least in the ways Shakespeare and Irving use it. Irving's epilogue does more than tidy up loose ends and bring things to a close; it propels the narrative into the future. Although Garp is dead, his energy, his life, continues to be felt by his children, his friends—and especially by his readers.

7

The Hotel New Hampshire
(1981)

The Hotel New Hampshire followed hard after *Garp* and was equally a commercial success, with an initial printing of 175,000 copies and a second printing of 100,000 copies. Dutton published the hardcover edition; Pocket Books acquired paperback reprint rights; it was also a Book-of-the-Month Club selection (Reilly 96). Reviewers and critics seem either to like the novel wholeheartedly or to condemn it outright. A movie, directed by Tony Richardson in 1984, and starring Jodie Foster, Rob Lowe, Beau Bridges, and Nastassja Kinski, retains much of the novel's plot but loses most of its fairy-tale qualities. Although the movie looks at many of the social, sexual, and political themes of the novel, the film becomes tedious (perhaps because of Richardson's determined emphasis on the bizarre), whereas the novel does not.

Readers of *Garp* were prepared for *The Hotel New Hampshire*, since Garp, near the end of his life, projects several forthcoming novels, the first of which would be *My Father's Illusions*. Garp's plot for his novel is similar to—although not exactly like—*Hotel*. In *Hotel*, the narrator, John Berry, refers so often to "my father's illusions" that it becomes an identifying "tag line" for Father.

Hotel contains many of the elements that appear in Irving's first four novels: bears, rape and random violence, family, "almost" orphans, Vienna, New England, academe, and loss and regain. There are, of course, some changes: the Under Toad in *Garp* becomes the dog Sorrow in *Hotel*;

wrestling becomes weight lifting; the dead father is now the dead mother; war is replaced by terrorism; love includes, but is not limited to, incest.

In an interview, Irving said that he got the idea for *Hotel* most directly out of *The Pension Grillparzer* in *Garp* (Miller 194). He wanted to create a "fairy tale," in which the story "[operates] most wholly on a symbolic level" (Miller 194). *Hotel* is a novel that "symbolically uses hotels, rape, dream, bears" (Miller 195). Unless we are willing to enter the novel's world on its own fictional—that is to say, symbolic—terms, we stand to miss its meaning.

Even though *Hotel* is a fairy tale, it is grounded in the material and historical situations of World War II, the Holocaust, the decadence of postwar Vienna, the violence of terrorism. Such "grounding" anchors Irving's novel, even as he demonstrates his commitment to use old forms, in this case the fairy tale and romance, in order to create what might be called a postmodern fairy tale. Irving's regenerative and restorative aesthetic impulse here lends itself to the twin themes of love and life that run through *The Hotel New Hampshire*.

Irving once again uses the first-person narrator, in this case John Berry, the middle child, who is the "least opinionated," according to him. He points out that he must make the family story clear. Although this story seemingly is seen through a child's eyes as he grows up (and John fears he will never grow up, never catch up to his sister Franny), the narration begins well after the events take place. The story starts with the parents' romance and courtship, but John tells it when he is past thirty and his older brother, Frank, is at least forty. Thus, in many ways, the narrative looks back to the past at the same time it has already moved into the future. Indeed, the narrative ends with John awaiting the birth of Franny's child.

Irving clearly wishes us to view John as a narrator who is similar to Nick Carraway in F. Scott Fitzgerald's *The Great Gatsby*, a novel alluded to throughout *Hotel*. Father is, in fact, called "a Gatsby" by Lilly, and as Edward Reilly notes, John is a "Carraway foil" to Father's Gatsby (*Understanding John Irving* 85). Both John and Nick learn as participants in their respective narrations; they grow and change as a result of experiencing numerous significant events in their lives. And both John and Nick tell stories colored by memory and imagination.

PLOT DEVELOPMENT

As with all of John Irving's novels, the plot of *Hotel* follows the formula of the Bildungsroman; the drive of the novel is toward the growth of the individual. *Hotel* is one of Irving's most tightly plotted novels (although this does not mean the plot is simple), and with two exceptions—the attention given to Donald Justice's poetry and the attack on academe—there is nothing extraneous. There are, however, some wonderful "loops" to the story, small bits that seem to be "throwaways," only to return much later in the plot. For example, when we first meet the man in the white dinner jacket, he offers a cigarette to Mother and Father, who refuse it. Late in the novel, when we meet the man again, he is dying of emphysema.

As Gabriel Miller argues, sometimes slavishly, *Hotel* is a fairy tale, a point Irving himself has admitted. The novel also follows the structure of the heroic monomyth (as described by Joseph Campbell in his *The Hero with a Thousand Faces*), at least as far as the characters of the children are concerned; there is "separation" from the life that is familiar; "initiation" into adventure and new life stages; and "return," changed and transfigured, to the world that was left.

The novel tells the story of the Berry family from Dairy, New Hampshire. The story begins with the courtship of Winslow Berry and Mary Bates, who meet in the summer of 1939 at the Arbuthnot-by-the Sea, a hotel in Maine. The story of their courtship, told over and over by the parents to their children, is repeated in a magical way by John Berry, who "imagines" the courtship story better than it ever happened (or so his father says).

Win Berry, the son of widowed Iowa Bob, the football coach at the Dairy School for Boys, plans to go to Harvard, while Mary Bates, daughter of old "Latin Emeritus," who once taught at the Dairy School, and his wife, plans simply to look after her aging parents until she is rescued by someone out of the ordinary: a Harvard man, who, she thinks, will take her to Boston and to a more romantic life than awaits her in Dairy. Win and Mary, summer employees at the Arbuthnot, fall in love immediately; they also encounter at the Arbuthnot two mysterious men who affect their future together. One is a wizened, gnomelike man named Freud (called "our Freud"—to distinguish him from Sigmund, the "other Freud"), who owns a motorcycle and a bear called State o' Maine. "Our Freud" is a Viennese Jew with a limp, who has been and done all kinds of things, from being a mechanic to a doctor. As a trainer of bears, Freud seems less than capable, and even worse as an entertainer with a bear. Freud has a great capacity for warmth, compassion, and love, however, and these qualities captivate Win Berry—so much so that eventually he buys both the motorcycle and the bear, and barnstorms the country as a not-too-successful entertainer.

Win and Mary also meet a mysterious man in a white dinner jacket, who arrives on a white sloop at the Arbuthnot's dock, appearing suddenly out of the fog. When the mystery man steps onto the dock, he asks if Freud and the bear have arrived, pointing out that it is a good thing Freud left Europe, since it will not be safe there for Jews. Nor will the world be safe for bears, he adds. These comments presage World War II and the Holocaust, as well as the death of State o' Maine, events that signal the end of what seemed a romantic era. As the man in the white dinner jacket prepares to leave, he says something else, but Win does not hear what it is; he will wonder for the rest of his life what was said.

Win learns that the man is Arbuthnot, the owner of the hotel. He says of Arbuthnot that his clothes were "perfect." "He had obscene confidence," Mary observes; Win adds, "He had money" (15). Berry's fascination with him (he misreads Arbuthnot, an anti-Semite, completely) leads to his equal fascination with hotels, and may account for his ending up buying three of them.

Because Freud is insulted and mistreated by an anti-Semitic German guest, he decides to return to Europe, and before he leaves, sells the bear, newly called Earl, and his motorcycle to Berry. Freud also exacts three promises from the couple: Win and Mary must get married right away; Win should go to Harvard; Mary must "forgive" Win (Freud does not say why forgiveness is necessary, but as the novel unfolds, readers discover forgiveness is necessary for Father's "illusions").

All three promises are kept. Marriage follows the magical courtship, as do children, five in all: Frank, Franny, John, Lilly, and Egg. Win and Mary become Father and Mother through most of the novel, which deals with the growing up of the children. Initially Father and Mother settle in Dairy, where Father, upon graduation from Harvard in 1946, after serving in World War II, teaches English at the Dairy School, and in Dairy he opens his first Hotel New Hampshire. This hotel, formerly a girls' school, seems a safe place to the children, although it is a poor hotel. Their grandfather, Iowa Bob, coach and weight lifter, moves in with them and as one of his tasks coaches John in weight lifting. Despite

Father's dreams for the hotel, it is not successful, though somehow they manage to keep it running.

During this period of time, John, Franny, and Frank discover sex. Frank learns he is homosexual, and is taunted and bullied at school; John has somewhat unsatisfactory sex with Ronda Ray, who works at the hotel; and Franny is gang-raped on Halloween, in the woods near the school, by Chipper Dove, the football quarterback, and two of his teammates. The black football players, led by Junior Jones, who is startlingly bearlike, try to rescue Franny but are too late. Although the "Black Arm of the Law" catches Chipper's teammates, he gets away; all three are, however, finally expelled from school.

Franny's rape proves to be one of the most significant scenes in the novel, although she initially suppresses it, saying only that she was "beaten up." The rape is associated with death, first of the children's dog, Sorrow, who is put to sleep, primarily because he "smelled bad," "farted," and "defecated" on the floor. In addition, Patrolman Tuck dies of a heart attack because of Franny's early evening Halloween prank; indeed, Franny and John are on their way to get help for Tuck when they are accosted by Chipper and his buddies. Later, Frank (whose hobby is taxidermy) will stuff Sorrow as a Christmas present for the youngest child, Egg. Irving uses Sorrow as a source of scatological humor but also as a symbol, associating the dog with sex and death. Frank hides the stuffed Sorrow in the closet of Iowa Bob's room, hoping to surprise Egg at Christmas. Unfortunately, Sorrow pops out of the closet and surprises Iowa Bob—literally to death.

Shortly after Iowa Bob dies, Father receives a letter from Freud, beseeching him to bring his family to Vienna in order to run Freud's hotel there. Although no one in the family, besides Father, wants to leave Dairy, particularly Egg and Lilly, Mother and Father decide to sell the Hotel New Hampshire and move to Vienna. They sell the hotel to a dwarf circus, a transaction that makes Lilly, herself small enough to be a dwarf (though the family euphemism for her dwarfism is that she just needs to "grow"), all the more reluctant to leave. (The dwarf circus will be expanded considerably in Irving's *A Son of the Circus*.) Egg agrees to the move only if he can take his beloved (stuffed) Sorrow with him.

Father and the four oldest Berry children leave for Vienna, with Mother and Egg—and Sorrow—to follow a day later. Father and the children arrive in Vienna to discover that Freud is blind, the result of Nazi experimentation in a concentration camp during the war. Freud uses a baseball bat as his walking stick and has a "seeing-eye" bear,

Susie, who is also a "smart" bear. Susie is actually a young woman who has donned a bear suit because she believes she is ugly. Like Franny, Susie has been raped. In Susie's case, the rapist put a bag over her head, claiming she was too ugly to look at. Unlike Franny, Susie has not suppressed the fact of her rape and expresses her rage about it often. She seems incapable, however, of getting beyond the "fact" of her ugliness; the bear suit is a "cover" for her hurt and a defensive barrier to keep people at a distance. Nonetheless, Susie becomes emotionally close to the Berry children and eventually a member of the family.

Freud's hotel, the Gasthaus Freud, is a disaster. Ill-kept—and ill-kempt—it is home to a group of prostitutes and so-called revolutionaries. That the two groups are similar is indicated by the fact that the older member of each group has the same name: Billig, which means "cheap." There is nothing cheap about Father's moving his family to Vienna, however; it costs them dearly. Mother and Egg, with Sorrow, never make it across the Atlantic. The plane crashes off the coast of France. Sorrow not only "strikes again," but it comes in many "poses." It even "floats," as it signals the spot in the ocean where the plane crashed. The deaths of Egg and Mother demonstrate to the children that Sorrow is everywhere; they know they have "arrived in a foreign country" (232).

Even Father's change of the hotel's name from Gasthaus Freud to the Hotel New Hampshire (to attract the Americans in Vienna) does not change the children's sense of isolation and alienation. Lillie does not "grow"; John continues his rather unsatisfactory sexual exploration and becomes enamored with the young Fraulein Fehlgeburt (Miss "Miscarriage"), one of the revolutionaries. Franny, too, continues her sexual experimentation, being especially attracted to Ernst, another of the revolutionaries and a lecturer on pornography. Only Frank seems to adapt to and be at home in Vienna. He learns its history and its language. Whatever his sex life, it is carried out discreetly. It is in Vienna that the children discover the folktale "The King of Mice," about the unhappy performer who one day quit "passing the open windows," and jumped out of them with his unwanted mice. "LIFE IS SERIOUS BUT ART IS FUN" is the king's message (285). The phrase "keep passing the open windows" becomes a sort of mantra for the Berry children. In Vienna, not only are the windows open, they are blown out in a bombing.

Fraulein Fehlgeburt alerts John concerning the revolutionaries' plan to blow up the State Opera. When Franny learns of this, she has sex with Ernst in order to find out just how the plan will work, although her motives for going to him are ambiguous: Is it out of horror, perhaps heroism, or fascination, or a combination of these? Whatever Franny's motives, Father, with Freud's Louisville Slugger, kills Ernst, who refers to Franny as merely a "necessary phase" and a "disappointment." The Berry family is held hostage by the revolutionaries, who elect to have the blind Freud drive the bomb car into something "hard," which will in turn set off a "sympathy" bomb at the Opera. The plan is subverted, however, when Freud, once again in possession of his baseball bat, hits the car with it, blowing up the car, himself, and most of the lobby of the hotel. In the meantime, John (whose years of weight lifting have paid off) squeezes one of the revolutionaries, Arbeiter, to death; Father is blinded by shards of glass from the broken windows and inherits Freud's bat. The bomb blast throws Franny and John together so that they can no longer ignore the love they feel for one another.

Without Freud, it is pointless to remain in Vienna, and the Berrys return to the States, to New York. Instead of owning a hotel, they now live in two: Father, Frank, and John, near Central Park; Lilly and Franny, at the Stanhope. Lilly has written the family biography up to the point where Mother and Egg die, and Frank, now her agent, sells it. Lilly believes writing will help her grow, even though it is hard work. Rich, as well as famous, Lilly shares her wealth with her family; after all, they *are* the story. And it is at the Stanhope that the Berry children work out two of the major traumas in the novel: Franny and John's incestuous desire for one another and Franny's rape by Chipper Dove.

Once in New York, Franny can turn her attention to the release of her brother and herself from their incestuous and obsessive love that has been shadowing them throughout their childhood and that threatens to destroy their adulthood. This she does by forcing John to have sex with her over and over, beyond the point of exhaustion and to the point of physical pain. It "cures" them of their obsession with one another, leaving each of them "free to live [his/her] life now" (381).

When John leaves Franny after their exhausting sexual encounter, he meets Chipper Dove by chance in the street. John picks him up and thinks of killing him in the same way he killed Arbeiter, but he carefully puts him down—and lets him know where Franny is staying. Dove calls Franny at the Stanhope, and for the second time in her life she is frightened. Lilly, John, Frank, and Susie rally around to protect Franny, and it is Lilly who takes charge. She writes a short drama that is enacted when Chipper calls on Franny. Susie, dressed in her bear suit, threatens Chipper with rape. The "almost" rape, brought to a halt by Franny at the last minute, reduces Chipper to a sniveling wretch and releases

Franny from her trauma. She says, with "awed affection": "here comes the rest of our lives" (403).

Only Lilly is incapable of living her life. She is the Berry child who cannot adapt or change in the face of new and different circumstances. Unable to grow—she does not grow at all after her mother and Egg's deaths—she cannot live. Although she tries to write in order to grow, she finds that she can no longer write anything of substance after her family biography. The biography, *Trying to Grow*, stopped at the point of the plane crash that killed Mother and Egg. Symbolically, life stops for Lilly at this moment in time, and she can write nothing further, except the brief playlet to restore her sister Franny to her life. Lilly quits passing the open windows and jumps to her death from her apartment at the Stanhope. Frank describes her view of the world as "real *Weltschmerz*" (world hurt).

The Hotel New Hampshire, like *Garp*, has an epilogue. Father wants to buy "one more" hotel, the Arbuthnot-by-the-Sea, which is now for sale. Frank and John journey to California to make the deal with Arbuthnot—the man in the white dinner jacket—now dying of emphysema. In a brilliantly executed scene, Arbuthnot is portrayed as a twisted and demented anti-Semite who does, however, sell his hotel. The last Hotel New Hampshire serves to sustain the illusions and dreams of the blind Father—blind all along to everyday life. As Iowa Bob tried to tell him, Father missed much of the present because he was always thinking of the future.

The third Hotel New Hampshire is never really a hotel; it is truly a home for Father and John—and finally Susie, whom John marries. Susie runs a rape crisis center at the hotel, and Frank remains in New York as a successful agent, managing his own and other people's lives. Franny becomes a movie star and marries Junior Jones, a successful attorney. When the novel ends, they await the birth of their child, whom they will give to Susie and John, *real* and perhaps *perfect* parents at last.

SETTING

Hotels provide the significant markers for setting in *The Hotel New Hampshire*, even before most of the important characters are born. The novel begins in the summer of 1939, when Mother and Father, both nineteen, meet as employees at the Arbuthnot-by-the-Sea, a resort hotel on the coast of Maine. This hotel, owned by the man in the white dinner jacket, seems a magical place. It is the scene of Mother and Father's courtship, and it is where Father meets "our Freud." More important, however, it is also where we discover Father's "illusions," which he will keep all of his life: that bears could live a life of human beings, and that human beings could live a life(time) in hotels.

The first Hotel New Hampshire represents the strength of these illusions. When Father and Mother marry, they live in their hometown of Dairy. The children begin their lives there, and the family as a cohesive unit is formed there. Hotels, with their numerous individual and closed-off rooms, usually suggest isolation, transiency, even loneliness and alienation. But the Berry hotel, fashioned out of a former girls' school, has the opposite effect on its family residents (there are very few hotel guests); the Berrys stick together as they share their rooms and their lives. Even Frank, more of a loner than the other children, can be counted upon to rally around his family.

The first Hotel New Hampshire is also appropriate symbolically. Its plumbing and furniture, installed for small schoolgirls, correspond to the young Berry children. The hotel represents a warm, comforting, and secure familial world. Iowa Bob says, "*Nothing* moves at the Hotel New Hampshire! We're screwed down here—for *life*" (132).

Although the hotel offers comfort and the town of Dairy seems safe, they are surrounded by dark and dangerous woods. Franny and John's going into the woods at Halloween leads to her gang rape, an event that traumatizes Franny for the rest of her growing-up years. It is nearly the end of the novel before her trauma is exorcised. Even in Dairy the Berrys are dogged by death and Sorrow.

The move to Vienna, to Freud's Gasthaus, which becomes the second Hotel New Hampshire, is accompanied by Mother and Egg's death. In Vienna, the hotel is a shabbier and sleazier version of the one in Dairy. It is also more dangerous: prostitutes use one floor; a group of revolutionaries, the other. The ever-present danger and sex, as well as the deaths of Fehlgeburt and Freud, force the children, with the exception of Lilly, to grow up. After Freud and the hotel are blown up, Franny and John comfort one another and cannot ignore what they have known and avoided all along: they are in love. But in Vienna, even love is not safe.

The Stanhope Hotel in New York City is a kind of way station when the Berrys return to the States. Lilly and Franny stay there, while Father, John, and Frank stay in a hotel on the other side of the city. The Stanhope is where Lilly's fairy-tale "opera" is performed to exact revenge on Chipper Dove and where Franny is set free at last from the trauma of her rape. The Stanhope is also where John and Franny make love (in a most circumspect and chaste scene) in order to let go of their obsession with one another. The Stanhope is also where Lilly stops trying to grow and stops passing the open windows.

The final setting for John and Father is the Arbuthnot-by-the-Sea, renamed the Hotel New Hampshire. With the purchase of the Arbuthnot, the novel comes full circle. Father realizes his dream, as his children make it come true for him. The third Hotel New Hampshire is not a "real" hotel; as John says, this hotel will never be a hotel. Indeed, the children turn the lobby into a game room—similar to the coffeehouse, Kaffee Mowatt, in Vienna—and convert the hotel restaurant and kitchen into a huge "country kitchen" (415).

Eventually, when Susie and John marry, the former hotel becomes a rape crisis center in which Father turns out to be the perfect hotelier, despite his blindness. He knows exactly what to say to the women who go there to be healed; in Father's comforting way, he is kin to Jenny Garp at Dog's Head Harbor. The women are healed, Father knows, because of the niceness of everyone in the hotel. When they leave the Hotel New Hampshire, they will be "whole again" (441). Such wholeness is "almost mystically accomplished," Father says.

This "mystical" accomplishment is visually represented in the final scene of the novel when Susie reenacts her bear routine for one of the very few paying guests, a family from Arizona who lost their way and stayed overnight at the "hotel." It had snowed overnight, and Susie the bear appears as if by magic, "as if [she] were the first bear on earth, and this the planet's first snow" (449).

The setting, like other elements of this novel, is used symbolically. Hotels are not merely hotels; they represent our world: sometimes they are home or a safe haven; sometimes they are dangerous, ready to blow up in our faces; and sometimes they are magical.

CHARACTER DEVELOPMENT

There are numerous wonderful, bizarre, eccentric characters in *The Hotel New Hampshire*, and as Gabriel Miller points out (so, too, does John Irving), the characters are used symbolically. They represent tale types (see Propp passim). "Our Freud," for example, is the magical guide who prepares the way for the quest of a dream; he exacts the conventional three promises from Mother and Father. Our Freud also has the important talisman, the bear, which embodies certain "magical," out-of-the-ordinary properties. In addition, of course, our Freud suggests through his name the body of knowledge disseminated by the "other" Freud, that is, Sigmund. If our Freud is a consumer and purveyor of dreams, Sigmund Freud not only wrote about them but also could be said to have started a whole dream industry.

The major characters, however, are the members of the Berry family themselves: Mother, Father, Frank, Franny, John, Lilly, and Egg. Mother and Father are a wonderfully romantic couple, as if a dream couple. Gabriel Miller notes that Mother is the classic heroine waiting to be rescued, or, as she puts it, waiting for her life to begin (her children will echo this sentiment themselves) when Father arrives on the scene. That they love one another is clear even to the cynical Franny.

Mother is the one who sorts out disputes, chastises John for swearing, and admonishes Frank after he displays the stuffed Sorrow: "I don't like Sorrow, Frank. . . . I don't find dead things amusing" (216). Franny and John are constantly amazed at Mother: they think she knows nothing, only to discover she knows everything. Although Mother agrees to buy the first Hotel New Hampshire with Father and later to go with him to Vienna, she nonetheless sees through Father's illusions: she studies about Vienna because she is well aware that Father is totally "unprepared" (204). And it is Mother who reminds them all that no matter where they are, they will always remain a family.

Mother—and her youngest child, Egg—is doomed to be a missing part of the family, an absence that is a deeply felt presence. Mother and Egg carry Sorrow with them on the plane that does not make it to Europe; although they do not make it to Vienna, Sorrow certainly arrives there.

Egg's very name suggests that he will remain an embryonic form in the family. His lack of development is similar to Lilly's lack of growth, which prepares us for her failure to keep passing the open windows. Although Lilly believes her writing will help her to grow, it is too much like her. Just as Lilly stops growing when Mother and Egg die, so her writing fails to grow: her family biography stops at the point of Mother and Egg's deaths.

Father is the dreamer of the family. From the moment the man in the white dinner jacket steps off the sloop at the Arbuthnot, Father is captivated by his confidence and money. Readers may recognize the similarity between Arbuthnot and Jay Gatsby in Fitzgerald's *The Great Gatsby*. Lilly also points out the similarity between Father and Gatsby when, in Vienna, Fehlgeburt reads Fitzgerald's novel to the children.

Indeed, Lilly cries, at the ending of Fitzgerald's novel, "Father is a *Gatsby*" (257). Frank misunderstands, and attempts to demonstrate the differences between Father and the events in Fitzgerald's novel, but Lilly has the linkages right, from the man in the white dinner jacket to father to Gatsby. There will always be an "*It*," she points out, referring to the "green light at the end of [the] dock," the dream Gatsby (and Father) pursues (Fitzgerald 182). Father will "keep going after it, and it's going to get away" (257). Lilly understands the pull of Father's dream, just as she understands that the man in the dinner jacket, who represents the dream, also represents death. She sees him in *her* dreams all the time.

Father does not calculatingly ignore his children in order to chase his dreams; it is worse. He is generally oblivious to them. When Mother dies, it is as if he forgets them most of the time. He is truly amazed to discover that they have completed college, that they have grown up in the seven years they are in Vienna. It is not that he does not love his children—a poignant scene with John in the Sacher Hotel bar demonstrates that he does—it is that Father himself never really grows up. It is unclear whether he ever understands who his children are.

Frank, the oldest child, is the most pragmatic—and circumspect—of the children. A homosexual who is exceedingly private—his siblings are unaware of any of his love affairs—he is shy concerning sexuality. However, he is extraordinarily perceptive and realizes that Franny and John love one another "too much." Frank and Franny are antagonistic toward one another but loyal in defending one another. For example, when Frank is being harassed by Chipper Dove for his homosexuality, Franny comes to his rescue, just as Frank does for her the first time Chipper (well before the rape) tries to have sex with Franny. Frank tries to do the caring thing—as with Sorrow—but often misses the mark. He has his signature obsessions, uniforms and taxidermy, which further tend to make him a loner.

Still, Frank is the most prepared for Vienna. He learns its history and politics, its art and literature. Perhaps it is not surprising that he studies economics; whereas Father is a capitalist dreamer, Frank is a capitalist entrepreneur—and realist. He becomes Lilly's agent, later Franny's, and soon is so successful at "managing" other lives that he could retire to the Arbuthnot if he wished. In short, Frank ends up "managing"—or, better, caring for—the Berry family.

Franny is the "leader" of the family, and everyone looks to her for her opinion—especially of moving to Vienna. She is also a fighter, literally and metaphorically (especially in the early years with Frank), and she is the most daring. She is also the most adventurous sexually. Chipper Dove's rape of Franny seems to set her on a course of even greater risk-taking. Although she attempts to suppress the rape, it is always present. Like the rape in *Garp*, it is an act that marks her; it violates her integrity, her wholeness as a person. The rape is Franny's encounter with evil, and it seems both to horrify and to fascinate her at the same time, which may account for her being drawn to Ernst the pornographer/terrorist.

Clearly, Franny replaces the dead mother in the family. It is Franny who looks after and nurtures her siblings. It is equally clear not only that she returns her brother John's love (that is "too much"), but also that she will not allow that love to destroy their lives. Her insistence on overdoing their lovemaking sets them free to pursue their individual lives. Appropriately, Franny marries Junior Jones, who is very much like her, fiercely independent and courageous. It is equally appropriate that, out of generosity, they will "give" their child to John and Susie, who will be "perfect" parents.

John narrates the family story, so we see everyone through his eyes. Even though he says he is the "least opinionated" of the family, it does not mean that he is unbiased. In some ways he is Franny's alter ego, a follower more than a leader, eager to please. In other ways, he is Franny's double, a sexual experimenter, a fighter when necessary. And he does love his sister "too much," just as she says. Certainly John's objectivity concerning his sister is open to question.

Because John loves Franny to the point of obsession, his sexual encounters are, as Miller points out, "strictly physical" (160). His relationships are either a transaction (as with Ronda Ray) or thwarted (as with Bitty Tuck, who, frightened by the stuffed Sorrow, faints while "diaphraming" herself). When he has sex with Fehlgeburt, John finds the experience as "desperate and joyless as any sex" in the second Hotel New Hampshire. Since Fehlgeburt commits suicide later that night, sex for John (as for Franny) is associated with danger and death.

John fears he will not grow up; he thinks he will always be fifteen, while Franny will continue to grow and change. She asks him how he can change if he never grows up. He has no real answer—he says he'll give up swearing—but he thinks he will never grow up enough to deal with the world. However, the incident with the revolutionaries forces him to grow up—at least somewhat—quickly. Physically strong (Iowa

Bob had seen to that with his weight-lifting program), John kills Arbeiter, one of the revolutionaries, who holds the family hostage with a gun. He squeezes him to death in what might be termed a bear hug.

Later, when John meets Chipper Dove in New York, he holds him in a bear hug that could be equally deadly, but he releases him. John is more than brute strength; he learns how to control his physical nature. Thus, it is fitting that this bear of a young man at last recognizes his love for Susie, who represents, as Irving has said, "the bear in us" all (Miller 195). Franny sees that John has changed, has grown up, enough to be a "perfect father," she says. "Or a mother, man," Junior Jones adds (443).

THEMATIC ISSUES

Numerous themes from Irving's earlier novels reappear in *The Hotel New Hampshire*, particularly random violence and death, loss and regain. There are, however, two major themes: the family and the American Dream.

The family itself dominates the action of the novel, from its beginning romance between Father and Mother to its end—which is really a beginning: a new generation of the family about to be born. The family is extended slightly to accommodate Iowa Bob, who provides it with a philosophy, and our Freud, who reinforces that philosophy.

Iowa Bob liked to tell the family that life is like being on a world cruise, but that no one is ever lost overboard because "the chairs are screwed down!" (131). To Iowa Bob, it was important to live each day in the present instead of the future, an idea his own son never accepted. The old coach knew that death was terrifying and too often "premature" (168). "So what," cries Father, thinking of the future. Iowa Bob, thinking of the present, says, "Right! . . . That's the point: So what?" For Iowa Bob and Father, there is no cause for depression or unhappiness, however, because "unhappy ending[s]" did not preclude a "rich" life. And both Iowa Bob and Father know that life has no "happy endings" (168). Frank calls this philosophy "happy fatalism."

It is just this "happy fatalism" that keeps the family together after Mother and Egg's death. When something awful happens in the family, one member or another steps up to bat. When the revolutionaries hold them hostage, Lilly throws up, unable to cope with the situation; Franny soothes and comforts her. Arbeiter says, "Americans are simply crazy about the idea of the family" (351). Taking an American family hostage will give the terrorists a worldwide audience. The revolutionaries are, of course, right.

The irony is that these violent revolutionaries, who think nothing of killing and maiming for an audience, hold hostage an American family itself full of "inner violence," as Mother, when alive, had disapprovingly noted (62). John also is aware of the family's violence: "Families must be like this—gore one minute, forgiveness the next" (65). The family may stay together out of love and forgiveness; when they fight together, they are formidable: witness Ernst, killed by Father; Arbeiter, by John.

In this family, once Mother is gone, the children must look after each other—and Father—because, as Franny notes, Father does not know what is going on. Father, like Gatsby, is too caught up in his dreams. A capitalist, but no realist, Father dreams of "making a go" of it one day, of having "obscene confidence," of having money. The man in the white dinner jacket represents the "perfect" dream, the American dream of a past romance that can be re-created over and over in the future. Like Gatsby, Father believes "in the green light, the orgiastic future that year by year recedes before us" (Fitzgerald 256). And like Gatsby, Father remains innocent of the death this dream carries. He never realizes, until possibly near the end of the novel, that the man in the white dinner jacket, Arbuthnot, is a representation not merely of dreams but of disease and death as well. Father does not want to meet with Arbuthnot to arrange buying the third Hotel New Hampshire. Perhaps this reluctance is only to protect the innocence of the dream he cannot let go.

There is no such reluctance on the part of John and Frank, however, and they meet with Arbuthnot to transact the business of buying the hotel. As Harter and Thompson remind us, the young man in the perfect clothes, tanned and fit, is now an old man dying of emphysema. He is a "[r]omantic figure transformed into horror movie monster" (120), unlike Fitzgerald's Gatsby, who retains "the qualities of innocence that allow him, among other things, to fraternize with Jewish gangsters in the anti-Semitic world of East and West Egg, Long Island" (Harter and Thompson 121). If Arbuthnot represents the dream, Irving seems to be saying that both are diseased and rotting "from the inside out" (Harter and Thompson 121).

Part of the dream in *Gatsby* is that, as Americans, we can invent ourselves the way Gatsby did; from Jimmie Gatz he becomes Jay Gatsby, owner of an estate as well as clothes that make one cry from the sheer romance of it all. At least, that make Daisy Buchanan cry. John Berry recognizes that we continue to dream and to create fictional lives: "We give ourselves a sainted mother, we make our father a hero" (449). But John has grown to be realist enough to know that if we invent "what we love," we also invent "what we fear" (449). In addition, he knows that dreams can evaporate as quickly and easily as they can be imagined.

Nevertheless, Father's sons keep his dreams alive. They create a third and totally different Hotel New Hampshire from the old Arbuthnot-by-the-Sea, which perhaps was never very desirable anyway: it was not "democratic" enough. Our Freud left because of anti-Semitism; Earl the Bear, aka State o' Maine, was shot in a senseless killing by a twelve-year-old boy. Father's hotel, at the end of the novel, is finally a "great" hotel because, like the "perfect" family, it provides the "space" for its guests "to grow their own way" (441). Father, as the hotelier, waves the Louisville Slugger (how American this symbol is!) like a "magic wand." Everything turns out "all right" in John's "fairy-tale hotel," but the last words of the novel are a somber reminder: "You have to keep passing the open windows" (450). "Happy fatalism," indeed.

A STRUCTURALIST ANALYSIS OF *THE HOTEL NEW HAMPSHIRE*

Nearly all critics point to the fairy-tale qualities of *The Hotel New Hampshire* (the narrator also tells us "it is a fairy-tale"); Harter and Thompson move beyond the analysis of the work as fairy tale to discuss it as romance in the American literary tradition. A number of critics point out the novel's weaknesses: the inclusion of Donald Justice's poetry, for example (Towers, "Reservations" 14–15). At the same time, critics seem to miss, for the most part, what is at the heart of the novel: transformation and how it is brought about.

A structuralist analysis of *The Hotel New Hampshire* helps us to see how Irving brings about transformation from incest and rape and how he uses "social drama" in his writing. Structuralists are interested in form over content, although content is not ignored. Structuralism looks at those parts or "segments" in narrative that, through their "functions," make meaning possible. For example, Propp in his *Morphology of the Folktale* (which includes fairy tales as well) studies *functions across texts* to discover systems capable of generating meanings that go beyond the boundaries of a given or individual work. (Roland Barthes's *Mythologies* and Claude Lévi-Strauss's *Structural Anthropology* also demonstrate Propp's methodologies.) Victor Turner, greatly influenced by Lévi-Strauss, writes of "social dramas," based on cultural paradigms (the nuclear family, for example). Often these dramas are ritualized, capable of generating meanings that may be in dialectic tension with what we understand as the social order.

The incestuous relationship between John and Franny arises out of the family drama and is linked to Franny's rape by Chipper Dove both in the positioning of scenes and in their functions. Chapter 11 makes this plain to readers by its title: "Being in Love with Franny; Dealing with Chipper Dove." The linkage between rape and incest is more subtly demonstrated in Chapter 4, "Franny Loses a Fight," where the rape, which occurs on Halloween, includes reference to John and Franny's "secret" place in the woods; the chapter ends with John listening to Franny drawing her bath (her third after the rape) and his whispering "I love you" through the locked door (122).

Although Franny is the leader and John the shadow–follower, both have foul mouths and are fond of scatological comments; are fascinated (if that is the correct term) by excrement; are sexual experimenters; and are independent. Franny is just ahead of her brother in knowing that he cares too much for her, and she *appears* to be more knowledgeable about sexual matters. Junior Jones, however, makes it clear that Franny is a "good" girl, if we need confirmation of this. Jones also makes it clear that Franny is John's double by asking John over and over what his sister wants.

The brother/sister relationship is more than a depiction of the Narcissus/Echo myth (that story ends in death); it is also an Oedipal relationship. Franny is the replacement of the dead Mother. Even before brother and sister make love, John asks her what the difference is between them. Franny answers that she will get over him but that he will not get over her unless she helps him. John knows Franny will not only manipulate their having sex, but will do it as part of her promise to "*mother*" the children after Mother's death. Franny says to John, "You and me need saving, kid. . . . But especially *you* need it" (368).

To save her brother from himself, to save them both, Franny ritualizes their intercourse. By ritual, I mean what Victor Turner describes as "prescribed formal behavior for occasions not given over to technological routine, having reference to beliefs in invisible beings or powers" (159). Such ritual may be regarded as an *enactment* of a social drama; in the case of Franny and John, it is their familial drama. Irving does not describe Franny and John's performance; he cannot do so because the very function of the performance is to transcend itself in its meaning. When Lilly returns to the Stanhope to find the apartment door locked, Franny tells her to go away because she is writing. Lilly rejects what she suspects is a lie, but in fact Franny is "performing" the "writing" of this play or drama. By the process of enactment, Franny intends for something new to be generated: a new relationship between herself and John that will release them from their obsession with one another.

Ritual enactment always follows a certain pattern, according to Van Gennep (*The Rites of Passage* 73): "preliminal, liminal, and postliminal" (one can, of course, see the sexual implications here). The liminal phase of Franny and John's performance is when they pass the threshold of pain. Their sexual meeting is not "fun," for it is deadly serious: "I want you a *lot* sore," she says. She wants them to cross a threshold, to enter a liminal time and space that is magical (Turner 161). It is there that "transformation occurs most radically in the ritual 'pupation' of liminal seclusion—at least in life-crisis rituals" (Turner 161). Out of Franny and John's "seclusion," out of their "human depths," comes the magic of a fairy tale. Franny forces John to understand that their love was "too much," that it would have been "the death" of them (373). What Franny does is to overdo it, and thus saves both of them.

At the end of the ritual, Franny says, "Hello, goodbye, my love," indicating that the process has been transformative. Moreover, this ritual that John and Franny have "lived out" is "artwork"; " 'That's it, that's all she wrote,' [Franny] murmured. 'That's the end of it. Now we're free. Now that's over' " (374). The postliminal phase will be the rest of their lives.

It is when John leaves Franny, after she has saved him, that he runs into Chipper Dove. It will now be John's turn to save his sister, although he needs the help, certainly, of Lilly—and, as it turns out, of Frank and Susie the Bear. The so-called revenge on Chipper Dove is, like the incest of Franny and John, ritualized. The drama, written by Lilly and enacted by Franny, Frank, John, Susie, a female stand-in for Junior Jones, and a few walk-ons from Susie's Washington Square players, is not so much to take revenge on Chipper as it is to transform Franny. Along the way, John, Frank, and Susie will also be transformed. Through the play Lilly provides, they not only can keep passing the windows, they can move beyond one of the most awful events in their lives—that of rape. Though Lilly writes the play, directs it (Franny, out of fear, loses much of her leadership role here), and acts in it, she, unfortunately, will not be transformed. (Irving's *Owen Meany* also will demonstrate that ritual does not work for everyone.)

Von Franz notes that fairy tales plumb the depths of archetype, myths, and psyche (*Interpretation of Fairytales* passim). Lilly's drama is a perfect fairy tale, plumbing the archetypal fear of rape and sexual violation. Chipper's "rape" is a ritualized reenactment of the Halloween rape of Franny.

Franny and John had been caught in a net by Chipper and his buddies. In the net, they also inadvertently caught a small trick-or-treater from town in a gorilla suit, but, because he is so small, the little boy looks like a spider monkey, one who is nearly frightened to death. Chipper lets the "spider monkey" go, but we recognize him as a symbol of death (Cirlot 202, 290). And the rape scene is a kind of death—for Franny, who is as afraid as the little trick-or-treater, and for John, who is afraid he will not get help in time to stop the rape (he does not). John and Franny have been linked by incestuous desires as well as by Chipper's rape. Brother and sister are caught in Chipper's net; brother and sister both feel deep fear. Moreover, John is implicated in the rape, insofar as he fails to save his sister.

Both Franny and John want Chipper to feel the same deathly fear they experienced. Franny does not want to kill Chipper; she wants him to be as scared as she was when he raped her. Moreover, she does not want to go too far in frightening him. The Berry siblings—and Susie, who is a member of the family long before she marries John—will enter liminal space and be transformed through the acting out of their play. They hope to change Chipper, but his transformation is of lesser importance in this social drama. However, there is no doubt that Chipper experiences fear.

When Chipper arrives at the door of the apartment, he is "propelled" into the room in much the same way that Franny and John were suddenly caught in the net. Franny has been given only one line: "Well, look who's here" (398), the exact repetition of Chipper's line when he saw her in the net. It is John who tells him that it is now Chipper's turn to be raped. Frank, who plays out the mad scene from Donizetti's opera *Lucia di Lammermoor* (while the music plays), bounces up and down on the bed, and screams that he isn't going to rape Chipper: "I like fucking mud puddles," an allusion to the time Chipper taunted Frank as a child for his homosexuality, and forced him to grind his body into a mud puddle. For Frank, this episode was tantamount to rape.

The repetition of the word "rape" in Lilly's drama signifies the drama's seriousness. Once Susie (who, we recall, also had been raped), makes her move, in her bear suit, on Chipper, Frank offers him advice: "*don't move*" (401).

When Dove is reduced to gibbering, "Please don't! Please!" (402), and when he screams, we recall the sound Franny made when she was raped, a sound that moved Harold Swallow, who was guarding John, to run for Junior Jones (108). At this point in the drama, Lilly was supposed to say, "There will be no more rapes . . . that's final" (402), for that "was all Lilly wrote." But there is indeterminacy here, and the "performance transforms itself," as Turner would say (160). Franny interrupts the scene and suddenly takes charge; she is no longer afraid. She tells Susie, "That's enough." And she tells Chipper to put his pants on, warning him that when he decides to take off his pants for anyone in the future, he should think of her. Frank adds, "Think of *all* of us," and John says, "Remember us" (402). Franny is not the only one set free. Susie takes off her bear's head: "she would never *need* to wear it again. From now on, the bear suit was just for fun" (402).

Critics who see this scene as misdirected, as silly, and even as trivializing rape (Harter and Thompson; Miller; Reilly) totally miss the point. Irving is underscoring the awfulness of rape. John points out that if the revenge "*had* been as awful" as the rape, "it would have been too much" (403). Going beyond the boundary Franny sets would have been to kill Dove. For Franny and her siblings (excluding Lilly but including Susie), ritualizing the threat of rape has been transformative. They cross the threshold into liminality, a space indeterminate but filled with potential for transformation. At the end of Lilly's drama, Franny says, in "awed affection": "Here comes the rest of our lives" (403). In *The Hotel New Hampshire*, ritual is both powerful and "magical"; we must wait until *Owen Meany* to see that ritual can also be "religious."

8

The Cider House Rules
(1985)

In his sixth novel, *The Cider House Rules*, John Irving asks his readers to consider with care the tangled question of abortion. Though Irving initially intended to make this a book only about orphans, abortion entered the novel about a year into his work on it. In one interview, he spoke of how the subject fit, and how he came to make Dr. Larch, one of the novel's protagonists, an abortionist as well as an obstetrician and pediatrician: "[W]hat doctor would be most sympathetic to performing abortions but the doctor who delivered unwanted babies, then cared for them in an orphanage?" (Fein 25).

Despite, or because of, its controversial nature, and because of Irving's successes with *The World According to Garp* and *The Hotel New Hampshire*, *The Cider House Rules* sold strongly, making the *New York Times* bestseller list. It was also a Book-of-the-Month Club selection. Like *Garp* and *The Hotel New Hampshire*, the novel was widely, if not always positively, reviewed. Benjamin DeMott and Christopher Lehmann-Haupt, in separate reviews in the *New York Times*, praised the book. DeMott was especially enthusiastic about Irving's examining so minutely in his fiction a topic as divisive as abortion. Paul Gray wrote in *Time Magazine*, "Irving's mastery of plot and pacing has never been more engagingly on display" (81).

Anthony Burgess reviewed *The Cider House Rules* negatively for *The Atlantic*, disparaging its length and characters, calling it "a little too plain for nearly six hundred pages: we long for tougher intellectual or aesthetic engagement than Mr. Irving is ready to give us. His characters are just not interesting enough" (98). More vituperative was Roger Lewis, who, in the *New Statesman*, described it as "a thick brick of a book" that should be "thrown back through John Irving's window" (29). In a more considered essay, Carol Harter and James Thompson find that Irving's treatment of abortion "fail[ed] to explore adequately the rich, if painful ambiguities of the issue," offering instead "a showy kind of concern for the subject itself" (137). Edward Reilly does not judge the novel's value vis-à-vis *Garp* or *The Hotel New Hampshire* but observes that in its settings, characters, situations, and themes, "*Cider House* marks a definite maturing in Irving's talents" (*Understanding John Irving* 119).

Interest in the novel has been fairly well sustained. It was dramatized in 1996, scripted by Peter Parnell, Jane Jones, and actor Tom Hulce. It was performed at the Seattle Repertory Theater and included in its cast Ethan Hawke as Homer, and Academy Award winner Linda Hunt as one of the nurses at St. Cloud's orphanage. Earlier readings featured Griffin Dunne, Isabella Rossellini, Frances Sternhagen, and Sam Waterston.

PLOT DEVELOPMENT

Irving plots *The Cider House Rules* with the care, complexity, and attention to detail of the nineteenth-century novels he loves. (These are also the only novels to which the orphan Homer Wells, Irving's chief protagonist, is exposed.) Dividing the novel into three parts and using the orphanage at St. Cloud's, Maine, as a narrative frame, Irving enables us to follow Homer Wells from his childhood in St. Cloud's to his adulthood in Heart's Haven and Heart's Rock, and then back to St. Cloud's in middle age. We see him grow up at St. Cloud's, becoming surrogate son and protégé to Dr. Wilbur Larch, who runs the orphanage/abortion clinic there. We watch him pull away from Larch, partly in disagreement with him over the morality of performing abortions and partly in pursuit of the love and friendship he has discovered with Candy Kendall and Wally Worthington. Finally, he returns to St. Cloud's to carry on Larch's work, taking Larch's moral stance as well.

The story is told in a mostly linear fashion; the only exception is Dr. Larch's backstory, which we are told just after we meet Homer. The novel features an omniscient narrator, who describes St. Cloud's as an isolated, virtually abandoned, Maine lumber town, named for its dreary weather rather than for any religious entity. In it is an orphanage where children are delivered of abandoned mothers and where, just as frequently, mothers are delivered of their unwanted pregnancies. How Dr. Wilbur Larch, obstetrician, pediatrician, and abortionist, arrives at St. Cloud's is an important plot element, as it prefigures Homer's eventual reconciliation to St. Cloud's as his real home, the one place he can truly be "of use."

As a young physician working at Boston's Lying-In Hospital just before World War I, Larch is shocked by the consequences of illegal abortion to poor women. Though he has seen women die horribly as a result of the awful measures they had to take to end a pregnancy, he refuses to perform an abortion for a desperate woman who comes to him. She is the daughter of Mrs. Eames, the prostitute whose company Larch's father paid for before his son entered medical school, and who recently had died from complications of a self-administered abortion. He refuses to help the daughter, the narrator tells us, because "he was too young" (49). Larch's fear of discovery overpowers his belief that he might be doing the right thing by assisting the daughter, and he sends her away. She is soon brought back, dying of complications from an abortion performed at an illegal clinic, one of several "Off Harrison."

The vague address "Off Harrison" refers to the questionable nature of the gynecological practices undertaken along that street, as opposed to the branch of Boston Lying-In that is *on* Harrison: the legitimate medical center, where Larch refuses to perform an abortion for Mrs. Eames's daughter. As a result of her death, Larch visits "Off Harrison" and learns about the varyingly effective, though never sterile, abortion techniques offered to poor women there and at "clinics" like it. Larch does not second-guess himself again when a thirteen-year-old, in her third pregnancy as a result of incest, presents herself. However, he knows he cannot continue to perform illegal abortions for long in a Boston hospital.

Upon returning home to Portland, Maine, Larch is invited to a meal with the Channing-Peabodys, a wealthy Boston family who summer there, and is asked to bring his medical bag. When he is requested to perform an abortion for the Channing-Peabodys' daughter, Missy, he begins truly to appreciate the fact that unwanted pregnancy knows no class boundary, but the availability of safe abortion does. He decides to find a place where obstetrics can be practiced in a more equitable fashion. As an obstetrician, he delivers babies, which colleagues call "the Lord's work." As an abortionist, he also delivers mothers, which is called "the

Devil's work" (67). Dr. Larch sees both kinds of delivery as "the Lord's work."

In St. Cloud's, Larch, with the assistance of his devoted staff, Nurse Edna and Nurse Angela, delivers babies and mothers without drawing attention. At night, Larch reads Dickens's *David Copperfield* or *Great Expectations*—stories about orphans—to the orphan boys before they fall asleep, while Mrs. Grogan, tending to the girls, reads Brontë's *Jane Eyre* to them. When Larch is not attending to orphans or mothers, he either expands his copious history of St. Cloud's or indulges in a quiet addiction to ether.

The status quo is maintained at St. Cloud's well into the 1930s, when Homer Wells, an oft-adopted orphan whose placements never work out, discovers an aborted fetus near the incinerator. Larch, for whom Homer is the closest to a son he will ever know, and who has hope that Homer may someday become a physician, has been training Homer as a midwife, and expects eventually to teach him to perform safe abortions. Larch tries, without success, to make Homer understand his point of view about abortion. Larch refers to the fetus as a "product of conception," but Homer sees it as a dead baby. It is only much later that Homer begins to agree with Larch that women deserve a choice concerning abortion.

While Homer grows up with Dickens, over in the girls' division, Melony is growing up with Charlotte Brontë. Melony shares more than orphan status with Jane Eyre; like Jane Eyre, Melony will find herself moving from place to place in search of a home and a hero. She learns something about survival from Jane, but their tactics differ. Whereas Jane Eyre's strength lies beneath a modestly compliant, even obsequious, exterior, Melony is a tough, strong girl physically and mentally. She teaches Homer the mechanics of sex, then makes him promise never to leave her. Eventually, Homer does leave, and Melony begins a relentless search for him, one that continues, unbeknownst to Homer, until they are both in middle age.

Homer leaves St. Cloud's after he befriends Wally Worthington and Candy Kendall, a happy young couple about his age who come to St. Cloud's for an abortion. Wally and Candy have nearly everything two young people could hope for: Wally's family lives on the coast of Maine and has a thriving orchard business called Ocean View, in a town called Heart's Rock; Candy's father is a lobsterman and gifted engine repairman in Heart's Haven. Candy and Wally will be married, but her pregnancy comes a bit too soon to be convenient.

When Wally invites Homer to accompany them to Ocean View to pick up plantings with which to start a small orchard at St. Cloud's, Larch encourages Homer to stay at the coast as long as he wants, though it breaks his heart to say so. He knows that Homer must leave if he is to have any chance to be a part of a world beyond the dreary confines of St. Cloud's, and, like a good father, he knows Homer deserves that chance. On his part, Homer is filled with new feelings: the beginning of a bond of friendship with Wally; the wide-eyed, engulfing attraction he feels for Candy; and the friction he feels growing between himself and Larch. The first section of the novel ends as Homer leaves St. Cloud's for the sunny, robust atmosphere of the orchards and the coast.

In the novel's second part, Homer establishes a home with the Worthingtons, finding himself consistently "of use" to the family and the business. He becomes an honorary member of the Worthington family, beloved and trusted by Wally and his parents, Olive and Senior Worthington. However, Homer can never be completely comfortable there; he worries about having left all the work of St. Cloud's to Larch, and he has trouble reconciling his growing love for Candy with his genuine affection for Wally. Candy recognizes Homer's love for her, and when Wally leaves to fight in World War II, she permits herself to accept her feelings for Homer as love.

When Wally's bomber is lost over Burma and he is presumed dead, Homer and Candy secretly conceive a child, Angel, who will be born, also in secret, at St. Cloud's, where Homer and Candy live happily during her pregnancy and over the winter after Angel is born. Eventually, Wally is found alive, paralyzed from the waist down, and he returns home. Homer and Candy return home as well, claiming to have adopted Angel together. Though Candy loves Homer quite sincerely, she still loves Wally, is loyal to him, and is torn about whether to marry him. When Homer presses her to decide between him and Wally, she says they must "wait and see." The phrase recurs throughout the rest of the novel, signaling the repeated ambiguities and ambivalences that have always shaped Homer's life. Candy marries Wally, and the three of them together raise Angel in a loving home, but one that cannot forever maintain the lie upon which the family is constructed. During this time, Homer and Wally remain close friends, and Homer and Candy meet for an occasional tryst.

At the same time, Larch, who never completely gives up hope that Homer will one day return to carry on his work, is preparing a new identity for Homer, in the event he should decide to step into Larch's shoes. In fabricating Homer's new identity, Larch uses the name of Fuzzy Stone, a contemporary of Homer's in the orphanage, who had died there many years earlier. With St. Cloud's increasingly conservative board of trustees in mind, Larch contrives "official" college and medical school records for Homer and an appropriate history as a missionary. "Fuzzy Stone," according to all reports submitted to St. Cloud's board, is a devoted, morally upright physician who, as a former orphan at St. Cloud's, is now prepared to give back what he received. Larch's last act in his intricate plan to bring back Homer is to send him a package containing a doctor's bag, marked "FS," that holds a new set of tools for the procedure known as dilation and curettage, the common procedure for early-term abortion. The contents of the package will be stored carefully and hidden until Homer is ethically prepared to put its contents to use.

Homer will take his place again at St. Cloud's, after a series of events at the orchard strip the facade from his life with Candy, Wally, and Angel. During apple-picking season, the orchard employs migrant workers, Southern blacks recruited by Mr. Rose, the crew boss. (Each year before the workers arrive, Wally's mother and—later—Homer type up and post a list of rules for the migrants, who all live in the cider house, rules that the returning crew expect and respectfully ignore, since no one but Mr. Rose can read.) Mr. Rose runs the crew efficiently and is known to be fast with a knife. The Worthingtons appreciate Mr. Rose, always friendly, if slightly menacing, for his supervisory abilities and leave him to manage the crew as he sees fit. One year, however, he is accompanied by his young daughter, Rose Rose, and her baby. Angel, then a teenager, falls in love with Rose, and they manage to spend some time together. Angel learns that the father of Rose's baby was cut up and driven away by Mr. Rose. He also learns that Rose is pregnant again, impregnated by her father. As the relationship between Mr. Rose and Rose Rose is exposed in a climactic series of events, the reality of the relationships among Homer, Candy, Wally, and Angel is also exposed. Handing Homer the stub of a candle left in the cider house, where he met Candy, Mr. Rose points out that Homer also has broken some rules.

In the chaos these hard truths generate, Rose Rose stabs her father. He refuses medical attention, preferring to die. Homer performs an abortion for Rose Rose, and she vanishes with her child. Earlier, Melony had appeared and instantly recognized Angel as Homer's son. She disparages Homer for having sunk so low as not to acknowledge his child; she thought he would do some "good" with his life, such as take Larch's place. Homer and Candy "wait and see" no longer. They confess everything to Wally and Angel. During the brief time it takes for these events to transpire, Dr. Larch expires when he accidentally overdoses on ether.

In its brief third section, the novel comes full circle, ending with an epilogue to tie up loose ends. Homer returns to St. Cloud's, "bringing the Lord's work with him." But now he is Fuzzy Stone, "because he knew that Homer Wells (like Rose Rose) was long gone" (584). Homer eventually forms a relationship with Nurse Caroline and spends his evenings reading to the orphans from *Jane Eyre*, *David Copperfield*, and *Great Expectations*. On his own time, he studies *Gray's Anatomy*. When all he lacks for further study, he believes, is a cadaver, a body appears. It is Melony's; she had left instructions that she be returned to St. Cloud's upon her death. Feeling she had been "used enough," Homer buries Melony in St. Cloud's new apple orchard (586). In this section, we also learn that Candy and Wally become fine apple farmers and good citizens, and that Angel becomes a novelist.

Following the epilogue is a fairly lengthy section of author's notes, some of which give background information about apples and orchards, or Alzheimer's disease, Senior Worthington's illness. Mostly, however, the notes acknowledge sources of medical information, including a great deal from Irving's grandfather, Dr. Frederick C. Irving, who at one time was chief of staff at Boston Lying-In. Other notes provide historical perspective on abortion in the United States: they include brief but dramatic case histories, as well as citations of treatises by respected physicians on the medical necessity of "premature delivery," code for abortion (591). This set of notes lends the novel—and its pro-choice tone—scholarly authority.

SETTING

The geographical settings of *Cider House* help to underscore the moral and ethical shadings that attend the issue of abortion. St. Cloud's had been a logging camp deep in the Maine woods, and the town grew up around it. The camp was originally called Clouds because of the low clouds shrouding the valley. As the logging business grew, so did the town. (Stripping the trees was the Ramses Paper Company, perhaps slyly named by Irving with reference both to the condom brand and to the Egyptian pharaoh Ramses II, who was most famous for greed, enslavement, and monuments to himself.) Clouds was changed to "St. Clouds," according to Dr. Larch's history, because of "the fervent backwoods

Catholic instinct to put a Saint before so many things" (3). The apostrophe was added later.

There was no seasonal relief to the dreariness: the climate in St. Cloud's consisted of frozen winters and stifling summers. As for fall, Larch wrote that it lasted for all of five minutes. Spring consisted of weeks of thawing mud, when it was impossible for people to go to work. Roads became unusable, and everyone stayed home. It was during spring that cabin fever hit. In spring, people in St. Cloud's turned to drinking and fighting, whoring and raping: "In spring, the seeds for an orphanage were planted and overplanted" (4).

The town that grew from the logging camp boomed for some time, but as the forest was cleared, the Ramses Paper Company moved downstream, and the town began to dissipate, leaving only older and plainer prostitutes and their children. In response to a plea from one of the prostitutes, Larch founded the orphanage at St. Cloud's. The buildings are old and dark, but not especially frightening. The depressing atmosphere, however, matches the scenes portraying women walking from the town in the gray morning, either to deliver or to be delivered. The gray represents both the desolation of the women arriving at St. Cloud's for either purpose, and the indeterminate—or is it irrelevant?—moral cast of the dilemma of each.

As in Dickens, names help tell the story. Whereas "St. Cloud's" represents the ambiguities inherent in an orphanage/abortion clinic, Heart's Haven and Heart's Rock are no less complicated. Their names only seem to represent the affirmation of life. Both towns, originally named Hart after Reginald Hart, who established the first farm in the area, had their names sweetened at some point.

Heart's Haven, the more affluent of the two, is located on the coast. In Heart's Haven is the Haven Club, where prosperous Havenites enjoy each other's company to the exclusion of everyone from Heart's Rock, except for the Worthingtons. Heart's Haven is more than a sunny oceanside town; it is a town that keeps its "spoiled and hard-to-please" citizenry untainted by outsiders (119). As the reader might expect, there is hypocrisy in Heart's Haven. Homer notices a small but representative example of it when Wally makes a condescending remark about the Pettigrew family just prior to greeting Debra Pettigrew warmly and affectionately.

Inland from Heart's Haven "squats" Heart's Rock. It was named for "the uninhabited rock island that appears to float like a dead whale in the otherwise perfect harbor of Heart's Haven" (118). The people of

Heart's Haven overlook the quaintly picturesque town stores of Heart's Rock, choosing instead to focus their judgments on Drinkwater Lake, a murky, mosquito-ridden lake whose "summer people" come from local towns. Its cottages and camps have "names of a striving wishfulness," such as Echo's End and Wee Three. Homer sees this "bog that separates Echo's End from Sherman's Hole in the Ground" as a sadly appropriate location for a summer camp for the St. Cloud's orphans, were there such a thing (119).

The people of Heart's Rock work hard on their tidy farms. If they are somewhat flintier than the Havenites, Heart's Rock's citizens spend a lot less time sitting in judgment of their neighbors in the next town. The Worthingtons' beautifully abundant Ocean View Orchard is in Heart's Rock, though the house and grounds, we are told, have a decidedly Heart's Haven look, and the name "Ocean View," though largely fallacious, has a Heart's Haven sound. Like Ray Kendall in Heart's Haven, the Worthingtons live in Heart's Rock, but they are not "of it."

CHARACTER DEVELOPMENT

Like Dickens and Brontë, who figure as literary backdrops in *The Cider House Rules*, Irving's long suit is the Bildungsroman; this novel follows Homer Wells from childhood to middle age. However, Wilbur Larch is nearly as much a protagonist in this novel as is Homer; in a sense, the two characters split the role, so parallel, if sequential, are their destinies. As Reilly points out, "While Homer grows up, the first five chapters treat Larch's life before and after he flees Boston for St. Cloud's. As Larch grows older, the last six chapters examine Homer's life after he flees St. Cloud's for Heart's Rock" (*Understanding John Irving* 105).

Larch's one experience with sex—his drunken father's gift, of time with a Portland prostitute named Mrs. Eames—had sent him to medical school with gonorrhea. Ether helped with the pain, and it would become Larch's one and only vice. His later experiences in trying to save Mrs. Eames and her daughter at Boston Lying-In, and his subsequent visits to "Off Harrison" help Larch conclude that sex is not for him, and he makes his way to Maine to try to give real help to mothers and children. Though he cares a great deal for all of his charges, love is a somewhat foreign concept to Larch. He does the best he can, however, and with the devoted Nurses Angela and Edna, he provides the orphans with stability and routine, reading to the boys' division, kissing them all good

night, and signing off each evening with the "benediction" "Goodnight,
you princes of Maine . . . you kings of New England!" (72).

Frequently referred to as St. Larch, Larch has a monastic quality. He
fulfills his mission to help abandoned women and children with focus
and dedication. And while he does not proselytize, he truly hopes that
Homer will follow his example and carry on his work. Reilly sees Larch
as "saintly, if not godlike," in that "he lives among the clouds and mists
of St. Cloud's; and he writes his chronicles that suggest gospels according
to St. Larch" (*Understanding John Irving* 104). Reilly points out that this
characterization is a significant element in the abortion discussion and
in the theme of "rules."

Larch's orphan–protégé, Homer Wells, develops cautiously, almost
painfully, as he is adopted again and again, only to be returned to St.
Cloud's again and again, through no fault of his own. For example, in
Homer's first adoptive home, he never cries, and the family returns him,
believing they have a "lemon" on their hands (7). His second family
returns him to St. Cloud's because he does cry—too loudly—after they
pinch and punch him. The final attempt at placement for Homer is with
a vigorous, athletic couple, who take Homer camping; while swimming,
the couple is killed by onrushing logs as Homer watches. Homer thus
becomes a permanent part of St. Cloud's, unofficially adopted by Larch,
and learns to assist in obstetric and pediatric procedures. Appropriately,
Homer also takes on the job of reading to the orphan boys at bedtime.

Homer accepts the fact that the orphanage is his home, but as he grows
older, he finds he cannot accept Larch's views on abortion. When Homer,
who sees being "of use" as the primary task of an orphan, finds a carelessly discarded fetus, he realizes he cannot morally be of use at St.
Cloud's. He loves Larch without reserve, but he is firm in his refusal to
perform abortions, though he observes them to oblige Larch.

As Homer moves slowly toward independence, Melony teaches him
the process of sex and extracts from him a promise that he will never
leave her. He has no reason to believe he will, but almost immediately
thereafter, Candy and Wally appear. They are a golden couple and seem
to represent temptation in their gleaming Cadillac with an apple logo on
its side. The orphan Curly Day, hopeful of adoption, sees them as "an-
gelic specimens" (181). Mrs. Grogan of the girls' division feels "charmed
to be looking at these lovely people" (184). Melony imagines them "too
perfect to need an abortion" (186). When Homer sees Candy, who *has*,
in fact, come to St. Cloud's for an abortion, he believes that "nothing
could interfere with her radiance" (193). "The boy has gone gaga on me,"

thinks Larch (197). Candy and Wally dazzle Homer with the romantic aura that emanates from them, and life takes on new meaning for the orphan. It seems right for Homer to leave with them. Here we find the center of the Bildungsroman—Homer leaves St. Cloud's to become his "own" man and to pursue the independent thinking that has caused his rift with Larch, until the day that he returns to St. Cloud's.

Candy Kendall is a familiar Irving heroine. Though she is devoted to her father, to Wally, and eventually to Homer, she is independent in her own way, and a caring mother. We watch Candy develop over the years, a child whose mother died giving birth to her and who was raised lovingly by her father, Ray Kendall. Candy has grown up to be not only beautiful but loyal and reliable. She appears without blemish, always polite and thoughtful. With her boyfriend, Wally Worthington, she arrives at St. Cloud's seeking an abortion, not because she is desperate but because she has become pregnant ahead of schedule.

Though Homer disapproves of abortion and would certainly disapprove of abortion on her terms, he is instantly in love with Candy. Her radiance renders his rules on abortion inoperative. The three young people become friends, but Candy's loyalty to Wally keeps Homer at a distance, though she loves him. When Wally's bomber is shot down and he is presumed lost, she allows herself to act on her love for Homer. When Wally returns, she continues to see Homer in secret, but her loyalty to and love for Wally demand that she marry him. Candy chooses to "wait and see" before making "final" decisions, a symbol, perhaps of the sometimes impossibly difficult nature of the choices brought to light in this novel.

Wally Worthington, like Candy, is blond and sunny. Though he seems a bit insubstantial, with his boyish playfulness and his ever-friendly manner, he is also stronger than he at first seems; as the story—and the web of relationships—unfolds, he proves to be a stabilizing factor. When Wally finally returns home from the war, he is paralyzed from the waist down and unable to father children. Though it is clear to him that Homer and Candy have turned to one another for support while he was gone, and even that Angel is their son, Wally, like Candy, takes a wait-and-see attitude. The light that emanates from Candy and Wally demonstrates that they are destined for one another, and Wally is right to wait and see. Candy makes the choice she must, and everything turns out for the best, as we might expect with this golden couple. But for fifteen years, the three adults together rear Angel, living in the same house "[l]ike a family" (457). The complexities of their triangular relationship are resonant of the complexities of the abortion debate. In neither case is there necessarily a right answer.

Melony is the opposite of Candy, though she is just as "good" in her way. As aggressive and pragmatic as Candy is cautious, Melony, hurt by Homer, is violent and relentless in her zeal to protect what she believes is hers, whether it is Homer or Lorna, the woman with whom she has a long and, at first, uneven relationship. Melony was older than most orphans when she came to St. Cloud's; no one knew her exact age. Like Homer, she was adopted and returned several times. Melony, too, has a firm grasp of rules—rules of her own making—born, no doubt of disappointment and rejection. Her clarity of purpose serves to mirror Homer's lack of it. For whatever reason, she wanted Homer to grow up to be some sort of hero (at least the hero of his own life), and when she finally finds him, she tells him freely and forcefully what a disappointment he is to her. Decisive, strident, a woman of action, she functions as a sharp counterpoint to Candy, who, while also strong, is gentle and kind, and waits and sees. Melony's rules are, however, as deeply felt as Candy's and, therefore, no less valid.

THEMATIC ISSUES

Nearly always central to Irving's fiction is the family, and its various versions in *Cider House* underscore his prevailing theme of "rules," both personal and societal. The attempts of the characters in their unorthodox families to create radically different rules help to contextualize the difficult theme of choice in abortion.

The closest Homer comes to a family of origin is St. Cloud's, whose "father" is Larch, while Nurses Edna and Angela and Mrs. Grogan, if not exactly mother figures, make some maternal contributions to the orphans' lives. All of them love Homer, but the "rules" of an orphanage work against even the most beloved orphan. The most tender moment of Homer's youth comes during his adolescence when Larch, thinking the orphan is asleep, kisses him twice and calls him "my boy." In the morning, Homer must change Dr. Larch's pillowcase because it is wet with tears. Larch's kisses are the only "fatherly kisses" Homer ever receives (135).

Though Larch is a reluctant father, his rules run St. Cloud's. Larch decides that, to spare orphans the potential pain of rejection, records of birth mothers will not be kept. Larch makes rules about when to deliver a baby and when to deliver a mother. And Larch determines that "the Devil's work," abortion, is as much "the Lord's work" as delivering orphans.

As for the orphans, most remain hopeful of adoption into a family more personal than that of St. Cloud's. Homer, who has no such hope, creates his own rules for living. To do so, he struggles against the rules of the family, the institutions, the society in which he lives. And at the same time, he *will* be "of use." He will be of use as Larch's assistant until he discovers a fetus near an incinerator and makes a new rule. Larch's rules about abortion no longer can be his. Homer decides that Larch can see the aborted child as a fetus if he wishes, but to Homer, it is a baby. If Larch chooses to do abortions, Homer can choose not to. Homer sees that rules change as situations change.

Similarly, the Kendall and Worthington families reconstruct the rules of family as they go along. Candy Kendall has no mother, and Wally might as well have no father (Wally's father, the victim of undiagnosed Alzheimer's disease, is more a child than a father). Candy's father, Ray, and Wally's mother, Olive, effectively join forces to look after Candy, Wally, and, eventually, Homer. The Worthington and Kendall "family" prepares us—along with Homer, Candy, and Wally—for the family to come.

The extraordinary family formed by Homer, Candy, and Wally, with Angel at its center, shakes the usual "rules" of family to their foundation. Yet this family flourishes. All three love Angel. All three understand that Angel is the natural child of Homer and Candy—including Wally, though he has never actually been told. After Angel is born—and just before Wally's return—Homer and Candy stand outside the cider house and establish rules about their son: "We both get to live with him. We get to be his family. Nobody ever moves out" (456).

For fifteen years, the four of them make the rules work. Wally and Candy maintain a happy marriage, while Homer and Candy continue, on occasion, to meet in secret. Because of the secrecy, the familial rules *appear* to be compatible with societal rules. Homer, Candy, and Wally have made their arrangement based on the information they have: Homer and Candy are Angel's parents, Candy is married to Wally, all four love each other. For those not involved in their situation, how are they to be judged?

Yet we do judge Mr. Rose, the crew boss of the migrant apple-pickers. He represents the phallic father of the nuclear family and the patriarchal society. As the undisputed leader of the migrant community at Ocean

View, his word, not the posted cider house rules, is the phallic law, enforced by his knife (see Moi 138, 140, 216). Indeed, Mr. Rose is well known for his quickness and efficacy with a knife; he needs only to show it to elicit the response he desires.

Mr. Rose makes it clear to Homer that the cider house rules posted each season are irrelevant to the crew. In posting the rules, Homer simply follows a tradition established by the Worthingtons. The fact that Olive, before Homer, typed and posted the rules may seem to obviate their paternalistic thrust, but she took over a job her husband could no longer do. Except that each rule begins with the word "please," they are paternalistic (281–282). Yet, none of the migrants can read, save Mr. Rose. " 'We got our own rules, too, Homer,' he said." The rules belong to Mr. Rose, and he literally, at times, inscribes them—sharply—on the bodies of "his" family of workers.

More insidious than Mr. Rose's work rules are his sexual rules for his daughter, Rose Rose. He has already laid down phallic law by cutting her boyfriend and claiming Rose Rose and her child as his own, his personal property. At Ocean View, his "law" of ownership cuts into and takes over Rose Rose's body for his own use; he impregnates it. When her pregnancy becomes known, Mr. Rose's power over his personal family as well as his migrant family begins to ebb. He has gone too far with his rules. After receiving an abortion from Homer, Rose Rose stabs her father to death with a knife given her by Muddy, one of the other migrants. For Homer, the "delivery" he performs for Rose Rose leads to a loss of innocence and a change in his rules about abortion.

A DIALOGIC READING OF *THE CIDER HOUSE RULES*

Discussion of abortion is nearly always hotly contested. In fact, "the abortion debate" probably is the most frequently employed phrase the media use to refer to the issue. However, Irving suggests that a "dialogue" about abortion may prove more productive than debate. In this novel, then, *dialogism* might help us to see the many layers of difficult questions that attend the making of "rules" for and the confrontation over abortion.

Dialogism generates meaning for the reader by examining a variety of voices. As developed by the Russian literary critic and theorist Mikhail Bakhtin, dialogism involves far more than the conversations of characters. David Lodge explains that "[t]he novel is . . . inherently 'dialogic' or, in an alternative formulation, 'polyphonic'—an orchestration of diverse discourses culled from both writing and oral speech" (76). Dialogue is the product of "the whole, complex, social situation," said Bakhtin, and includes the reader (qtd. in Todorov 30). It consists of all utterances, including inner tensions and collaborations, occurring even "between the lines" or in the gaps; such utterances exist not only in novels, of course, but in life as well.

For example, readers of *Cider House* come to it with their own opinions about abortion, opinions based on the rules they live by and the information they have acquired during their lives. The novel, with its attention to the shifting of rules, invites us into its dialogues and negotiates meaning with us. It does this by drawing us into the issue of "choice" throughout the novel. Choice is at the foundation of abortion, but the characters also make important choices, as well as rules, about other issues, too: "The larger significance of 'choice' involves the tension between freedom and restraint in a whole range of human situations, and Irving would appear to have set out to examine the 'rules' that result from that tension, the abortion law being only one" (Harter and Thompson 137). The dialogue in *Cider House*, then, is comprised of the "voices" from many different discourses, as well as the participation of the reader's own life-"voice."

Irving is particularly adept at getting us to see the gaps between different voices, to see that things are not often as they seem. In a discussion of the orphans' nightly reading of Dickens, the narrator reminds us that it is not just the story the boys hear: "[T]he boys' division was an audience like any other: self-interest, personal memories, their secret anxieties crept into their perceptions of what they heard (regardless of what Dickens had done)" (qtd. in Harter and Thompson 132). This subtle passage demonstrates a central point: that language, no matter how it is used, can never be neutral. Each of us, including the novel's characters and narrator, brings a history to every language experience. Similarly, each of the characters in *Cider House*—including the narrator—brings a history.

Viewed dialogically, then, *Cider House* is about rules and how, through its characters, rules surrounding issues such as abortion are negotiated. Those who are against abortion defend their rules: a fetus is a life (Homer's position); to abort a fetus is to kill; to kill is immoral (the "Devil's work," against God) and, at the time the novel takes place, illegal. On the pro-choice side is the opposite position: a fetus is not a life in the first trimester, or until the fetus is "quick" (Larch does not perform abortions after the first trimester); thus, to abort a fetus is not to take a life. For much of *Cider House*, Homer is squarely in the anti-abortion group; he cannot be otherwise until circumstances force him consciously to re-negotiate his position. However, even when the subject of abortion seems absent, the *dialogue* is present; it is always ongoing.

We can see Irving's discussion of abortion through the "dialogue" present in the term "fetus." For Homer, this word is never neutral, and he must negotiate its meaning for himself. As an adolescent, Homer finds a fetus by the incinerator and learns about abortions, that they are being performed at St. Cloud's. Later, Larch asks him to prepare a nearly full-term fetus, stabbed along with its mother, for autopsy, and Homer is made literally sick. He ponders the question of when a fetus has life. He rejects Larch's rule that there is a point in the fourth month when a fetus has life (before that, the fetus remains, in Larch's distancing phrase, among "the products of conception" [115]). Homer rejects Larch's logic that he is delivering mothers as well as babies; indeed, Homer rejects the idea of performing abortions at all.

But Irving will not allow Homer—or the reader—to make rules contrary to Larch's too easily. Throughout the novel, we see other "fetuses"—all damaged. The terminally ill Fuzzy Stone with his almost transparent, "caved-in shape," looks to Homer like a "walking, talking fetus" (110). At the movies with Wally and Candy, Homer sees his first camel and is horrified, seeing it as possibly "some fetus-phase of a horse" (254). Homer, masturbating in the cider house, discovers that Grace Lynch, a shadow of a person, has been there the whole time. She is curled up silently on one of the cots, "like a fetus" (250). The defeated victim of a brutal husband, Grace tells Homer that she has been to St. Cloud's for an abortion.

It is clear that Irving wishes us to see that Larch truly does "deliver mothers" as well as babies. Significantly, when Rose Rose tells Angel that she is pregnant by her father, she lies in the grass in "what Angel could not help observing was a fetal position" (557). When Angel brings her to his father, Homer's rules change. He does not want to be an abortionist any more than Larch did when he was young, but his ongoing negotiation of the meaning of "fetus" leads him to alter his rules. He takes on the rules that belonged to his "father," Larch, who also had, in his past, negotiated the meaning of fetus between "Off Harrison" and "on Harrison."

Irving demonstrates the difficulties of negotiating rules for abortion through a number of families, but nowhere more tellingly than in Homer's family with Candy and Wally, and in Rose Rose's family. Homer, Candy, and Wally negotiate the meaning of family in large part because of the choice Homer and Candy make about abortion. Their decision not to abort Angel leads to their unorthodox family. Indeed, the very presence of Angel, the delight and love he brings to those around him, and even his name suggest that Homer's rule against abortion has been the "correct" one.

Rose Rose also has a family, but her situation is far worse than Angel's in his unconventional, though loving, family. Indeed, Rose Rose is worse off than any orphan at St. Cloud's. If the staff of St. Cloud's could not give each orphan enough attention, neither did they abuse the children. Mr. Rose, in fact, gives his daughter *too much* attention. She cries out for an abortion (as she apparently did not when pregnant by her lover) because her father's "rules" bind her body, her very self, to him, to the exclusion of all else. Mr. Rose *is* the rule—the law—carried to its most egregious and dead end.

Rose Rose's pregnancy as a result of incest overtakes Homer's mono-logic, "absolute" rule that abortion is always wrong. Homer's new understanding that abortion sometimes may be right sends him back to St. Cloud's to continue Larch's work. It is perhaps irrelevant whether Homer believes it is "the Lord's work." He sees that the choice to have a baby or an abortion is not his to make: if he can operate on Rose Rose, he cannot refuse any woman. "How could he refuse anyone? Only a god makes that kind of decision" (568). With this statement, Homer's dialogue is seemingly at an end. But is the reader's?

Irving ties up all the loose ends, but not in the life-affirming sense of most of his earlier novels and, as we shall see, of *Owen Meany* and *A Son of the Circus*. *The Cider House Rules* ends with compromise all around; the world of St. Cloud's remains gray; much has been lost by everyone involved. Homer, as Fuzzy Stone, returns to St. Cloud's, where he delivers children and mothers—the latter somewhat grimly. He becomes involved with Nurse Caroline, but his love remains Candy. Candy continues to live fairly happily with Wally—they are a golden couple again—but losing Homer is part of the compromise for both of them. When Melony's body is returned to St. Cloud's, Lorna writes to Homer that Melony "died a *relatively* happy woman" (emphasis mine; 586). Only Angel (whose parents chose *not* to abort him) lives in love and happiness, though even he must split his time between Homer and Candy.

Harter and Thompson point out that "[t]he rules of society and those we establish for ourselves are at best uneasy compromises between con-

9

A Prayer for Owen Meany
(1989)

With a remarkable first sentence, the story begins: "I am doomed to remember a boy with a wrecked voice—not because of his voice, or because he was the smallest person I ever knew, or even because he was the instrument of my mother's death, but because he is the reason I believe in God; I am a Christian because of Owen Meany" (1). In this one haunting sentence, Irving introduces many of the themes of *A Prayer for Owen Meany*: free will and determinism, memory and forgetting, death and resurrection, faith and doubt. There are other themes in the book, to be sure: most obviously, the Vietnam War and the venal carelessness of politicians and other "powerful men." Nevertheless, if the title were not enough to suggest that religious issues would take center stage, the opening sentence should leave no doubt.

Like *The World According to Garp* or *The Hotel New Hampshire, Owen Meany* can rightly be called a coming-of-age novel. It follows Owen Meany and his best friend, Johnny Wheelwright (the narrator), from Sunday school and Little League through Gravesend Academy, the University of New Hampshire, and beyond. As with most such novels, the quest for identity is a central concern, especially for the narrator. Even this, however, is framed in religious terms. Late in the novel, the narrator describes the focal points of his life, churchgoing and schoolteaching, as "devotions" (570).

As for Owen Meany, his identity is only slowly revealed to the narrator and to the reader, but for Owen himself his identity is never in doubt. For Owen, the quest is not to discover his identity but to live out his destiny, to fulfill the difficult calling that, he believes, had been revealed to him by God.

PLOT DEVELOPMENT

The narrative is framed by two deaths. In the first chapter, Tabby Wheelwright, the narrator's mother, is killed by a foul ball hit by Owen Meany in a Little League game. In the last chapter, Owen Meany himself is killed in a heroic act of self-sacrifice. The hands that had been, at least to Owen's mind, God's instrument of death for Tabby become God's instrument of life for a group of Vietnamese children. The funerals for Tabby and for Owen are reported in detail, with hymns, Scriptures, and prayers quoted extensively and commented upon by the narrator. The funerals thus provide the occasion for extensive religious reflection, both at the beginning and at the end of the novel.

Between the two deaths, the narrative advances, broadly, in chronological order, following the boys through the rhythms of growing up. That sounds straightforward, but Irving's narration is actually subtle and complex. By using a first-person narrator, who looks back on the events of childhood and adolescence from the perspective of middle age, Irving tells his tale with rich texture and depth.

Johnny Wheelwright goes to Canada the year of Owen's death (1968), a year when many Americans resisting the Vietnam War moved north, but Johnny actually begins his story twenty years after he left the United States. As he says, it took him "years" to face his memory of how Owen died (506). Johnny's narrative, then, embraces not only the present but also the past, including his growing-up years with Owen.

As the narrative advances, the specific transitions from one scene to another are often thematic and reflect the way human memory works. For example, the narrator describes Hurd's Church, the nondenominational chapel at Gravesend Academy, as so dark that a funeral seemed more fitting there than a wedding. Nevertheless, he adds, "my mother had both" there (116). Irving then proceeds to describe both rituals, moving directly from one to the other, even though many events that occurred in the years between the two ceremonies are narrated elsewhere. The narrator describes how Mr. Chickering, his Little League coach, wept at Tabby Wheelwright's funeral; on the same page the adult narrator tells of visiting Mr. Chickering in the nursing home, where, despite his Alzheimer's disease, the former coach still remembers Tabby's death on the Little League field (126).

As the narration moves back and forth across time, Irving directs the reader's attention, and builds suspense, by careful foreshadowing. Sometimes this is explicit: "As you shall see" is a phrase the narrator employs repeatedly (e.g., 7, 87). At other times, the foreshadowing tantalizes with hints and unanswered questions. A classic example is "The Shot." Owen Meany, who at maturity would stand barely five feet tall, is obsessed with slam-dunking a basketball. Over and over, Owen and Johnny practice a maneuver where Johnny passes the ball to Owen, who dribbles back toward Johnny and jumps into his arms; Johnny then boosts Owen high enough to dunk the ball. When Johnny gets bored and complains that it is silly to practice a play that could never be used in a game, Owen, "who had his own reasons for everything," says simply that it is not for a game, with no further explanation. Later, while practicing The Shot, Owen tells Johnny, "I AM GOD'S INSTRUMENT" (338). Astounded, Johnny lets Owen fall and demands to know why God's instrument should need Johnny's help to slam-dunk a basketball. Owen does not answer. Two long chapters after The Shot is first introduced, the boys are still practicing, working to complete the shot in ever shorter time. Finally, Owen dunks the ball in under three seconds. When Johnny sarcastically asks if they now have to aim for under two seconds, Owen tells him not to be ridiculous, three seconds is good enough. Only in the final, horrifying scene of Owen's heroic death does the reader learn why three seconds is fast enough, why Johnny needs to help Owen, and what The Shot is really for.

Irving has used first-person narration, with its rich possibilities for narrative loops and foreshadowing, in other books. Unique to *Owen Meany*, however, are the dated entries from the adult narrator's diary, such as those for 1987, many of which are critical of U.S. President Reagan and his covert support for the contras in the Nicaraguan civil war. The diary entries serve several functions. They allow Irving to draw thematic parallels between the Vietnam War, which is prominent in his primary narrative, and the Iran-contra affair, which was making headlines as he wrote. The entries also allow Irving to loop back into the primary narrative at a different point than he left it. Most important, perhaps, they allow the reader to see clearly the kind of person the narrator has become, an outgrowth out of the events related in the primary narrative.

One other narrative technique—both obvious and memorable—deserves mention. To characterize the "wrecked voice" of Owen Meany, Irving presents everything he says in ALL CAPITAL LETTERS. At Gravesend Academy, Owen's strange voice leads to his being nicknamed "The Voice." Owen adopts this title for his columns in the school newspaper and decides that everything he writes will also be published in all capitals. Thus, every word from Owen in the novel, whether written or spoken, appears in all capitals. Anyone who has read an edition of the Bible where the words of Jesus are printed in red will recognize the parallels.

The two major plot developments have to do with Johnny's search for his father and with Owen's destiny as the "instrument" of God. Interpolated into the plots are significant references to the Vietnam War and the Iran-contra affair, with their moral and political fallout.

Johnny and Owen set out as adolescents to discover the identity of Johnny's father, an adventure that we follow throughout the text. At first, their investigations only lead to more confusion. All that Tabitha Wheelwright, killed when both boys were only eleven, ever told Johnny about his father was that she had met him on the train to Boston, where she went once a week for singing lessons. Naturally, the boys go to Boston to seek clues. Owen, whose own mother is a noncommunicative recluse, is enamored of Johnny's mother. He has kept a red dress that belonged to her (as well as her dressmaker's dummy) but that they never saw her wear. Using the label from the dress, they find the shop where it was made.

They find more than they bargained for. They learn that Johnny's mother had lied to them. She had gone to Boston for voice lessons, as she had said, but there was more to the story. In Boston, she had sung in a supper club as "The Lady in Red," always wearing the red dress that she never wore in Gravesend. In Boston, she had a completely different identity than in Gravesend; she had deliberately bought a dress that was unlike her. In Boston, Tabitha seems to be kin to Hester Prynne in *The Scarlet Letter*. While he is seeking his father's identity, Johnny's first discovery is about his mother, which leaves him feeling confused. As Owen points out, Johnny no longer knows who she was, either.

Boston never leads to the discovery of Johnny's father. Eventually, Johnny learns the disappointing truth that his father has been in Gravesend all along: the Reverend Merrill, the doubt-ridden, stuttering, rather nice but innocuous pastor of the Congregational church, who later becomes the Gravesend Academy chaplain. Instead of being a mysterious stranger, Johnny's father is "an insipid soup of a man," in no way different from Johnny himself (570–571).

Owen does not need to search for his identity so much as to understand his destiny. He believes he is God's "instrument," although he does not know for what purpose. There are two plot episodes that not only build suspense in connection with Owen's purpose on earth but also underscore issues of character and theme.

In 1953, Owen plays key roles in two of Gravesend's ritual dramas of Christmas: the church Christmas pageant and the community theater production of Dickens's *A Christmas Carol*. The Christmas pageant reveals Owen's identity to anyone with eyes to see; in *A Christmas Carol*, his destiny is revealed to him alone. Irving interlaces the two dramas in the telling. Each one is complex enough on its own, but suffice it to say that Owen manages to have himself cast as the Christ Child in the pageant, and as the Ghost of Christmas Yet to Come in Dickens. His performance in these roles is enough to "remodel Christmas" (201).

In the Christmas pageant, Owen, with his commanding self-confidence, takes control; he calls the shots and casts himself as the Christ Child, thus becoming, in Johnny's phrase, both "the star and the director" of the Nativity (184). Owen casts everyone else and reshapes the presentation of the drama. Throughout the rehearsals, as the other children sulk or squabble, Owen exudes the calm assurance of "a deity to be reckoned with" (168).

At the performance, everything that can go wrong, does. Actors forget their lines, children in their costumes faint, Mary collapses onto the Christ Child, and Owen has to move her aside. Yet, Owen, with a commanding "presence," manages to command and keep the audience's attention. When he sees his parents in the audience, however, he loses his composure. He suddenly sits up and angrily screams at them, demanding to know what they were doing there. He banishes his parents from the church and demands that Joseph and Mary carry him out, too.

Some regular churchgoers are incensed or confused by the disaster; for Mr. Fish, not a churchgoer, all that happens is a convincing part of the drama. When Owen, from the manger, audibly tells a forgetful angel what to say; when he throws the Virgin Mother aside; when he screams at his parents—to Mr. Fish, these are dramatic ways of presenting the theme that Jesus is truly Lord. Indeed, Owen is revealed, in the narrator's words, as "an unpredictable Prince of Peace" (219), as a "special Christ" who knows not only his own role but also "all the other vital parts of the story" (217).

Thus, it is fitting that Owen also plays the Ghost of Christmas Yet to Come in *A Christmas Carol*, because it is a role in which the future is foreseen. In portraying this role, Owen says, if the actor really appears to know everything about the future, the audience will be scared witless. And in this role, Owen proves as compelling as when he is the Christ Child: onstage, he does not seem at all human, and his authority is "supernatural" (203). In this drama, Owen foresees his own future, his name on the gravestone and the date of his death. The sight scares him to the point of fainting.

By using these two dramas, Irving emphasizes the importance of Owen's destiny and also maintains suspense surrounding it. Irving also is able to make clear and believable the extraordinariness of Owen Meany. As the audience—and Johnny Wheelwright—is impressed by Owen's presence, so are we. The two dramas reinforce Owen's sense of being caught up in a larger destiny that he must fulfill, just as the dramas make clear that Johnny, although a bystander (a real "Joseph"), is most importantly a witness to the meaning of Owen Meany's life.

Interpolated in the above two plots concerning identity and destiny are running commentaries on the Vietnam War and Iran-contra. The buildup of the war is given in flat, reportorial observations of events that occurred. The terrible devastation of the war, in terms of the dead and wrecked human lives, is, however, built into the plot; the war touches and changes Gravesend forever. Johnny Wheelwright leaves his ancestral home for Canada; other "boys" from the town are killed, including Owen. Indeed, the moral vacuity, the violence, in this country that accompany the war are brought home in a dirty, temporary men's room in the Phoenix airport; here Owen dies a hero and finally understands his destiny. In Owen's death, we see the horrifying effects of the war, its moral confusion, its chaos, and its victims; in Owen's death, we also see heroism. The Iran-contra affair is seen by Johnny after he has moved to Canada. To him, the affair is simply more of the lies and sordidness he and others had believed surrounded the Vietnam War.

SETTING

The most important settings are Gravesend, New Hampshire, where both boys grow up and attend Gravesend Academy, and Toronto, where the narrator lives, teaching at Bishop Strachan School and worshiping at Grace Church on the Hill.

Gravesend, on the surface, is a bucolic New England town, but beneath the surface, the town is deeply divided by class. When Johnny's mother first suggests that Owen will one day attend Gravesend Academy, ten-year-old Owen protests that the Academy is not for boys like him. The Meanys are blue-collar, granite quarriers. At a town meeting, Mr. Meany once pronounced that the interests of the town and of the Academy had nothing in common.

Johnny Wheelwright is a member of the town's most prominant family. Descended on his grandfather's side from the founding pastor of the town, and on his grandmother's from folk who came over on the *Mayflower*, Johnny says that, as a Wheelright, he was automatically "a New England snob" (582).

Both boys eventually attend Gravesend Academy, but both are outsiders there. Although Johnny is from a locally prominent family, he (an undiagnosed dyslexic) is a poor student and is admitted only because his stepfather, Dan Needham, is an Academy teacher. Owen, although a brilliant student, is not from the upper class. Both are "day boys," not part of the student life in the dormitories. When Owen, in his senior year, offends the headmaster (in a wildly comic scene), he is expelled from the school; he is especially vulnerable to such punishment because he is dependent on getting a scholarship to college.

Gravesend is also a place of innocuous, undemanding religion. Hurd's Church (on the campus) has the plain appearance of a civil service office; it is a place of "reassuring numbness" (132). The Congregationalists, along with their pastor, Rev. Lewis Merrill, require little in the way of either participation or belief, while the Episcopal rector, an ex-airline captain named Wiggin, is a master of boredom. Owen is convinced that all these churches believe less than he does (22). Thus the setting serves as a contrast to Owen's faith, which is fervent, certain, and demanding.

In addition, the very name Gravesend points to the religious theme of death and resurrection that runs through the novel. Is the grave the end, or is religious faith the end of the grave? The miracle of resurrection holds special interest for Owen, as indeed, by the end of Owen's life, it does for many of the townspeople.

Whatever else Gravesend represents, it is a place of great change, brought about in no small measure by the Vietnam War. Johnny Wheelwright leaves the town for Toronto. Owen dies as a result of the war, and so, too, indirectly, does Mrs. Meany. In addition, Harry Hoyt dies in Vietnam, not in combat, as it turns out, but a "victim" of the war even so, his mother says. Buzzy Thurston, who tries to stay out of the draft by drinking and taking drugs, runs his car into a bridge abutment a short distance from the Meany quarry. Like many other American small towns, Gravesend's face is changed forever by Vietnam.

Toronto is important not so much for what it is as for what it is not: it is not the United States. Toronto is where the narrator has lived since deliberately renouncing his own country. "I left my country . . . once and for all" (2). His decision to move to Canada was a way of making a political statement against the Vietnam War (454), and he uses Canada as a foil for criticizing all that is wrong with the United States. Some criticisms are trivial—Canadians are more polite than Americans and give directions more readily. Some are weightier, as when the narrator asks who can pardon the United States for what it did in Vietnam and in Nicaragua, for the way it contributes to nuclear proliferation.

Repeatedly, the narrator uses his comments about Canada to set himself apart from "my former fellow Americans" (126). Ironically, his very passion about these issues is recognized by his Canadian acquaintances as typically American (224). Irving uses Toronto to show just how American John Wheelwright really is. Even the trivial differences show him up. After bragging about how "we" in Canada offer directions more willingly than Americans, the narrator refuses to give directions to Americans lost in Toronto, denouncing them as idiots (363).

CHARACTER DEVELOPMENT

Johnny Wheelwright and Owen Meany are the twin stars around which the rest of the characters orbit. Both are shaped heavily by their families, even though Owen's parents are obscure figures. His father is described by Johnny's stepfather as a mystery, and Owen's mother is an unspeaking recluse. One thing is sure: the Meanys are working class, granite quarriers.

The Wheelwrights, on the other hand, are New England patricians; Johnny's grandmother is a strong-willed and opinionated family matriarch. Johnny and his mother live with his grandmother in the Wheelwright family's imposing house. Johnny was born out of wedlock, a fact that is presented as a key to his identity: "I was little Johnny Wheelwright, father unknown" (9). His mother calls him "My little fling" (15).

Discovering his father is of little help to Johnny Wheelwright in forging his own identity, however; it merely confirms that "I am my sorry father's sorry son" (549), vacillating between faith and doubt, inspiration and despair (571). While staying with friends at their summer cabin, John overhears the husband tell his wife that Wheelwright might be "a non-practicing homosexual." When the wife protests that she doesn't think he is gay, the husband says nonpracticing homosexuals don't always know what they are. All he has learned from his eavesdropping, Wheelwright wryly comments, is that "I don't know *what* I am" (423).

Indeed, he does not. Outside of his family, Owen Meany seems to have been the only person Johnny Wheelwright ever loved, but there is not the least suggestion of sexual intimacy between the two. Johnny always was—and remains—fascinated by his cousin, pop star Hester the Molester, but he never was in love with her; her love is for—and is returned by—Owen. Sexuality aside, Johnny still does not know what he is, even at the end of the novel: an American who keeps insisting he is Canadian; a fervent believer who takes no comfort in his faith, who believes that all religion is an account of "vengeance toward the innocent" (7); a self-professed Christian who admittedly lacks forgiveness (547).

Although a keen observer of others, John Wheelwright remains "an insipid soup of a man," as he called the Reverend Merrill. In his friendship with Owen, Johnny was always the follower, Owen always the leader. It was Owen who led the search for Johnny's father. It was Owen who taught Johnny how to overcome his dyslexia and be a good student. It was Owen who provided the way for Johnny to keep from being drafted. It was Owen who prompted him to move to Canada. It was Owen, Johnny tells us, who started Johnny's master's thesis for him. It was Owen who challenged Johnny to take charge of his life, to "MAKE A *DECISION*," to "FIND A LITTLE COURAGE" (502). Johnny never really does.

Owen Meany, on the other hand, found all the courage he needed to face the death that he knew awaited him. Even as a child, Owen was decisive; he took charge, presiding over a dog's funeral, Johnny says, as Owen did over all rituals and ceremonies.

There is no point in trying to describe Owen Meany as an ordinary character. Right from the start, the narrator drops hints that Owen was extraordinary. As a child, the narrator used to think that Owen's voice was from another planet. As an adult, he is sure that Owen's voice was not from this world. Even as a child, Johnny would often wonder if Owen were more than human, recalling a scene where Owen stood in a beam of light streaming through an attic skylight, looking like "a tiny but fiery god, sent to adjudicate the errors of our ways" (69). In case the reader should forget this description of Owen, Irving has the narrator recall the scene, and repeat the description word for word, over 400 pages later (488).

Owen Meany, simply put, is a Christ figure. Late in the novel, Johnny learns from Mr. Meany that Owen's parents believe that Owen was born, as Mr. Meany puts it, "like the Christ Child," without sexual intercourse having occurred. Johnny never fully accepts this story of Owen's virgin birth, but that is not important. Owen had been told the story when he was ten or eleven years old, and he, apparently, never doubted its truth.

For the narrator, and the reader, this story of a virgin birth comes almost as an afterthought, for Owen's remarkable character has already been amply revealed in the novel. There are small epiphanies all along in the book, but it is at Christmas 1953, when the boys are eleven years old, that two major revelations occur. Owen's performance in the Nativity pageant confirms his "difference"; as Mr. Fish states, there is no doubt that he is Jesus from "Day One." And in Dickens's *A Christmas Carol*, Owen learns not only that he will die, but that he will die 1Lt. Paul O. Meany, Jr., in 1968.

THEMATIC ISSUES

There are numerous thematic issues in *Owen Meany*, many of which Irving has developed in other novels: issues of family and growing up, of violence and death, of memory and forgetting. It can be argued that Johnny Wheelwright's quest for identity is an important theme (especially in connection with his character), but even it is enveloped in the two major themes in *Owen Meany*: the religious and the political. Both of these themes are intertwined.

The religious theme that runs through *Owen Meany* is reinforced by the religious symbolism clustered around Owen: his "miraculous" (or at least mysterious) conception and birth; his stature; his Voice; his prophetic pronouncements; and the way he "touches" those around him. Tabitha, who "adores" Owen, is linked to Mary Magdalene, as "the Lady in Red" and through her "little fling"; Hester the Molester, Johnny's cousin, with her wild life, her sexual energy, and her wonderfully rich and luxuriant hair, is a younger version of Tabitha/Mary Magdelene. She, like others, recognizes the extraordinariness of Owen. She also loves him—whether carnally or not is irrelevant—and offers to marry him, to follow him from army base to army base, and to bear his children. The only thing she refuses to do is attend his funeral. Because Owen sees into his future, he never asks her to marry him, though he loves her; as he says, it would not be "fair" to marry her.

In addition to the symbolism in the text, certain events in the plot reinforce religious themes. Primarily the events revolve around belief and unbelief, faith and doubt. Pastor Merrill represents the difficulty of faith in the twentieth century, as well as the skepticism of personal revelation. Both Pastor Merrill and Johnny Wheelwright demand logical "proof" of miracles; they seek answers to uneasy questions.

One of the key elements in the religious thematics of the novel concerns a fear of the future; as Owen says about *A Christmas Carol*, nothing is so frightening as the future. Yet Owen not only accepts his future, he has faith in it, affirming that God will help him faithfully meet his destiny, no matter how difficult Owen finds it. As Owen approaches the foreseen date of his death, he writes in his journal that although he is not afraid, he is nervous. Torn between wishing he knew less about what was to come and wishing he knew more, Owen concludes pages of questions by writing "I MUST TRUST IN THE LORD" (585).

Owen's trust *is* his faith, which is hard, demanding, difficult, and costs everything—his very life—and is in direct contrast to Johnny's unbelief. Even after Johnny becomes a believer because of Owen, saying that "unbelief" now seems so much harder to him than believing, he nevertheless maintains that religious belief raises "many unanswerable questions" (571).

The narrator finds no comfort in his belief, ending with the same sort of "faith" that his father, Pastor Merrill, had so long demonstrated: vacillating between doubt and conviction, hope and despair. Ironically, Pastor Merrill, at the end of the book, achieves a faith that is "absolute and unshakable" (571), causing him to lose his stutter and become a crackerjack preacher. Only Johnny knows that Pastor Merrill's new faith is based on a fake miracle that Johnny has "tricked" his father into believing.

Although Irving seems to use faith and belief interchangeably, there also seems to be an important distinction. The "belief" of both the narrator and his father requires tangible proof: Pastor Merrill believes he sees Tabitha, come back from the grave to forgive him (Johnny has taken his mother's dressmaker dummy, dressed it in the red dress, and set it up in the shadows to "trick" his father into belief); the narrator witnesses Owen's death, reads his diary, hears his VOICE, even from beyond the grave. Both Merrill and Johnny pray for God to return Owen to them. At Owen's funeral the Reverend Merrill cries out to God to give Owen back. The last line of the narrator—and the novel—echoes Merrill's prayer. What would be the response of Owen, who required no proof of miracles to believe and who had said that although he could not see God, he knew beyond a doubt that God was present?

The religious theme of faith is linked to the political issues of the Vietnam War and Iran-contra affair. Of the two issues, the war is more important. The linkage to the Vietnam War is made in a number of ways; perhaps the most important are through Owen's service in the army as a casualty assistance officer (he is in the "dying business," an escort to the "remains" of those killed as a result of the war) and through his cutting off Johnny's index finger so that he will not be drafted. In addition, interpolated into the text are matter-of-fact statistics "reporting" the escalation of the war and the rising body count. The assassinations of John and Robert Kennedy and of Martin Luther King, Jr., are also in the background, and reinforce the lack of moral center in the United States.

The lies of Johnson and Nixon blur into the later lies of Reagan about Iran-contra. They are all "made for television," Johnny's grandmother, Harriet Wheelwright, would say. One of Irving's most brilliant images is of Marilyn Monroe, linked with John Kennedy early in the novel. When the narrator hears of her death, he is afraid, but wonders what Monroe's death has to do with him. Owen explains that Marilyn's death has to do with every American because she was a living symbol of the country: "NOT QUITE YOUNG ANYMORE, BUT NOT OLD EITHER: A LITTLE BREATHLESS, VERY BEAUTIFUL, MAYBE A LITTLE STUPID. MAYBE A LOT SMARTER THAN SHE SEEMED" (430). Owen believed that Marilyn, like America, wanted to be good, but that all the men in her life—Joe Dimaggio, Arthur Miller, and the Kennedys—used her, used her up. Owen sees these men, especially the Kennedys, as "CARELESS," "TREATING THEMSELVES TO A THRILL," just as they carelessly used the country for their own thrills. Owen's long speech is one of Irving's most serious indictments of this country.

Owen never loses his faith in God, but he certainly loses faith in his country. The kind of men who used Marilyn Monroe appeared moral. In fact, Owen (as did many others) thought Kennedy was a moralist, but concludes that he was only a skilled "SEDUCER" (430). Owen feels tricked, and like Marilyn Monroe, he, too, will be "USED *UP*." Later, as the Vietnam War grinds on, and as he gets closer to his own death, Owen equates contemporary religion with the appalling carelessness and chicanery of government leaders, of powerful men. Religion is being taken over by the television preachers, who, Owen exclaims, are peddling spiritual junk food with unholy self-certainty. He goes on to predict that future American presidents will be just like these television evangelists: slick, careless, immoral, and above all, guilty of oversimplifying everything: "THIS COUNTRY IS HEADED . . . TOWARD OVERSIMPLIFI-CATION" (603). Ignoring life's complexities leads both preachers and politicians to the same mistake: "THEY'RE SO SURE THEY'RE *RIGHT!* . . . THE FUTURE, I THINK, IS PRETTY SCARY" (603). We recall this line about the future from Owen's analysis of *A Christmas Carol*. The future in that play presaged Owen's death.

A HERMENEUTIC READING OF *A PRAYER FOR OWEN MEANY*

A Prayer for Owen Meany is rich in scenes that, seemingly insignificant, turn out to be highly important in retrospect. Owen himself has a "genius" for directing and choreographing, as well as acting in, a good many of the dramas and rituals in the novel. As Johnny Wheelwright reminds us, Owen presides over all ceremonies and rites of passage. It is not enough that Owen calls the "shots" in the 1953 Nativity pageant at Christ's Church, wresting control from Rector Wiggin and his wife, Barb; he does pretty much the same with Dan Needham's amateur players' production of *A Christmas Carol*. If the Nativity reinforces the character of Owen as a Christ figure, Dickens's *Carol* poses certain questions: Why did Irving include it, and how does it relate to the overall meanings of the novel?

A hermeneutic reading of Irving's use of *A Christmas Carol* may help to answer these questions. According to Roland Barthes, hermeneutics involves problems of interpretation that are raised in a segment—or segments—of the plot. Under what Barthes calls the "hermeneutic code," he lists various terms ("formal" or structural) by which an enigma is raised, held in suspense, and ultimately made known (*S/Z* 18). The segment itself, in this case *A Christmas Carol*, may be seen as part of the "hermeneutic circle," a term used to express the paradox that the whole can be understood only through an understanding of its parts. And we can understand these parts (retrospectively) only through an understanding of the whole to which they belong (Hirsch passim).

Owen's role in Dickens's *Carol* begins when the postmaster, Mr. Morrison, quits his role of the Ghost of Christmas Yet to Come because it is not a speaking part. Owen tries to convince him that this role, the

"*GHOST OF THE FUTURE,*" is not only important but the most frightening of all. And, as Owen points out, a great actor doesn't have to talk; a great actor doesn't even need a face. Simply showing Scrooge the fate that will befall him if he refuses to keep Christmas, simply showing people their own grave, is more frighteningly powerful than anything else.

Owen goes on to tell Mr. Morrison that this role requires an actor with great stage presence, who can convey that the future is the most frightening thing of all. There is no doubt that this role is made not for the postmaster, but for Owen himself, who here perceptively analyzes Dickens's character of the Spirit of the Future. Thus, when Morrison adamantly refuses to play the role, Owen immediately calls Dan Needham, the director, and demands to play the Ghost himself. Owen links the role, and rightly so, with that of the Christ Child that he is playing in the Nativity: both parts require an actor who can control a scene without speaking, and Owen is confident that he is just such an actor.

As soon as Owen convinces Dan that there is no need to look further for a Spirit of the Future, Owen begins to take charge, just as he does in the Nativity play. His interpretation of the Ghost of Christmas Yet to Come is translated into the technical aspects of drama; he controls his makeup, using white baby powder to cover his face and hands. His eye sockets are black-lined to make them look "hollow." He arranges his costume to delay the sight of his face; his hand will slowly protrude from the sleeve of his cloak. He is so successful with the mechanics of the drama that no one in the small town can recognize which of their neighbors is playing the part. The actor disappears totally into the role; Owen appears to *be* a ghost. Owen *is* a presence—as he plays "absence" in the form of a ghost. Mr. Fish, who plays Scrooge, speaks for himself and the audience when he tells the Ghost of the Future that he is more frightening than any of the other ghosts in the drama. The audience responds to Owen's presence with dread; even Harriet Wheelwright, usually detached and superior, visibly shivers, as does the rest of the audience.

Owen, who is onstage with a bad case of flu, coughs, but the sound is not what Dan is by then hoping for, an everyday sound that will break the dread spell of Owen's performance. Instead, the cough sounds so much like a death rattle that members of the audience jump. Maureen Early wets herself. A moment later, as Owen points with a hand made deathly pale by baby powder, Mr. Fish, playing Scrooge, "flinched." The audience is struck dumb. Among the papier-mâché gravestones, Owen leads Mr. Fish/Scrooge by pointing and pointing. Owen steps closer to the gravestone (on which Scrooge's name is supposedly written) so that Mr. Fish, amateur actor that he is, will stop dawdling and read Scrooge's name on the grave. But as Owen steps closer to the grave and appears to read the name, he faints.

Owen's fainting stops the show, but not quickly enough. Before the curtain is brought down, Owen revives, screaming in terror, provoking near-panic in the audience. Dramatic illusion becomes "reality." Dickens's play is transformed: Scrooge is upstaged and the Ghost of the Future scares himself. Still, no one knows, at first, what Owen had seen that scared him so. *A Christmas Carol*, both Dickens's novel and the play based on it, works off repetition, delay, and recognition, the very techniques Irving uses in his own novel. Moreover, *A Christmas Carol* is about visions, both of the grave and of hope, as well as of transformations, just as Irving's novel is about these things.

We have to wait a while to discover that Owen has seen his own name on the grave. The Reverend Merrill, supposedly a Christian of some—even if not complete—faith, tries to make of the vision something logical and "natural," telling Owen that his vision of his own name on a gravestone was just a bad dream, something that happens to nearly everyone. Reverend Merrill has seen one of the points of the play but has missed its meaning entirely.

It is not until nearly ten pages after this scene that we learn more of what Owen saw. It was not just Owen's name, not the way he "*EVER*" wrote it, he tells Johnny. It was not the way Owen had written his name in baby powder in the dressing room before going on stage. It was, he tells Johnny, his "REAL NAME" in full. Owen's "real" name is Paul O. Meany, Jr. (as Johnny says, he was named after a saint), and Owen repeats that the gravestone revealed "THE WHOLE THING"—and lies to Johnny when he says that no date was given.

It is a hundred pages before we discover that Owen knows *when* he will die, though he doesn't know *how*. We also discover that Owen's faith gives confidence that God will reveal to him what it is that he must do. Connected with these discoveries is the knowledge that Owen talks with Pastor Merrill "ABOUT LIFE AFTER DEATH" (385), and that Owen has had a "dream" that apparently is disturbing enough to reduce him to tears. These bits and pieces of Owen's future—that he will be a hero, that Johnny is in his dream, that he will save a group of Vietnamese children—are interpolated in the plot as we move to the end of the novel. The interpolations force us to recall *A Christmas Carol*, as well as Owen's role in it, and constantly to readjust our reading of it; these readjustments simultaneously resonate in our reading as we move forward in the narrative.

Owen's faith in his vision of his own gravestone—as well as in a subsequent dream—and his acceptance of himself as an instrument of God lead him to join the army during the Vietnam War and to keep Johnny out of it. He assumes—incorrectly, it turns out (Owen does not know everything)—that he goes into combat and there saves the Vietnamese children (472–473). But it is in his assignment as a casualty assistance officer that Owen's vision of his gravestone in *A Christmas Carol* and his dream coalesce in a bizarre fashion in a temporary men's room, not in Vietnam but in the airport in Phoenix, Arizona. There Owen fulfills his "dream" in a heroic action, saving a group of Vietnamese orphans who are traveling with a nun.

Dick Jarvitts, the younger brother of a soldier killed in Vietnam, bursts into the men's room and threatens to kill everyone; he tosses a grenade that will detonate in four seconds. Owen has learned enough Vietnamese to tell the children to lie down, and not to be afraid. It is at this point that Owen and Johnny's practice of The Shot comes into play. As Owen had told Johnny when they were children, The Shot never was intended for a game. Johnny, who is visiting Owen, lifts him in just under three seconds, and Owen is able to "slam-dunk" the grenade onto a high window ledge—not, however, quite before it blows off his hands and half his arms. Owen points out that he knows why he has his strange "VOICE"—it gets the children's attention, and they obey it. He also knows how he comes to be a hero: his hands, which Owen believed to be an instrument of God, save the children, as he had foreseen in his dream, and rescue Johnny, just as he promises to do throughout the novel. Owen's salvific act and subsequent death, envisioned by him earlier in *A Christmas Carol* and in his dream, are finally fulfilled in both a bizarre *and* a miraculous fashion.

A Christmas Carol is a tale about conversions, about endings and beginnings. Dickens's *Carol* reminds us of our own grave end and the possible end of the grave; it is not, to a person of faith, a "bad" dream, as Pastor Merrill suggests.

Owen's funeral, which comes in the novel *before* his death is described, recalls for us the immediacy of his revelation in *A Christmas Carol*; it also reminds us of the strength of doubt and the difficulty of faith. Still, Pastor Merrill, who has been a man of great doubt, is converted to faith, perhaps not so much because of Owen Meany as because of a miracle Merrill's own son gives him. Merrill preaches at Owen's funeral and follows "An Order for Burial" in the Book of Common Prayer. The narrator calls attention to the prayer book's note that the funeral liturgy is a liturgy of Easter, drawing its meaning from the hope of resurrection. Yet Reverend Merrill departs briefly from the established order, begging God, in a prayer, "give us back Owen Meany" (566), lines that Johnny will echo at the very end of the novel. Pastor Merrill's conversion, as we know, is not the only one in Irving's novel. The novel begins with a reference to Johnny's own conversion; he is "doomed" to remember Owen because Owen is the reason he believes in God and is a Christian.

At one point in the novel, Owen Meany teaches Johnny how to read by using Thomas Hardy's *Tess of the D'Urbervilles* (a work, in its own way, also about destiny, faith, and conversion) to demonstrate "that any good book is always in motion—from the general to the specific, from the particular to the whole, and back again. . . . Good reading . . . moves the same way" (324). The relationship of *A Christmas Carol* to Irving's novel, then, is not merely to move the plot forward—it hardly does that—but to resonate the profound meanings in the text. We do not fully understand the meanings of Dickens's *Carol* in Irving's text until we understand the "whole" of *Owen Meany*, and we do not understand Irving's novel half so well until, retrospectively, we understand the crucial part Dickens's *Carol* plays in it.

10

A Son of the Circus
(1994)

John Irving's eighth novel, *A Son of the Circus*, has been misread and undervalued by most reviewers, who fail to see his experimentation with such forms as the crime novel and the thriller. *Circus* is Irving's homage to Graham Greene, especially to *The Heart of the Matter* and *The Power and the Glory*. In his tribute to Greene, Irving has written his own allegory for our time.

A Son of the Circus was published to reviews such as the author has received for all of his books: mixed—from accolades to faint praise to righteous outrage. The novel, a *New York Times* best-seller, was reviewed by Robert Towers, who gets the description of the novel's complexity of plot right and who finds *Circus* to be Irving's "most entertaining novel since Garp" ("*A Son of the Circus*" 1). Webster Johnson, in the *Times Literary Supplement*, notes that the characters of *Circus* lack the "quirkiness" with which Irving endows his more "privileged characters" (11). And Walter Kirn, in *New York* magazine, simply calls the novel "Freak Chic," drawing attention to what he calls the book's slow and "regressive" story (113).

Only Sharon Locy, in *America*, seems to understand that *Circus* has to do with identity in a world that increasingly isolates and alienates us from each other and from ourselves. In addition, Locy sees that Irving's "circus presents a metaphor for human life that considers both its imperfection and its hopes" (27).

PLOT DEVELOPMENT

John Irving has always been fond of the convoluted plot with multiple spin-offs, seeming digressions, loops, and riffs, but the plot in *A Son of the Circus* nearly defies description. Thus far in Irving's published works, the plot in *Circus* is his most congested. On the surface, *Circus* is a novel of detection and a thriller. The novel's focus is on murder and on the discovery and capture of a killer, events that provide a framework for Irving to explore questions of identity. There are three intersecting main narratives in *Circus*: (1) the major plot, the story of Dr. Farrokh Daruwalla, who feels "displaced" in the world; (2) the story of Vinod and his family, circus dwarfs; and (3) the story of the twins separated at birth. All three of these plots are linked to varying degrees with the murder at the beginning of the novel. In addition, from these major plots loop at least a half-dozen subplots.

Although the action is set mainly in Bombay, India, with some few excursions outside the teeming city, it is not, as the author says in his prefatory "Author's Notes," "about" India. It is, instead, "about" Dr. Farrokh Daruwalla, fifty-nine, an orthopedic surgeon, born a Parsi in Bombay but nevertheless not "really" an Indian.

Daruwalla was educated by Jesuits in Bombay (at St. Ignatius School), then trained as a doctor in Germany. He married Julia, a Viennese Roman Catholic, and they live most of the year in Toronto, returning "every few years" to Bombay, where Daruwalla donates his services as an honorary consultant surgeon at the Hospital for Crippled Children. Here he also pursues the genetic markers that he hopes will explain achondroplastia—dwarfism. In order to undertake this research, he draws blood samples from circus dwarfs. When the doctor is not working at the hospital or visiting the circus for blood, he is at the Duckworth Club, drinking Kingfisher beer and eating.

In addition, Daruwalla is a "closet" screenplay writer, having written the notorious Inspector Dhar movies, the latest of which is based on a murder Daruwalla learned of some twenty years earlier. The Dhar movies star the doctor's young brother, John D., the son of an American film actress (Veronica Rose, who is sexually uninhibited) and either a British actor (Neville Eden, who is gay) or an American screenwriter (Danny Mills, an alcoholic). John D. had been adopted, at the request of his mother, by Dr. Lowji Daruwalla, Farrokh's father. Farrokh thinks of John D., so much younger than he, as his son, "the dear boy." At the time

Circus begins, Daruwalla is awaiting the arrival of John D.'s identical twin, Martin Mills, who was separated at birth from his brother by Veronica Rose (one child is more than enough for her); Veronica marries Danny Mills, primarily because he is willing. Martin Mills, a would-be Jesuit priest who has not yet taken his final vows, has been sent to St. Ignatius School and Mission. Also, when the novel opens, there has been a murder—of Mr. Lal, a member of the Duckworth Club.

All of the above is jammed into a very few pages of the novel's opening scenes, so it may be little wonder that the the reader can only hope things will get clearer—and simpler. They do not. If anything, the novel, with its flashbacks and sidebars, its loops, its lengthy descriptions, its not so humorous riffs on orthopedic and sexual surgery, becomes increasingly crowded. Even the plots appear to multiply.

The main action of *Circus*, however, is relatively simple, even though we lose sight of it from time to time. It is a plot of detection: Who killed Mr. Lal at the Duckworth? Much of the action of this plot focuses on the quest to discover and then to trap Lal's murderer, who may also be the serial killer of the "cage-girl" prostitutes (so called because they are exhibited in cages in the alleys of Bombay's red-light district). The killer of the prostitutes always draws a cartoon on their bellies of an elephant head, with one eye formed by the navel. The elephant appears to be winking as it sprays water in the direction of the cage-girl's pubic area.

The murderer of Lal did not draw a cartoon on his belly but instead left a two-rupee note in his mouth as a warning that unless Dhar is eliminated from the club, more members will die. Dhar, a fictional movie character whose image appears everywhere—not only in the enormously popular movies but also on billboards and in advertisements—is perceived as a "real" person in India; of course, John D. is the club member, not Dhar. The note-writing murderer has simply absorbed John D. into his movie persona, a role that John plays, or perhaps hides behind, whenever he appears in public in India.

Both Dr. Daruwalla and John D./Dhar "inspect" the body of Lal and thus are brought into the case by an actual detective, Inspector Patel. Although acting as a coroner is not part of Daruwalla's duties or expertise, he had performed the same function twenty years earlier when he inspected the body of a murdered girl and had seen the disturbing picture of the mocking elephant on her belly. Indeed, Dr. Daruwalla had appropriated the image as the basis of his most recent movie, *Inspector Dhar and the Cage-girl Killer*, the result of which was to provoke further murders.

Because the two-rupee note calls for the dismissal of Dhar, it is assumed Lal's murder is somehow connected to the cage-girl murders, since Dhar seems to be the object of the killer's deadly rage. What earlier appeared to be one of Irving's subplots, a digression about the cage-girls, now intersects with the main plot. When Daruwalla first saw the cartoonish elephant inscribed on the dead girl's body, he also attended to the badly cut foot of a young American hippie, Nancy. Unknown to Daruwalla, Nancy had been a witness to the murder of the girl, Beth, as well as to the murder of Nancy's lover, Dieter. Nancy never saw the face of the killer, but she believed that the murderer had both breasts and a penis. Nancy is memorable to Daruwalla not so much because of her cut foot (a result of stepping on broken glass when she attempted to clean up the aftermath of the murders) but because she carried an enormous dildo with her.

The dildo had a substantial amount of money in deutsche marks in it and provided a means to smuggle money into India. Dieter, in India for a drug transaction, used Nancy, with her clean-cut American good looks, to carry the dildo through customs. Nancy, who never knew what was in the dildo until after Dieter's death, keeps the money but forever feels guilty. After Daruwalla has patched up her foot and she prepares to leave the area, Nancy meets John D., to whom she is immediately attracted. To her chagrin, he ignores her, seeming, at the same time, to sneer at her. This same Nancy is now the wife of the deputy commissioner of police, Inspector Patel.

If Lal and the cage-girl murders are linked to blood, so, too, is Dr. Daruwalla's obsessive interest in the circus and in collecting blood from dwarfs as he pursues the genetic marker for dwarfism. Vinod, the circus dwarf once treated by Daruwalla, is the doctor's guide to collecting blood, as well as his and John D.'s unofficial chauffeur and bodyguard. Vinod's positions with the Daruwallas bring him into the murder narrative; he figures in the entrapment plot set to snare the killer.

Daruwalla knows Vinod and his wife, Deepa, initially from an embarrassing incident at the circus. Deepa, not a dwarf, had been sold to the Great Blue Nile Circus as a girl and married Vinod (she had no dowry). A novice trapeze artist, Deepa fell into the safety net during a circus performance, dislocating her hip. When Daruwalla crawled into the net to help her, somehow he fell on her, his nose landing somewhere in her pubic area: "this encounter . . . would be . . . his single extramarital experience. Farrokh would never forget it" (7–8). Farrokh's rather bizarre "nose" fantasy links him to the killer, whose equally bizarre fantasy is inscribed on the bellies of his women victims. The killer acts out his fantasy; Farrokh merely recalls his visually.

Vinod and Deepa work to rescue children from a life of prostitution and crime, a mission they carry out with the help of Mr. Garg, a pimp and owner of the Wetness Cabaret in the red-light district. Two of these children, Ganesh, a crippled beggar whose foot was stepped on by an elephant, and Madhu, one of Garg's girls, are rescued and taken to the Great Blue Nile Circus, where supposedly they will be trained for some circus work: Madhu, perhaps as a "boneless" girl, a contortionist; Ganesh, as a cook's helper and general roustabout.

This plot intersects with the twins-separated-at-birth plot when Vinod rescues Martin Mills, mistaken for Dhar, from being beaten senseless in the red-light district. Vinod, too, believes Martin is Inspector Dhar, suffering brain damage from his beating. Martin, along with Daruwalla, becomes part of Vinod's efforts to rescue Ganesh and Madhu. Martin, who has arrived in India to report to the Jesuit Mission and School of St. Ignatius, is suffering a religious crisis. Unsure of his vocation as a priest, he debates whether to take his final vows.

Patel, Daruwalla, and John D. discover that the cage-girl killer is Rahul, a transsexual well known to the Daruwallas (the killer's identity is hardly a secret to the readers of the novel). Rahul, now the second Mrs. Dogar of the Duckworth Club, has always been smitten with John D. And so Patel and Daruwalla set up an elaborate entrapment scene, with John as the bait, for New Year's Eve at the Duckworth Club, where Mrs. Dogar is arrested.

Shortly after the arrest, Dr. Daruwalla decides to leave for Toronto, never to return to India. But not before writing one more scenario: sending Martin and John D. on the same plane to Zurich. The twins meet, as if in a movie of their own, in the sky. The recognition scene, however, takes place off-camera, though the twins recount it often and with great embellishment.

The epilogue to *Circus* gives a summary of what happens to the major characters in the novel. The twins remain in Zurich, where John D. has small roles at the Schauspielhaus; Martin teaches at the university and visits various Jesuit centers, where he lectures. Sometimes, as a prank, the twins trade places. Ganesh dies in a failed attempt to be a "sky-walker" (a person who "walks" across the top of the tent, without a net) in the circus. Garg, who buys Madhu back from the circus, dies of AIDS, and Madhu disappears, likely dying as well. Patel and Nancy move into the Daruwallas' Bombay apartment and join the Duckworth Club. Mrs. Dogar dies in prison, beaten to death by the guards.

Vinod is killed in one of the bombings that take place on India's Independence Day. His wife, Deepa, and their son, Shivaji, move up from the Great Blue Nile to the Great Royal Circus. And Dr. Daruwalla, with his wife Julia, continues to live in Toronto. The doctor puts away his screenplays as well as all of his research on dwarfism. He continues to work as an orthopedist. His longtime friend and colleague, Dr. Macfarlane, suffering from AIDS, persuades Daruwalla to become a volunteer at the AIDS hospice in Toronto.

Irving uses an omniscient narrator in *Circus*, possibly in an attempt to keep control over the many plots, loops, and digressions in the novel; the result is less than happy. The omniscient narrator tends to distance the reader from both plot and character, at times to the point where it is difficult to care much what happens or to whom. Walter Kirn's criticism of the novel—that the plots move forward by taking two steps backward—is inaccurate, however, and fails to recognize that Irving is working with formulaic structures of the novel of detection and the thriller.

From these genres, Irving adopts and adapts such plot devices as retardation (the "regression" Kirn mocks), the prolonging of suspense, and seeming diversions. The plot is constructed in such a way as to cause readers to be confused; concealment, pursuit, detection, recognition, and confrontation are primary elements. And, without doubt, Irving relies on coincidence, a primary technique of the crime novel. Indeed, the twins' meeting on the plane to Zurich repeats nearly all of the plot devices, as well as the themes, of Irving's novel. Although Daruwalla scripts John and Martin's meeting, they improvise on it. The twins' recounting of their discovery scene—their recognition and confrontation of one another—uses a basic plot repeated throughout the novel: a plot with a variety of seemingly confusing details and digressions that obscure and conceal the event.

Although two of Irving's novels, *Garp* and *The Hotel New Hampshire*, have been made into movies, *A Son of the Circus* seems to be the most cinematic of all his novels to date. That is, *Circus* has a graphic, cinematic quality about it, with the narrator as the camera eye zooming in for the close-up, panning broad scenes, moving back for the long shot, and giving odd-angle shots even Hitchcock would be proud of.

SETTING

Most of *Circus* takes place in India, with an important closing scene in Toronto. Mention is made of Iowa (Nancy is from there, and it is a place, significantly, to which she does not want to return), Vienna, and Zurich, but the novel focuses primarily on Bombay, with a major side trip to Goa.

Irving makes little attempt to map the city of Bombay, but he does make us see the poverty of the place and smell its stench. We also have a sense of the hordes of people jammed into the city, the numbers of beggars, as well as their aggression. Class distinctions are maintained not only at the Duckworth but reach everywhere, including the Daruwallas' apartment building, where a sign reads:

> SERVANTS ARE NOT ALLOWED
> TO USE THE LIFT
> UNLESS ACCOMPANIED BY CHILDREN (642)

Vinod defies this rule every chance he gets, much to the dismay of the dogs in the building and the upper-class apartment dwellers. Daruwalla's servants, who once worked for his father, and who are getting old and feeble, always use the stairs, despite the effort it costs them.

In Bombay, a central setting is the Duckworth Club, a holdover from the days of the Raj. The Duckworth Club allows Irving an opportunity for irony. The club is comprised of 6,000 carefully selected Indians, with a waiting period of years to become a member. The class snobbery is as obvious as the ostentatious plumbing in the Duckworth: the men's room features ornate tiger plumbing; the women's room, (unwinking) elephants, the source of the cartoon images Rahul draws on his victims. When he was a little boy, Rahul was taken by his aunt, Promila Rai, to the women's room, where he sat on her lap while she urinated; then little Rahul would urinate. Afterward, they washed their hands by pulling the elephant's tusk that controlled the flow of water.

The Duckworth is a vestige of colonialism, appropriated by upperclass Indians for their own postcolonialist satisfaction. Dr. Daruwalla and his family (including the fair-skinned John D.) are members because his father, Lowji, had been a member (Lowji was killed outside the club by a car bomb). Membership, along with other privileges, is inherited. To

John D.'s credit, at the end of the novel he resigns his membership and place to Inspector Patel and his wife, Nancy. Under ordinary circumstances, the Patels would never have been selected as members. Even though they meet the criterion of having contributed significantly to the life of the community, the Patels are a biracial couple and lack "proper" class standing. We remember, however, that the killer, Mrs. Dogar, once Rahul, had been considered doubly "proper" enough to be a member of the club. She married a member of the club (Mr. Dogar), and she had inherited a membership through her Aunt Promila.

Goa is the resort on the coast where Daruwalla and his family vacation. Like the Duckworth and the apartment with its sign, Goa remains part of the past and its traditions. It, too, is divided by class distinctions. But Goa has gone slightly to seed and has become a place for drug-buying. Here Dieter, Nancy, and Beth wait to pull off a drug deal. In Goa, Rahul, in the middle of his sex change, and thus with breasts and a penis, desires the handsome movie star John D./Dhar, but cannot arrange a tryst. It is also in Goa that Rahul snuggles against Nancy, who is in bed with a high fever, and viciously kills Dieter and Beth. Daruwalla cleans and bandages Nancy's infected foot, injured when she stepped on glass as she cleaned up the carnage from the murder before burying her lover and her friend.

Nancy, like Rahul, desires John D., but he willfully ignores her, which she takes not only as rejection but also as some sort of moral judgment. She never gets over the way John D. looks at her and makes her feel cheap. Goa, then, is traumatic for Nancy in more ways than one. She remains "infected" from the place.

The Jesuit Mission and School of St. Ignatius has some importance as well, since this is where Martin reports and feels his spiritual crisis most deeply. Daruwalla had been educated at this boys' school, which remains tradition-bound in its own way; the priests, who come from all over the world, are old and seem not to know or care about the world around them or its people. Martin is to them a disruptive figure dressed in loud Hawaiian shirts. He feels as much a misfit in the mission as Daruwalla feels in Toronto and Bombay. Martin's crisis of faith, his belief that he lacks God's grace, mirrors that of other characters in the novel.

But perhaps the circus is ultimately the most significant setting in the novel. It is, as Locy reminds us, a metaphor for the world. Whenever "any circus," from the Great Blue Nile to the Great Royal, is in Bombay, Dr. Daruwalla has a front-row seat (27). Indeed, he is "an adopted son of the circus" (27). To Daruwalla, "the circus was an orderly well-kept oasis surrounded by a world of disease and chaos" (27). Circus people boil their water and milk; areas are swept often, and the order pleases the doctor.

Yet, Dr. Daruwalla is mistaken about the circus; its world reflects our own. Disease and chaos exist in both. Deepa becomes sick; Vinod is injured. The children Daruwalla and Martin bring to the circus to be "saved" remain lost: Madhu is bought and sold and has AIDS, and Ganesh not only remains crippled but dies while attempting to skywalk without a net. A circus chimpanzee that bites Martin's ear represents the sudden eruption of inexplicable violence that occurs in Goa, in Bombay, even in Toronto. The chimp's master returns the animal's violence with "rehabilitative" beatings. The chimp learns nothing; it dies from rabies.

If there is horror at the circus, there is also hope and beauty. Ganesh hopes to be a skywalker, to shed his beggar's clothes as well as his infirmity. In Daruwalla's imagination, Ganesh succeeds. We all live in the circus; we all, at some time, must work without a net. Perhaps it is possible . . . we, too, might just be able to walk the sky. At least we hope so.

CHARACTER DEVELOPMENT

Irving usually creates energetic characters who not only surprise and delight us but also are memorable: consider Garp, Roberta Muldoon, Franny Berry, Owen Meany. In *Circus*, however, the characters, with the possible exception of Nancy Patel, are underdeveloped and have little psychological resonance. Such underdevelopment may be appropriate, however, for two reasons. First, in crime detection or thriller novels, the focus tends to be on plot and landscape rather than on characters, who frequently run to type or are allegorical. Moreover, in a novel where the major question has to do with identity itself, characters may well appear to be tenuous.

Dr. Farrokh Daruwalla, the central character, is a kind person who feels, we are told over and over, alienated from his country of origin, India, and from his country of adoption, Canada. He is a devoted father to two daughters and husband to Julia. Indeed, he can be a passionate husband when stimulated by such writing as that of James Salter, whose work apparently excites the good doctor and his wife. Farrokh is obsessed with finding a genetic marker for dwarfism, partly out of his love for the circus and partly out of his love for medicine and a desire to make his own "mark" in the world. It is at the circus that he feels most at home. If circus folks, especially dwarfs, are "outsiders," or alien, Daruwalla feels that he is one of them.

In addition to the circus, his other great love is his "beloved boy," John D. One gets the distinct impression that Daruwalla cares more for him than for his own daughters, who, along with his wife, Julia, are little more than props in the novel. Daruwalla has not only helped to bring John D. up, he has, in effect, "created" an identity for him, that of Inspector Dhar. At least Dhar is John D.'s identity when he is in India; outside of India, John D.'s identity remains a mystery to Farrokh, much to his frustration.

Daruwalla, who writes awful, hard-boiled detective movies for Dhar, filled with sex and violence, has a rich "interior" life, Julia believes, but we catch only glimpses of it—perhaps more clearly at the end of the novel. He recognizes his movies as "trash" but calls them "ironic." Quite how an intelligent man, one we are told is sensitive, can view the racism, sexism, and savage violence in his creations as ironic is never made clear. One suspects that he feels guilty over his screenplays, which make him a great deal of money. His guilt may account for his desire to write an "artistic" screenplay, which he does, calling it *Limo Roulette*. It ends up unproduceable, lying in a bureau drawer—because it lacks the trashy elements of a Dhar movie.

Just as he scripts Dhar's life, and creates a career for John D., so does Daruwalla script the arrest of the serial killer and the meeting of the twins separated at birth. In both cases the scripts get away from him; he cannot control them; improvisation takes over.

After the arrest of Mrs. Dogar/Rahul, Daruwalla determines to leave India for good and to remain in Toronto, with trips to Zurich to see the twins. It is not that Daruwalla feels at home in Toronto—racism and stupidity abound there, as in Bombay—but he undergoes a kind of conversion.

In Goa many years before, he had a conversion based on a silly incident concerning his "big toe." Rahul had climbed to the balcony of the Daruwallas' hotel room, believing that John D. was sleeping there. When Rahul saw a foot sticking outside the mosquito netting, he not only sucked the big toe, he bit it in some sort of sexual ecstasy. Farrokh's cry of pain scared and disgusted Rahul, who left immediately, but Farrokh, who had been dreaming he was St. Francis (whose "miraculously preserved body" was bitten by a "crazed pilgrim"), underwent a conversion. From unbelief, he became a believer. When Farrokh learned Rahul was responsible for his toe being bitten—that he was not kin to St. Francis, after all—Daruwalla was "unconverted."

In Toronto, he is converted once again—this time more convincingly and more subtly—when he learns that his best friend and colleague, Dr. Macfarlane, suffers from AIDS; at the same time, he learns that the twins are homosexual. Thus, Farrokh, who claimed not to be homophobic, but who certainly was, becomes a volunteer at the AIDS hospice in Toronto. One night a woman calls the hospice, asking to speak to someone in charge, saying, "I want to speak to a *doctor*! . . . Who *are* you, anyway? *What* are you?" (652). Farrokh answers "with such conviction and pride that he surprised himself. 'I'm a volunteer' " (652). Whatever else this scene shows us about Farrokh, it signifies spiritual growth for him; it is an epiphanic moment.

For the twins, John D. and Martin Mills, racial assimilation may not seem a problem, but it is nonetheless linked to their identity. In India, the blond, pale John D. is Inspector Dhar, supposedly a Parsi, his brother/father's creation. He has no "real" identity in India except the fictional one Farrokh creates for him, and the Dhar creation is so incredible, so patronizing of Indians, that it offends everyone. Still, the fictional Dhar serves a purpose; John D., by turns arrogant, cold, contemptuous, can hide behind the public persona of Dhar, keeping everyone, including his family, at a distance. The only time John D. appears engaging is when Daruwalla's children are young, and John D. plays with them. Only then does he not play a role.

His unscripted life in Zurich remains a secret from his family. John D. has a Swiss passport; Dhar has a fake Indian passport. Together, the passports symbolize John D.'s divided self. In Zurich, John D. lives an openly gay life with an older man, his longtime companion, Mathias Frei, who toward the end of the novel dies of a heart attack. John D. is also an actor in the theater, taking small roles at the Schauspielhaus.

John D. is reluctant to meet his identical twin because he fears the delicate balance of his dual lives will be upset. However, once the meeting takes place, John D. becomes more playful, more likable. He comes to life, ironically, through transatlantic phone calls to Daruwalla in Toronto.

For all that Martin is John D.'s identical twin, he is in many ways his opposite. Whereas John D. is taciturn, secretive, cynical, Martin is talkative (he never shuts up), open, curious. John D. is an elegantly dressed man who also moves elegantly; his brother wears outrageous Hawaiian shirts and stumbles and careens through life. Martin, who perhaps has sought the priesthood because of his terrible parents, Veronica Rose and the drunken Danny Mills (perhaps also because he feels somewhat responsible for his best friend's death), is, like his brother, not at ease with himself or in India. A man who injures others inadvertently, Martin is forever *being* injured by himself or others; he indulges in self-flagellation, and others beat him as well. He is even bitten by a rabid chimpanzee. It is a wonder he lives long enough to meet his twin. However, Martin comes across with more energy than most of the characters in *Circus*.

The brothers have hearts of gold. Martin shows his own heart self-consciously in his desire to "save" India, one person at a time; first with the prostitutes in Bombay's red-light district, for which he is beaten nearly senseless, and then with Madhu and Ganesh, the children he "delivers" to the circus. Unfortunately, Madhu, HIV-positive, leaves with the pimp Garg; Ganesh dies. John D.'s heart is not so obviously displayed, but he is more successful than his brother in doing good. It is his idea for the Daruwallas to let the Patels have their Bombay apartment at a price they can afford; the view would be "good" for Nancy, John D. says. And it is John D. who resigns his membership at the Duckworth Club so that the Patels not only can "belong" but can enjoy belonging.

One would think that in a novel that has at its center a murder, the killer would be more interesting than Rahul, but he is curiously flat. The description of Rahul, the second Mrs. Dogar, reveals her eyes are "cold"; she is arrogant; she "feels" nothing. To be sure, there are similarities between Mrs. Dogar and Inspector Dhar; the line between killer and detective is stereotypically blurred.

Mrs. Dogar's motivation for murder remains unknown. She may be motivated by Aunt Promila's sexual fondling or being taken into the women's room when Rahul was a child; or by the failure to seduce John D.; or by being rejected by the art school he wanted to attend; or by a hatred of women—and men; or by any combination of these. As Patel explains, there is never a simple motivation that explains murder; we get that only in the movies. Whatever the motivation(s), Mrs. Dogar demonstrates the sheer "satisfaction" she gains from killing. It makes her "younger," even "girlish."

Even though Nancy and Patel are minor characters in *Circus*, they turn out to be especially interesting. Patel, who has worked his way up to inspector, has, like all Indian police, been able to do so only by bribing certain officials. Thus, although he represents the law, he also signifies its corruption, a fact he is well aware of when he "bribes" Dhar. It is also Patel who recognizes that the state will not mete out justice to Mrs.

Dogar; since the state is also corrupt and complicit in the violence of killing, it cannot judge the killers. The only justice Mrs. Dogar will suffer is poetic justice.

Patel's care and intense love for Nancy are touching to readers. We have the sense that there is a passionate life beneath the surface of this couple, as well as a great deal of suffering and sadness. Nancy is in many ways a child–woman and linked with Madhu, Garg's woman–child, who disappears. Both are victims. Nancy fears she has lost her innocence; Madhu *has* lost hers.

THEMATIC ISSUES

Many of John Irving's concerns reappear in *Circus*: children, violence, random death, religion, class, disease (the great attention given to AIDS is new to this novel). Although we don't get bears in this novel, we do get a chimpanzee and elephants. The circus and dwarfs that appeared in *The Hotel New Hampshire* return in expanded form in this novel.

Of overriding concern in *Circus*, however, is the theme of identity: racial and ethnic, as well as sexual. All the major characters feel a sense of alienation from their homeland, their family, their very origins, and themselves. Nowhere is this made clearer than with the main character, Farrokh Daruwalla.

Farrokh, born into privilege, is a man who seemingly has everything he could desire—an expensive home (later two homes), a good education, a successful and lucrative orthopedic practice, a beautiful wife, and smart, attractive children. He also has a secret, yet successful, career as a screenwriter. Nevertheless, Daruwalla feels alienated in all of the places where he lives, including his heart. His creation of a career, by which he means a "life," for John D. is far more ironic than his pathetic attempt at irony in his movies: his casting a fair-skinned Anglo as a Parsi who solves violent crimes in India, all the while sneering cynically at everything that *is* India and, at the same time, being pursued by Indian women. Daruwalla fails to understand that this fantasy reveals his own anxieties and self-hatred as it demonstrates the depth of his alienation.

Even in Toronto, Farrokh can not escape his sense of isolation, his feeling of not belonging. He is taunted by those who yell "go home" or, worse, harassed by young thugs who rough him up. In one of the final scenes in the novel, an Anglo boy (a little "gentleman," Farrokh thinks) asks him where he is from. Farrokh answers, "I'm from the circus" (680).

The child is instantly delighted: "What [Farrokh] saw in the boy's happy face was something he'd never felt before in his cold, adopted country" (680). The "uncritical acceptance" is the "most satisfying pleasure" any "immigrant of color would ever know" (680). Farrokh often remembers his father saying "Immigrants are immigrants for life"; for an instant Farrokh can forget his father's comment.

Farrokh's dis-ease, his sense of alienation, appears also in the twins separated at birth: Martin, who talks nonstop and cannot walk across a room without harming himself, and John D. who "un-Dhars" himself as he flies to Zurich by shaving off his mustache. Perhaps Rahul is the most obvious representation of the alienated self. As Rahul, in Goa, he appears with breasts and penis, and as Mrs. Dogar, at the Duckworth, she arrives with breasts and hard muscles. The transsexual killer reveals the multiple anxieties and divisions of the alienated self.

Nancy, told by her parents she is a "bad" girl, is, like Martin, clumsy, and, like John D., often moody and taciturn. Perhaps of all the characters, Nancy is the most profoundly aware of the implications of a divided self: "She'd embraced evil; she'd found it lacking" (269). Her belief that she has lost the better part of her self moves her to look to Patel for reintegration, for "salvation." To her, Patel symbolizes the order of law and justice, the "incorruptible policeman [who] could restore her essential goodness" (269).

But Nancy does not know "how far from home Vijay Patel" is (230). He is a Gujarati, from a merchant family that left Gujarat for Kenya to do business there. He is "as cut off from them . . . as Nancy was from Iowa" (230). Patel came to Bombay to make his way on a Maharashtrian police force (230). To become D.C.P. Patel, he was forced to pay a small bribe—once and only once. But it was enough. He reminds Nancy that such order as she desires no longer exists, if it ever did. Order in the world has been replaced by the chaos of the isolated, betrayed, and fragmented self.

A FORMULAIC READING OF *A SON OF THE CIRCUS*

In *A Son of the Circus*, Irving refers several times to the novels of Graham Greene, especially to *The Heart of the Matter* and *The Power and the Glory*. Indeed, Farrokh and Martin argue over whether they are "Catholic" novels, that is, specifically related to church dogma. Their argument aside, Irving, who admires Greene, finds in these novels—and in

Greene's so-called entertainments—a number of formulae that suit his purpose in the "mystery" of *Circus*.

For readers of *Circus*, a formulaic analysis helps to illuminate the multilayered meanings of Irving's intricate and complex novel. John Cawelti defines a formula as a "combination or synthesis of a number of specific cultural *Conventions* with a more universal story form or archetype" (qtd. in Yanarella and Sigelman 7; see also Cawelti passim). For Cawelti, such formulae have particular cultural significance; through repetition, they become the conventional way in which certain images, symbols, myths, and themes are represented. Through the use of such formulae—or conventions—we can infer collective fantasies and anxieties shared by readers. Formulaic literature is not necessarily constraining: for example, both Shakespeare and Emily Brontë—as well as Graham Greene—used formulae at the same time they transcended them.

Irving adapts a number of formulae found in the crime novel and the thriller: sensationalism, repetition, delay and deliberate retardation of plot, alternation of plot lines to prolong suspense, landscape, and identity (recognition and confrontation), to name only a few. Of these formulae, two seem to be of particular significance in *Circus*: landscape as a moral index and questions of identity (recognition and confrontation). No more than Greene, however, does Irving use these formulae simply to write a "who dunnit." Like Greene, Irving believes, for the most part, that "we *all* dunnit." From his first to his most recent novel, Irving makes it clear that we are responsible to each other. And we are all, in one way or another, guilty of the evils of the modern world. Greene, too, wrote of our collective guilt, as well as our lost innocence, in *The Lost Childhood and Other Essays*: "Violence comes to us more easily because it was so long expected—not only by the political sense, but by the moral sense" (189). How could our world be other than it is? A fallen world, without grace.

Violence in Irving's *Circus* springs not so much out of individual character as it does out of society's collective viciousness. Such viciousness is expressed in the very landscape that Irving depicts. Indeed, the landscape itself becomes a character; it assails us at every turn, just as victims disappear into or become part of the landscape (Madhu, for example). Killers, too, blend into the landscape, as Nancy knows; she looks for Rahul around every corner, in every street.

The violence that erupts in both Bombay and Toronto demonstrates just how thin the veneer of civilization is. Irving's representation of Bombay hardly entices any would-be tourist. The cacophony of the city is horrendous; Bombay boils and seethes in the stench of its own excrement. Filth and poverty reach everywhere, even to the streets in front of the most exclusive and pricey hotels. Animals and people clog the streets, but there are also animals, barking dogs, in the upper-class apartment building in which the Daruwallas live. And there are dogs—barking Dobermans—at the police station; their excrement can be found amid police "order" (357).

Irving gives us no garden imagery in this landscape, no beautiful flowers, to counteract the appalling wasteland that is Bombay. To be sure, the lawns at the exclusive Duckworth Club are cool, green, and manicured. But the flowers of the bougainvillea are being killed off, and in their midst is a corpse fed upon by vultures. Even the circus, which Daruwalla finds an "oasis" of order amid anarchy, remains a matter of perception: his children never liked the circus; it was too dirty.

Out of such a landscape arises brutality that cuts across all classes from children, to prostitutes, to pimps, to wealthy apartment owners, to members of the social elite, even to the arms of the law. In such a landscape, riddled with class, religious, and ethnic hatreds, it is no wonder that individuals feel isolated and alienated. The India that Irving gives us may seem exotic, quite foreign, but the author wants us to recognize this as clearly our world, with no exaggeration. It exists in Canada, in Toronto's "cold" landscape and its Little India, where Farrokh is kidnapped and roughed up. In Little India, he discovers in a shop the elephant faucet that so inspired the "artist" in Rahul. It also exists in the viciousness of Hollywood, transported to India, and in Boston, where Veronica Rose seduces her son's best friend, driving him to suicide. And it exists in America's heartland, in Iowa, where a young girl is judged evil because she becomes pregnant.

In such a world, how can we feel other than displaced? Farrokh, the central figure (the "hero," if there is one in *Circus*), is alienated from both India and Canada. He claims to be at home only in the circus and at the unchanging Duckworth, where he holds on to "the illusion" that he is "comfortable being in India."

As Sharon Locy notes in her review of Irving's novel, Farrokh's divided self (she refers to it as an "identity crisis," a woefully inadequate phrase) is doubled in the twins, John D. and Martin. John D. must "un-Dhar" himself each time he leaves India; Martin must accept that the priesthood is not his vocation. Nancy, too, is divided, in her sexual loyalties and in the battle she wages within herself between good and evil.

It is not coincidental that Rahul/Mrs. Dogar is Daruwalla's double.

His/her sexual division is obvious; Daruwalla's, more subtle—and represented in a different fashion. Farrokh loves his wife, Julia, but becomes passionate only by reading James Salter's masturbatory, titillating *A Sport and a Pastime.* Reading of a certain kind arouses Farrokh, who at one point says that writing is a "ruthless" business; murder is equally arousing for Rahul—and ruthless.

Rahul never forgets his desires for John D., just as Farrokh never forgets his sexual fantasies about Vinod's wife, Deepa. Nor, presumably, will he forget his desire for the child prostitute Madhu. Whereas Rahul acts out his fantasies and brutal desires in killing, Farrokh projects his fantasies of lust and violence into his enormously popular Dhar movies. The movies implicate the moviegoing public, whose own fantasies are aroused and who, in turn, want to "kill" the pale, non-Indian Dhar.

For Irving, as for Graham Greene, the alienated and split self is indicative of the lack of a moral center. When Martin confesses his spiritual doubt, his sin of pride, his very despair, the father confessor at St. Ignatius is so bored that he falls asleep! Martin's sense of his divided self, torn between love of God and doubt, is reflected in his own gracelessness; he bumps into, collides with unmovable objects, cutting, bruising, and injuring himself constantly. He is, as Daruwalla says, a man "dangerous" to himself and others.

Nancy, like Martin, keenly doubts whether there is any morality—by which she means spirituality—in herself or the world. Her gracelessness, though it may not match Martin's, is represented in her awkwardness, in the way she dresses, in the way she enters a room, in the way she fails to socialize. She fears she has been totally corrupted, that she has lost her innocence, just as her parents—and neighbors—told her. Nancy's fascination with and repulsion for John D. and Rahul (thus linking these two) reflect her self-doubt. She is like Madhu, not only in terms of lost innocence but also because they are both child–victims. Madhu loses her life; Nancy survives—barely.

Nancy seeks both "salvation" in the love of her husband, Patel, for her and security in the "order" she believes he represents. To hold fast her belief, she must minimize the fact that the institution he represents is rife with bribe givers and bribe takers. Indeed, he has engaged in bribery. Yet, for all Nancy's love of Patel, she suffers few illusions. She knows she cannot "go home" again; the view from her apartment (which, if pursued far enough, leads to her origins, her childhood in Iowa) is "sort of fading now," she tells Farrokh near the end of the novel (667). The "retired Inspector Dhar" can imitate "the exact degree of deadness in Nancy's voice," and he does, over and over, until the "ex-screenwriter" says, "Stop it" (667). Nancy realistically knows there is little chance for joy in life—she will remain grace-less.

Because the "deadness" of Nancy's voice comes near the close of the novel, it appears to undercut what might be seen as Irving's affirmative ending. Farrokh tells the little boy who asks where he is from, "I'm from the circus," and in his mind—and heart—he *is* at the circus. He sees in his imagination the "elephant-footed" boy, Ganesh, who is dressed no longer as a beggar, as he was in life, but is "in his singlet with the blue-green sequins" (681). Ganesh descends "in the spotlight" with "the completion of another successful Skywalk, which in reality had never happened and never would" (681). Farrokh knows that "[t]he *real* cripple was dead" (681). "Yet in his mind's eye," he sees "the elephant boy walk without a limp across the sky" (681). To Farrokh, this India is "as real" as the one he left behind. In short, Farrokh indicates his hope of both human goodness and the possibility of grace in the world.

There is, then, a doubleness in the ending of *Circus*: on the one hand, "deadness"; on the other, hope. We recall an earlier scene with Farrokh, a scene that comes in the very center of John Irving's novel. Farrokh is at St. Ignatius Church, and he cannot resist "snooping at [the] Lectionary . . . open to the Second Epistle of Paul to the Corinthians" (377): "Therefore, since we have this ministry, as we have received mercy, we do not lose heart" (II Cor. 4:1), writes Paul, who himself was converted. Farrokh skips ahead:

> We are hard pressed on every side, yet not crushed; we are perplexed, but not in despair; persecuted, but not forsaken; struck down, but not destroyed—always carrying about in the body the dying of the Lord Jesus, that the life of Jesus may also be manifested in our body. (4:8–10)

Like Graham Greene's *The Heart of the Matter* and *The Power and the Glory*, John Irving's *Circus* is about the power of grace manifested even in the landscape of our fallen world.

11

A Widow for One Year
(1998)

John Irving's ninth novel, *A Widow for One Year*, is his riskiest and most experimental novel to date. For the first time, Irving creates a female protagonist, Ruth Cole, but Ruth's femininity is complex. He describes her as handsome, not pretty, in a somewhat "masculine" way, a woman deemed "difficult" by men, a woman who admits to being a writer first, a woman second. Nevertheless, Ruth also desires marriage and a child, and it is her relationships with men, starting with her father, that often propel the narrative. Irving's choice of protagonist is directly tied to the second major risk he takes. Irving, a self-acknowledged follower of nineteenth-century literary tradition, presents once again a narrative of traditional power structures such as the Oedipal plot—dominated by the father, inherited by the sons. Or so it seems. But he tells the story in such a way that the reader is invited to explore that narrative and call it into question.

To be sure, *A Widow for One Year* contains many motifs from Irving's earlier novels: familial and sexual love; loss and recovery; adultery and random violence; and subjectivity and voice. And as he has done in the past, Irving includes a range of genres and mediums: postcards, letters, pieces of a diary, biography, poetry, children's stories, thrillers, and romance. In *A Widow*, Irving's interlacing of genres clearly not only challenges our expectations as readers but also seems to challenge literary traditions as well. The mixed fictions repeatedly draw attention both to multiple perspectives and to the process of fiction-making itself.

But the process of writing is only half of the story. We don't read fiction, generally speaking, to find out how it is made. We read it for the particulars of individual experience and for ways of knowing and understanding that experience. As readers we are interested in the exploration of character, in crossing boundaries and envisioning new horizons. Irving's *A Widow for One Year*, above all, provides us with the opportunity.

PLOT DEVELOPMENT

A Widow for One Year is the story of Ruth Cole as she grows up to discover love and herself. The novel provides three views of her, taken at different times: the summer of 1958, when she is four; the fall of 1990, when she is thirty-six and a successful writer; and the fall of 1995, when she is a recent widow of forty-one. The obsession with time in the novel seems to be conventionally linear, marching forward in orderly progression, dominated by Ruth's father, Ted Cole, who not only sets the story in motion but keeps it running for much of the novel.

Yet, the linear emphasis on time goes awry and fails repeatedly in the novel. Within this time frame, only limited stories such as romances and mysteries can be told, and they peter out; their endings fail to be conclusive. The Cole family itself turns out to be irregular in its structure and seems to negate lineal time. Linearity is disrupted by the past and its memory. Although we see that time passes and inevitably presses on, it proves to be circular as well. Irving's emphasis on the flow of linear time begins with the title of the novel, but the title refers to a time near the end of the novel.

Even the omniscient narrator speaks from the perspective of the ending. The narrator's voice, through asides, rhetorical commentary, and addresses to the reader, forces us outside of any narrative continuity. The constant opposition between continuity and discontinuity encourages us to suspend or revise judgments and to entertain the possibility of multiple meanings. The very complexity of Irving's use of time, which insistently reminds us of the season, the year, the ages of characters, also emphasizes moments that are delayed, remembered, revised. We are shown both diachronic and synchronic studies of time; that is, we are aware of events evolving over time even while we are concerned passionately with particular moments of time.

In *A Widow for One Year*, Ruth Cole, the daughter of Ted and Marion Cole, is the replacement child for her two brothers, Thomas and Timothy, who were killed at ages sixteen and fifteen in a terrible automobile accident, the facts of which are made known to us some 150 pages into the book. Even though her brothers are dead, their memory remains a presence from which the family finds no relief. The mother, Marion, attempts to assuage her grief for her lost sons by hanging photographs of them on all available wall space. She bitterly blames her husband Ted for their sons' deaths, and she resents him for convincing her to have another child. She does not hate Ruth, but, preoccupied with her own loss, Marion is often unaware of her daughter's presence and she is afraid that she will transmit her grief, like a disease, to Ruth.

Ted recognizes his wife's despair but is angered by it. A man of chronic philandering and drinking (both pursuits begun long before his sons died), Ted's sense of love and responsibility is expressed only for Ruth. Ted writes and illustrates children's stories, several of which are summarized in *A Widow*. *The Mouse Crawling Between the Walls* and *The Door in the Floor* were both written for his sons—one before they died, one expressing the anguish of nothingness after they were killed. Both reveal a horror of potential violence and death, of the unknown. The story Ted writes for Ruth, *A Sound Like Someone Trying Not to Make a Sound*, is retold in its entirety in *A Widow*, and its illustrations described. All of the children's stories are cautionary tales, but Ruth's is especially so. It is about a moleman, truly a man/animal, who kidnaps little girls to take them to his underground lair, where he keeps them. The psychological aspects of the tale, the aggression of the male, his desire to possess and punish the female, to bury her, are clear. The girl's alternating fear and desire for the moleman are equally clear, as are the Oedipal implications in the story of the daughter's love for her father/hero who saves her. Irving strategically uses the story of the moleman as part of a larger tale of a "real" moleman who captures his female and keeps her forever by first killing her and then photographing her body.

Ted plots more than just children's stories; he plots to be rid of his wife and to acquire sole custody of Ruth. Thus, he is more—or less—than the father/hero; he is squarely in the camp of the moleman. In the summer of 1958, Ted hires Eddie O'Hare, who is sixteen and resembles Thomas, to be his general assistant and driver (since Ted, because of his alcoholism, is not allowed to drive). Eddie, from Ted and the boys' *alma mater*, Exeter Academy, wants to be a writer and looks forward to spending the summer with Ted Cole in the Hamptons on Long Island. What Eddie cannot know when he arrives on the Island is that he and thirty-nine-year-old Marion Cole will have a passionate love affair from which neither of them will recover over the next thirty-seven years.

Ted, who assumes that Marion will love Eddie because of his resemblance to Thomas, intends to be rid of Marion on the grounds of adultery. In this case, however, he has over-plotted the story; Marion has already decided to divorce Ted and to leave Ruth with him. Marion goes to Canada where eventually (using her mother's name, Alice Somerset), she becomes a writer of detective novels. She never corresponds or communicates with her daughter or Eddie. When Marion leaves her family, she takes with her all of the photographs of her sons except for one in which they are standing in front of a building at Exeter Academy. On the building is an inscription in Latin, which translates as, "Come hither boys and become men." This ironic photo—her boys will never grow up to be men, and even though Ted has grown older, he is still a boy—Marion leaves for Ted. Marion also leaves all of the picture hooks on the wall where the photos had been.

When Ruth is four in that summer of 1958, she witnesses a primal scene, not between her parents but between her mother and Eddie O'Hare. She never forgets it, though she forgets some of the details. Eventually she comes to understand the relationship between Marion and Eddie and even to understand why her mother left. Ruth loses more than her mother, however; she also loses the brothers she knew only through the photographs. Each picture "told" a story, and when the memory of the photograph fades, Ruth is forced to create a story to go with the hook on the wall. It is no wonder that Ruth becomes a writer. Eventually, the pictures of her brothers are replaced with Ruth's pictures, which tell stories of her own life and development. These photos are her biography, so to speak.

Ruth, like her brothers and father before her, goes to Exeter (and, indeed, has her photo taken before the same building her brothers did). At Exeter, her best friend is Hannah Grant, Ruth's opposite and alter ego. Whereas Ruth is good-looking in a "masculine" way, Hannah is stereotypically feminine with fashionable clothes, beautifully coiffed hair, manicured nails, and made-up face. Ruth remains largely innocent and wary of men; Hannah is sexually knowing and aggressive. Ruth is aggressive only when playing squash, a game her father taught her. In this novel, squash is a metaphor for discipline, rules, and order, just as wrestling is in earlier Irving novels, such as *The World According to Garp*.

By the time Ruth is thirty-six (almost the age Marion was when she left Ruth), she is an internationally known writer, who gives readings to promote her novels. At one of these readings in New York City, she meets Eddie O'Hare again. Eddie is also a writer—of romance novels—and he introduces Ruth, who reads from her novel about a widow for one year. (Irving's reflexivity may be noted here: On October 18, 1996, he gave a reading at Arlington Street Church, Boston, of his then unfinished novel, *A Widow for One Year*.)

It remains a rueful running joke throughout much of Irving's novel that his protagonist may have discipline and order in her written work, but that her own life is chaotic and empty. She has few women friends—it seems only Hannah—and her male acquaintances are merely interested in ogling her well-developed breasts and bedding an acclaimed novelist. For example, Scott Saunders, who is superficially charming and handsome, wants to have sex with Ruth and ends up raping and beating her. Ruth retaliates by breaking Saunders' knee and his collarbone with a squash racket.

What Ruth longs for—especially after the Saunders episode—is order in her life and a child to fill it. For both desires, she looks to Allan Albright, her editor; as she suggests, she needs more than a book editor, she needs someone to edit her life. Allan, although not sexually attractive to her, is polite, caring, articulate, well-read, non-aggressive with women, and loyal. In short, Allan is safe. Ruth promises to marry him when she returns from an international tour promoting her newest book.

Before Ruth leaves, however, she finally beats her father at the game he taught her, squash, and tells him about being raped. She also tells him that, as a child, she found pornographic Polaroids in his work-table drawer, as well as condoms and lubricating jelly in his nightstand. She tells him she knows that he had planned for Marion and Eddie's affair and that he had a one-night stand with her best friend, Hannah. Ruth, in fact, not only beats Ted on the squash court, she beats him at life. Ruth's bitter triumph over her father does not assuage her own pain and loneliness, but she does break Ted's heart and may be partly to blame for his suicide.

Ruth's book tour in Amsterdam leads to an idea for her next novel, a book about a writer who chooses bad boyfriends. She decides to call the novel *My Last Bad Boyfriend*. One of these boyfriends, who is much younger than the writer, persuades the novelist to watch a prostitute having sex with a customer. Something happens during the act that so degrades the writer she decides to change her life. It is not coincidental that Ruth decides for the first time in her career to write this novel with a first-person narrator. Irving creates all of this with the deftness of a magician, as he blurs the distinctions between writer and character, writing and living, art and reality.

The plot that unfolds takes us into the world of prostitution in Amsterdam, where women advertise themselves in shop windows as men go shopping for sex. Ruth becomes a character in her own novel, but as a character she is no longer writing. Thus she merges with us, the readers; she too wants to know what will happen next. When Ruth pays a prostitute, Red Dolores (better known as Rooie), so that she can watch her with a customer, Ruth, like the customer, makes use of Rooie. We join Ruth as she hides behind the curtain in Rooie's room as witness to the evil "moleman," who "takes" Rooie by snapping her neck. He then photographs the dead woman to keep her underground forever. Ruth, not unlike some readers, holds her breath, not daring to breathe, "making a sound of not making a sound."

After Ruth witnesses the murder, she feels her own complicit guilt; she has done nothing, made no outcry, has not tried to save Rooie. Out of her guilt, Ruth cons her young would-be lover (Wim Jongbloed) to write, in Dutch, a description of the events she saw and mails the statement to Detective Sergeant Harry Hoekstra. Even after the murderer is discovered and the mysterious, missing witness is no longer needed by the police, Harry Hoekstra wants to find her. And he finally does, several years later, for he is much more than a consummate detective: he is an "old-fashioned reader." He knows how to read clues and gather meanings, how to understand plots and characters.

Witnessing Rooie's murder changes Ruth's life. She hurries home to Allan Albright and marries him. Although she may not feel great passion for Allan, she nonetheless loves the safe life he gives her. She also loves, intensely, the son she has with Allan, a son she names Graham, after Graham Greene. The marriage is shortlived; Allan dies of a heart attack when Graham is three and Ruth just forty.

When Ruth publishes *My Last Bad Boyfriend*, Harry purchases it and immediately recognizes that the novel recounts, among other things, the murder of Rooie. Harry realizes he has found his witness at last. When Ruth returns to Amsterdam to give a reading of the book and meets Harry, the mystery of the missing witness is over. The ending of the mystery for Harry is the beginning of Harry and Ruth's love and marriage.

But Harry and Ruth's marriage is not the end of Irving's novel. As soon as Ruth puts the Cole house in the Hamptons up for sale, Marion returns, not because of Ruth's marriage, but because she would like to buy the house. Although Eddie and Marion seem to meet by chance after she returns, it is reasonably clear that Marion intended to return to him. As Marion tells Eddie, she never left him or the house. She left because she knew her grief over her lost sons was contagious, and she did not want Ruth or Eddie to catch it. What Marion and Eddie caught was love; for them it lasts forever.

It is significant that Irving ends his novel on Thanksgiving weekend, just as he ended *The Water-Method Man* on Throgshafen, the old Norse equivalent to the American holiday. Thanksgiving is truly a holiday for families, and thus it is especially poignant that Marion and Eddie, Ruth and Graham, all come together during this time. Ruth, who hardly ever cries, does so when she is reunited with her mother. As Eddie and Marion are reunited in love, so too are mother and daughter. Past, present, and future collapse, as Eddie, perhaps more than anyone else present, recognizes that the significant moments of life are those in which, for an instant, time stops.

SETTING

There are two major settings in *A Widow*: the Hamptons, Long Island, in particular the Cole house, and Amsterdam, especially de Wallen, the area of prostitution. To be sure, other settings come into play: Toronto, to which Marion retreats; New York City; Paris, Berlin, and other European cities, where Ruth gives readings; Vermont, where Ruth has a house in the country; and Exeter Academy, the *alma mater* of Ted Cole, Eddie O'Hare, Ruth Cole, and her friend Hannah Grant. But these places are way-stations before the characters return to Long Island or set out for Amsterdam. The novel opens at the Cole house in the Hamptons in the summer of 1958 and closes there in the fall of 1995.

The Cole family house is full of secrets and anguish, of desires, hatreds, and violence. When the novel opens, the house has been turned into a memorial to the sons, Thomas and Timothy, who were killed in an auto accident. All available wall space is covered with their photos at various stages of their brief lives, and each photo tells a story of the brothers. Ruth, conceived to replace the boys, can recite by memory these stories by the time she is four. After her mother, Marion, takes the photos off the wall, leaving only the picture hooks behind, Ruth can still re-tell the stories. When memories of the photos fade, the sight of the hooks stimulates Ruth's imagination to make up stories about her dead brothers.

The image of the dead boys in the photos reminds us of the vulnerability of youth and the randomness of death, but the image of the empty hooks is even more powerful. The hooks arouse our deepest feelings of forlornness, of the kind of loss that seems to go on forever. The presence of the hooks creates a not-quite empty wallspace that seems much worse than clean, bare space. Therefore, Ruth's father begins to use the hooks and covers the spaces with photographs of Ruth as she grows up. Whatever else the photos and hooks do, they impress upon us the passage of time.

The Cole house, like most of our own houses, contains secrets and imaginary—or not so imaginary—monsters and monstrousness. The house contains numerous doors; on the other side of the doors is the frightening unknown. As a child growing up in the Long Island house, Ruth finds the truth of Ted Cole's children's books all too apparent. There is *The Mouse Crawling Between the Walls*, which Ruth thinks she hears. The monster in the walls is furry, with no arms or legs—almost, but not quite, scarier than the dress in Mommy's closet, the dress that comes alive, trying to get off the hanger, forming a woman *inside* itself. No wonder Ruth grows up hating to wear dresses.

The Long Island house is in many ways closely linked with the maternal, with Marion Cole, even though Ted owns it and keeps it after Marion leaves. For Ruth, the space of the house is identified with her mother; it is the womb where Ruth's life begins. The house envelops her and is the threshold of her life into a larger world.

Ted's first book, *The Door in the Floor*, published after his sons' deaths, suggests his attempt to wrest control of the house from the maternal. The door itself, of course, is in the wrong place; it is never called a trap door, yet it surely is one, ready to spring open. The story is about a baby boy, in his mother's womb, who does not know if he wants to be born. His mother is also not sure if she wants him to be born. The isolation of mother and child, who have only each other (they live in a cabin in the woods, on an island, with no one around) is in itself both reassuring and frightening. Once there were other children, but they opened the door in the floor and disappeared forever into a dark hole. Beneath the door, horrifying things exist, enough to turn the mother's hair white in an instant. The child in Marion's womb, the one she is not sure she wants to give birth to, is Ruth, and under the floor of Marion's house are the dangerous and awful secrets waiting to swallow her and her child.

One of the most powerful and awful secrets of the novel has to do with male lust (a recurring theme of Irving's). Ted's story of the moleman coming up the stairs after Ruth depicts a frightening image of such lust. Ruth discovers Ted's own moleman activities when she opens the drawer in his nightstand and finds condoms. In his workroom studio in the house, she finds pornographic photos and drawings of the young mothers he used for purposes other than illustrating his children's stories. Later, Ruth herself is attacked in the Cole house by Scott Saunders, the moleman-date she brings home who viciously rapes and beats her and in turn is beaten by her.

The Cole house is also the place where Ted teaches Ruth to play squash. Ruth's ability with a squash racket enables her to take revenge on Saunders. Ruth also beats her father on the squash court and cries because she knows that she both loves and hates him and that he loves her more than anyone else. Squash, like life, has its "dead spot"; her father hits that dead spot over and over in their final game. The sound the ball makes as it hits the dead spot remains in Ruth's memory a long time after the game is over.

It is also at the Cole house that Ruth learns to drive. Her driving lesson is, like many other events in her family, connected to a story, the story of her brothers' deaths and the culpability of her parents. As Ruth is taught by her father never to take her eyes off the road when driving, Ted tells the horrific story of the deadly accident that took the lives of Thomas and Timothy. So, too, when Ruth has her father drive her to the airport, she reminds him of his own driving lesson—never take your eyes off the road—because she knows that if Ted is driving, she can say *anything* to him and he cannot look at her. She tells him she knows all about the plot he set up concerning Eddie O'Hare and Marion, that when she was ten she discovered the condoms and lubricating jelly in his bedroom and the pornographic photographs in his workroom, that Scott Saunders raped her, and that she retaliated by beating him with a squash racket. Her father is reduced to tears just as Ruth was reduced to tears by his story about her brothers. Family houses and privileged settings, even in the Hamptons, are not safe havens for children or parents, we learn.

The other major setting in *A Widow* is Amsterdam, and it too is no safe haven. Ruth's third visit to Amsterdam is to help promote the Dutch translation of her novel, ironically titled *Not for Children*. Her real excitement in this city, however, is to research her next novel, *My Last Bad Boyfriend*. In Amsterdam, Ruth enters not only de Wallen—the world of the prostitute, with its S&M sex shops, its blatant, midday advertisement, of women for sale in the windows and doorways—but also the very room of one of the prostitutes, Dolores Ruiter, known as Red Dolores or Rooie. Rooie wears red as her signature; her hair, too, is red, just as her room is red, with maroon curtains, a blood-red carpet, and varying shades of red-pink in the bedspread and towels. The small room is filled with mirrors at various angles so that someone entering it sees not just one Rooie but many.

Ruth pays Rooie to talk with her about sex. Thus, in this mirrored red room, Ruth participates, no matter how vicariously, in the world of prostitution. The writer stations herself complicitly as a voyeur, a spy in the house of sex. This room, however, turns out to be literally more murderous than the bedrooms in the Long Island Cole house. If Ruth believed that Ted Cole and Scott Saunders, seeing themselves as lady/women killers, were users of women, in Amsterdam she witnesses a "real" woman killer, a man she identifies as the moleman, a man whose squinty eyes make him look as blind as a mole. Irving makes sure that we, as readers, do not miss the linkages among Rooie, Ruth, and Marion; all three women assume the exact same sexual position in less than ideal situations.

From a hiding place in the wardrobe in Rooie's room, Ruth watches Rooie's customer/killer crush her throat. At this moment, Ruth becomes the child in the illustration of Ted's story, *A Sound Like Someone Trying Not to Make a Sound*; her silence is the only sound in the room, and although it works to save Ruth's life, it does not save Rooie. The wardrobe contains not just Rooie's clothes, but her life. As Ruth hides in this intimate atmosphere, she becomes linked to the prostitute. Only in the wardrobe is there any order: the shoes are lined up neatly, Ruth's among them, with her feet planted firmly in them. As we watch with Ruth, we too share in the intimacy of Rooie and her wardrobe.

In all of Irving's novels, he has been able to use space and its objects with precision, imagination, and great psychological perception. In *A Widow for One Year*, he reveals the brilliance of his writing skill as he opens the houses, not only of his characters, but of our lives, forcing us to examine our own fantasies, our secret drawers, and our most intimate wardrobes.

CHARACTER DEVELOPMENT

Irving's novels feature characters who are strange to the point of weirdness, characters who are frightening or at least unpleasant, and characters who are sympathetic, all of whom we recognize in one way or another. There are four major characters in *A Widow*: Ted and Marion Cole, their daughter Ruth, and Eddie O'Hare. Although Ruth is the novel's protagonist, Ted, Marion, and Eddie are of nearly equal importance. It would also be a mistake to omit or minimize Ruth's brothers, Thomas and Timothy; their deaths, and thus their physical absence from the novel, remain a presence to be reckoned with.

Ted Cole, writer and illustrator of children's novels, is a perpetual philanderer, obsessed with the young mothers he uses as models for his books. When Ted begins work on his book illustrations, he photographs, very legitimately, mothers with their children, usually their little boys. Soon he switches to photographing the mothers alone. These mothers then become more than models for Ted's books; they become objects of seduction and he photographs these women in pornographic poses. These photos always turn out to be sad; the women look ashamed. It is impossible to mistake the Oedipal triangle here, with the father figure asserting his control over the mother, capturing her attention from her child.

Although an alcoholic, as well as seducer and pornographic photographer in his off hours from working on children's books, Ted is, ironically, a "good" father to Ruth. Like many fathers in Irving's novels, however—for example, Severin Winter and the unnamed father-narrator in *The 158-Pound Marriage* or even Garp in *The World According to Garp*—Ted Cole is, to put it mildly, often irresponsible. At times, this irresponsibility leads to disaster, as in the case of his own sons. Ted is drunk, so he cannot drive in a snowstorm. Because Marion, who would usually drive in this kind of situation, also has been drinking (something she rarely does), Thomas ends up driving, with his brother, Timothy, in the front seat, their parents in the rear of the car. A head-on collision with a snowplow kills both boys instantly. In Ted's own family, he manages (however inadvertently) to remove his sons from the picture.

Even had his sons lived, Ted would have continued to substitute younger women for Marion, women who would give Ted their undivided attention, if only for a short time. Ted's preoccupation with younger women became apparent shortly after he married Marion, and he never changes. He even seduces Hannah Grant, who is young enough to be his daughter and who is in fact, his daughter's best friend.

Whatever Ted's charm may be for other women, he is despicable toward Marion. Setting up Marion's romance with Eddie O'Hare to create grounds for divorce seems laughable given Ted's own track record of illicit affairs. But an affair with Eddie, who is only sixteen at the time, might be tougher for Marion to excuse than the young (but older than sixteen) mothers Ted cavorts with. His motivation, Ted claims, is to save Ruth from "catching" her mother's despair over the deaths of her sons. If Ted is charming and seductive to most women, he is equally so to his daughter Ruth. Ted's plan to drive Marion away may be in part a desire to protect and nurture Ruth, but it is also a desire to keep Ruth for himself.

One might call Ted a great gamesman, with good strategy and timing—until he gets older and becomes a bit "off his game." In fact, Ted pushes his sexual scoring too far when he sleeps with Hannah Grant. Hannah, Ruth's alter ego in a number of ways, is perhaps too close to Ted's own daughter for comfort; the flirtation with incest in the novel is barely papered over in the Ted-Ruth-Hannah triangle. In fact, Ted's tryst with Hannah damages Ruth's friendship with her and drives Ruth to leave her father nearly broken-hearted (it seems to be the *only* affair over which he suffers), and he never recovers.

The greatest gift Ted (and, inadvertently, Marion) gives his daughter is in the realm of imagination. Each picture of Ruth's dead brothers has a story and in turn stimulates the creation of other stories. When Marion removes the pictures, leaving only the hooks in the wall, the blank spaces where the photos had been encourage Ruth's imagination even further. Ted's illustrated children's books also encourage Ruth to imagine worlds other than her own, no matter how violent and nightmarish. Indeed, the children's books, like fairytales, ironically turn out to be all too similar depictions of Ruth's world. Yet, also like fairytales, they prepare her to live in her own world. They save her life.

Ted's wife, Marion, is one of Irving's more mysterious and enigmatic characters. She disappears rather early in the novel, when she leaves for Canada and becomes a writer herself. Once she is out of the picture, so to speak, Irving portrays Marion largely through her mystery novels, which center around a woman detective.

Marion is tall, willowy, beautiful, and sophisticated; she is, in fact, a vision, a dream woman, the wonderful lost mother of fairytales. Whatever her existence before her sons' deaths, after the deadly accident, for which she feels terribly responsible, Marion is lethargic and zombie-like. In her sorrow, she did not want another child. Although she loves her daughter, Marion's grief so overwhelms her that she has too few emotional resources to nurture Ruth.

When Eddie O'Hare arrives at the Cole house, he represents not so much Marion's sons (though he resembles Thomas) as he does the *life* they will never enjoy. It is too easy to look at Marion's relationship with Eddie only from an Oedipal point of view, although Irving wants us to recognize the Freudian implications. In Marion's sexual encounter with Eddie, however, she sets clear emotional boundaries. She does not hide the fact that she sees him as an anodyne to her great sense of loss—and as revenge against Ted. Nor does she neglect to tell Eddie that the affair will end and that she intends to leave. Indeed, she enlists Eddie's help on the day that she leaves.

Among Marion's admirable traits are her tender displays of feeling with both Eddie and Ruth and her absolute honesty with herself. Marion is aware that she must leave in order to save Ruth. Thus, Marion is in direct contrast to Ted, who brings up his daughter with love but also with duplicity.

Like her sons, Marion becomes more interesting in her absence. The mystery novels she writes have a woman hero (as does *A Widow for One Year*), Margaret McDermid. Like Marion, Margaret is not so interested in finding murderers as in seeking out and understanding victims. In fact, Margaret would rather work in Missing Persons than Homicide; then she might find the persons before they became victims. In Missing Persons her work involves studying photographs of missing children, photographs that haunt her. Most of all, the images of two boys, Americans who disappeared during the Vietnam War, haunt her. Obviously Marion's mystery novels are cognates for her own life. Margaret's obsessions are Marion's: the photos of Margaret's lost children and of children who are victimized represent Marion's own lost children.

Marion makes no attempt to contact her daughter or Eddie O'Hare. Even at the end of the novel, Marion returns to buy the Cole house because she hears that it is on the market; she does not expect to find Ruth there. Nevertheless, throughout the novel, Marion's desire to protect Ruth is evident, if only in Marion's command to Ted never to drive when drunk. If he does so, Marion will see to it that he loses Ruth. In giving up Ruth, Marion demonstrates the depth of her feelings for her daughter as well as her indomitable strength.

Of equal if not greater interest than Marion is Eddie O'Hare. Eddie, only sixteen when he meets and has an affair of the heart with Marion, never gets over his love for her. Although his passion for Marion seems excessive and obsessive—he keeps bits of her clothing after she leaves—Eddie's romance is central to the novel. His love and loyalty for Marion never waver through time.

Like nearly everyone else in this novel, Eddie too is a writer. Not surprisingly, Eddie writes romances, thinly disguised novels of his own life and love for Marion. Although it is easy to criticize the romance of these two characters—a boy being initiated sexually by an older, experienced woman—it is not so easy to dismiss the love the two feel for each other. Irving wisely has the narrator raise any Freudian or psychological issues, saving the reader the bother. In addition, Irving also defuses any snide laughter about such a relationship by having the narrator aware of the potential for jokes. Irving reinforces this relationship with references to popular culture, especially to films: such as *The Summer of '42*, which relates a similar story, except that the young woman's husband has been killed in the war; and *Tea and Sympathy*, a play by Robert Anderson about an older woman and a schoolboy, which was later made into a movie. Eddie's first novel is called *Summer Job*; his second, *Coffee and Doughnuts*. Irving's own playfulness is evident here, as the narrator notes that Robert Anderson (like Eddie O'Hare, and Irving) was a graduate of Exeter Academy.

Offsetting the humor, Irving invests Marion and Eddie's relationship with an intensity that forces the reader to pay attention to it. Moreover, their relationship stands in contrast to the sordid affairs of Ted Cole. Hannah Grant's numerous affairs are less than attractive, as well, and even Ruth's relationships with men before she marries Allan Albright come off as tawdry, violent, or manipulative. In short, through the narrator's voice and through other characters in the novel, Irving is able to erase, or at least dissipate, any of the stigma that may fall on Marion and Eddie's love for each other.

Marion and Eddie's love remains a mystery. There is no unravelling it to reveal some rational and simple explanation. Eddie remains true to his love for Marion over a period of thirty-seven years. As he says at one point, he loves the "whole" woman. Like Shakespeare, Irving knows that the real interest in a story is in the psychology of characters, but, like Shakespeare, he also recognizes that the heart's mystery, finally, cannot be "plumbed."

Although the triangular relationship of Ted, Marion, and Eddie offers fascinating character studies, Ruth Cole is the focus of the novel. She is Irving's first female protagonist, although arguably not his first female hero (for example, there is Franny in *The Hotel New Hampshire*). Like all of Irving's protagonists, Ruth grows up over the course of this coming-of-age novel. She is aware that she was conceived as a replacement for her dead brothers, Thomas and Timothy. She knows her parents wanted her to be a boy, and as a child, she strives mightily to dress and behave like one. She hates dresses, believing that they mold and shape one to be a girl/woman. Ruth is adept at sports, especially squash, her father's own game, and eventually she beats him at it.

Ruth's dead brothers provide the impetus for Ruth's imaginative recreation of them in stories. Although photos of her eventually fill the spaces left by the removal of the boys' pictures, it is they who live on in her writing. Ruth longs for her mother while growing up, wishing she could talk with Marion about her fears and her dreams. The only time Ruth feels unafraid is when she is writing; indeed, she writes to work out her life, to make sense of it.

Although Ruth can create order in her writing, she seems incapable of doing so in her life. She has a knack for choosing "bad" boyfriends and moves from one short-lived, sour affair to another. Yet, for all of Ruth's bad choices in men, she remains hopeful that one day she will find someone worthy of her love.

Having lost her mother, Ruth also fears losing her father. When so many other women, with a mere blink of the eye or a flattering gesture, appear to command Ted Cole's undivided attention (if not forever, at least for a night), Ruth feels overlooked. She desperately tries to claim her father's attention. Scott Saunders, a charming, good-looking, lawyer who plays squash with Ted on occasion, is one way to get her father to look at her, Ruth thinks, especially after she has caught Ted in bed with her friend Hannah Grant.

Ruth is both angry and vulnerable as she takes Saunders on a little tour through the Cole house, into her father's workshop and then his bedroom, all the while matter-of-factly recounting her childhood traumas. First she tells Saunders that she had discovered Ted's black and white pornographic polaroids of models in his workshop and that, shortly after, she discovered the condoms and lubricating jelly in the nightstand near his bed. She asks Saunders if this *"boy's stuff"* turns him on, goading him to respond (although he is too dense to understand), and she reminds him again that this is all boy's stuff.

Ruth's walk through the family artifacts—if one may call them that— results in sex with Saunders, during which Ruth wishes her father would come home and see his daughter "now." If he did, Ruth would have the perfect revenge, she thinks, for all of the women, and especially Hannah, whom he brought home. But Ted does not arrive home in time to see his daughter, and sex with Saunders ends with his raping and beating Ruth. This scene is not followed by a drama with a pretend-bear, as in *The Hotel New Hampshire*; instead Ruth beats Saunders unmercifully with a squash racket, using every swing she learned from Ted on the squash court.

Although Ruth's anger at her father may be what causes her to choose such "bad" boyfriends, as she calls them, at the same time there is no doubt that she loves her father dearly. Moreover, it is precisely this love that leaves her open to the possibility of love with a "good" man. In addition, Ruth would like a child. Witnessing Rooie's murder in Amsterdam sends Ruth nearly running into the arms of Allan Albright, her editor, who offers her his love—and safety—if not sexual passion.

Irving is not especially interested in the character of Allan. As a "nice guy," there is little more that can be said about him. Allan gives Ruth the child she desires, and then after three years of marriage, he conveniently dies.

Irving is, however, interested in Ruth's second husband, Detective Sergeant Harry Hoekstra, who is much more than a Dutch policeman, more than any mere man, perhaps: he is a *reader*. Physically, he is more attractive than Allan, and Harry and Ruth fall quickly and passionately in love. After being a widow for one year (following the opening line from one of her own novels), Ruth marries Detective Hoekstra. Harry and Ruth make love during the day and read to each other at night; both activities express their passion for each other. Hannah, anti-intellectual journalist that she is, finds both activities baffling and perverse.

Harry's remarkable and intelligent perception moves him to stay out of the way at the reunion of Ruth and Marion at the end of the novel. These two women over the great distance of thirty-seven years reflect the strong bond between mother and daughter. Both mother and daughter have matching flaws in their eyes which can suddenly change their eye color. These flaws in the eye/I of each also reflect the transforming power of love each feels for the other. As Eddie and Marion are reunited in love, so too are mother and daughter. The novel comes full circle.

THEMATIC ISSUES

The themes in *A Widow for One Year* are similar to those in all of John Irving's novels: the family, with special attention to children; issues of gender; sexual cruelty, including rape; random violence and death; pornography; and, of course, love. All of these have been discussed above. The novel is also concerned with the telling, writing, and reading of stories. *A Widow* is perhaps Irving's most literary novel, though that is a tough claim to make, since all of his novels work off of and allude to many other literary works.

As in *A Son of the Circus*, homage is paid to Graham Greene, although perhaps not in so direct a fashion; in *A Widow*, more attention is paid to Norman Sherry's biography of Greene and to Greene's autobiography, *A Sort of Life*, than to Greene's fiction (to be sure, *The Ministry of Fear* and *The Power and the Glory* are mentioned). George Eliot's *Adam Bede* (a novel about love and marriage, among other things) is quoted. So are two of Yeats' poems; one is read at Allan Albright's funeral, another at Ruth's wedding to Harry Hoekstra. The first poem, "When You are Old," appropriately has to do with loss, and the second, "He Wishes for the Cloths of Heaven," has to do with the hope and promise of love. These two poems, along with Eliot's great commentary on marriage— "to be one with each other in silent unspeakable memories at the moment of the last parting"—provide perhaps a wonderful summation of Irving's thoughts on *eros* and *thanatos*, love and death—and love beyond death.

In addition to the major themes of love and marriage, *A Widow* is a novel about storytellers, storytelling, and told stories. It is also a novel about the very public business of publishing, not only about the private life of the writer. And it is a novel about readers.

It is not new for Irving to people his novel with writers: he does this from his earlier novels to his latest, but most notably in *The World According to Garp*, *The Hotel New Hampshire*, and *A Son of the Circus*. In *A Widow*, nearly everyone writes something: Ted and Marion Cole, Eddie O'Hare, Ruth, even Hannah Grant. Ruth first learns about listening to and telling stories from her father and mother. The very "sound" of storytelling is comforting to Ruth, as her parents tell her stories about her dead brothers.

Much of *A Widow* deals with finding one's voice, not only for the oral tale but for writing. Eddie finds his voice in the summer of 1958 after falling in love with Marion Cole. Yet Eddie's voice is limited to the autobiographical, which he writes with a certain power and simplicity. He cannot *imagine* or create. Marion Cole, like Eddie, relies on memory in her writing; her detective, Margaret McDirmid, is a thinly disguised Marion, forever seeking the lost children. In fact, when Marion writes her last novel concerning the retirement of her detective, we know that Marion has come to terms with the deaths of her sons. Ted Cole's voice is limited to children's stories because he himself remains a boy, concerned only with "boy's stuff." Hannah's writing appears not worth discussing, as there is little said about it in *A Widow*.

Ruth, in comparison to these writers, commands it all: language, complex plots and characters, and narrative energy. She is truly a *writer*, and, as she puts it, a writer "first," before a woman. She towers above the other writers in her family, as well as Eddie and Hannah. If her attributes as a writer seem very much like Irving's, they are. Irving has said that he always begins with characters and situations when he writes a novel, just as Ruth does. Both Irving and Ruth claim to be writers of comedy, and both claim not to be autobiographical in their work. One is reminded of Helen Holm telling readers to read the work, not the man, in *The World According to Garp*.

Ruth is unafraid of life only when she writes. We recall that she marries Allan Albright because she needs someone to edit her life, not her novels. She comes to love Allan only after they are married for the comforting life he gives her. Ruth's diary, counterpointed by her postcards to Allan, emphasizes the conflict she feels between her life and her work as a writer. She fears most of all that marriage will be the death of her freedom to observe the world. The interlacing of postcards, diary, and the "lived" part of Ruth's life gives Irving an opportunity to move between omniscient and first-person narrator and to do so in an effortless and fluid fashion.

To a large extent, Ruth's life *is* her writing. Even at promotional readings, Ruth would rather talk about writing, not read from her novels. Nevertheless, at a reading in Germany, she refrains from telling the audience that she plans to write a novel about a writer; as she knows, nothing would bore her audience more quickly. One recognizes an edginess Irving himself may feel here; that is, he understands that as a writer he too is taking a risk with his own novel.

All of the things that Irving cares deeply and seriously about as a writer are interwoven in this novel of romance. Not least of his concerns is the reader, a concern Irving grappled with earlier in *The World According to Garp*. There Jillsey Sloper, a cleaning lady, turns out to be the model reader. In *A Widow for One Year*, the model reader, Harry Hoekstra, is a detective. Who better to be interested in stories and their complexities? Just as Harry knows that there are no simple solutions to violence in the world, he also knows that "plot summaries" are gross distortions of novels. Indeed Harry would warn the scholarly critic to beware of attempting to summarize Irving's plots any more than, say, Shakespeare's or Dickens'. All three writers provide us with a narrative too rich for simple summary. No wonder Ruth falls passionately in love with Harry. He understands that he can never see the whole story—or even the only story—in her work or in her life. Nor can we in Irving's.

A NARRATOLOGICAL READING OF *A WIDOW FOR ONE YEAR*

Narratologists are critics who focus primarily on plot and story, on the temporal sequence of events, with an emphasis on causality and on character. An analysis of narrativity, the telling of stories, attempts to uncover various models of narrative formation. Peter Brooks puts it very well in his book, *Reading for Plot: Design and Intention in Narrative*: "Plot starts (or must give the illusion of starting) from the moment at which story, or 'life' is stimulated from quiescence into a state of narratability, into a tension, a kind of irritation, which demands narration [storytelling]" (103).

Storytelling, the very process of narration itself, drives *A Widow for One Year*. Nearly all of the characters, from Ruth Cole, her parents Ted and Marion, and Marion's lover Eddie O'Hare, to relatively minor characters like the prostitute Rooie, tell stories; indeed, they live their own narratives, in part, if not in whole. At first glance, *A Widow* seems to follow the narrative structure of other Irving novels: a coming-of-age story from childhood to maturity. As in *The Water-Method Man*, *The World According to Garp*, and *The Hotel New Hampshire*, the maturity of the protagonist leads to heterosexual love, marriage, and reproduction. In these earlier novels, lineal, generational, and paternal plots propel the narratives. What makes *A Widow* different is Irving's shift in focus to a female protagonist, a shift that should alert careful readers to the possibility of additional narrative changes.

A quick reading of *A Widow* seems merely to confirm that the novel follows the classic Freudian Oedipal narrative. Such a narrative, dominated by a paternal presence, contains a plot that pulls us in a linear direction. The repetition of chronology—the emphasis on the dates of events and the ages of characters—reinforces this linear pull. Initially, *A Widow* focuses on the triangular nuclear family with a continuous flow of events emanating from it in a straight line. The sons' deaths threaten to alter the linearity of the narrative as the Cole family is realigned to accommodate the loss of the boys. The narration early on is pushed by the boys' deaths into a skewed family plot.

After the death of his sons, Ted calculatingly sets about to rearrange his family according to his desires. He pushes Marion to have another child—Ruth. He drives a wedge between mother and daughter and brings Ruth up as he sees fit, even though this leads ultimately to his losing her. The shift from nuclear family—mother, father, child—to Daddy and his daughter is not a happy one. In his work as a writer, Ted is also a powerful paternal presence. He separates the young mothers and sons he uses as models for his book illustrations; it takes little time for him to be rid of the little boys and to begin photographing (in pornographic poses) the seduced mothers. Ted's children's stories replicate the plots of his life: monsters lurk in the walls of houses, under trapdoors, and underground, waiting to steal children from their mothers. The reshaping of family, whether in Ted's life or his books, remains under the father/husband/lover's control.

The tripartite divisions of *A Widow* seem to present an orderly progression: "Summer of 1958"; "Fall of 1990"; "Fall of 1996." Yet within these divisions, order is disrupted and discontinuous. The divisions themselves are strangely off-center and suggest Irving's subversion of his own paternal plot structure. As readers, we begin to notice that divisions of time and lineal sequencing of events are not nearly so important as moments of disruption and neglected, overlooked gaps in time.

In Irving's dedication of *A Widow* to his wife, he calls his novel "a love story." Love stories, by definition, draw attention to the centrality of disruption and to the possibility of more complex narrative structures than linearity. The heart of *A Widow* is love: the love of Marion Cole and Eddie O'Hare, as well as the love of Ruth Cole and Harry Hoekstra; the love of Marion for her lost sons, as well as the love of Ted Cole for his daughter; the love/hate of Ruth for her father and Ruth's overwhelming love for her son Graham. Nevertheless, the central love story in this novel concerns the intense bonding between Marion and her daughter Ruth despite abandonment, grief, and suffering over thirty-seven years. The narrative of Marion and Ruth revises the partrilineal plot, which ends in a marriage guaranteed to repeat the older generation's familial structure, and provides us with a radically feminist narrative.

Embedded in Marion and Ruth's narrative are older, similar stories: the Biblical story of Naomi and Ruth and the Homeric story of Demeter and Persephone. In the Biblical tale, mother and daughter-in-law are widows, and although Naomi tells Ruth to leave and return to her home-land to remarry, Ruth refuses. Instead, the two women journey to Beth-lehem, Naomi's birth land, where they live together until Ruth eventually marries Boaz, a kinsman of Naomi. The Biblical story takes place in a male-dominated society that deals heavily with women (es-pecially single older women), a fact underscored by Naomi's insistence that her people call her Mara, a name that means bitterness, for God the Father has dealt "bitterly" with her.

It is hardly a coincidence that Irving names his characters Marion (cf. Mara) and Ruth. After all, Irving has refashioned Biblical stories before, as in *Owen Meany*. Both *A Widow for One Year* and *The Book of Ruth* contain marriage plots that on the surface are lineal and genealogical, but the alliances that matter in *The Book of Ruth* (as in *A Widow*) are matrilineal, not patrilineal. The marriage plot in *The Book of Ruth* is straightforward and uninteresting. What gives the narrative life is the story of the two women. The memorable lines have nothing to do with Boaz, the husband-to-be—the marriage is merely contractual—but everything to do with Ruth and Naomi. Ruth says to her mother-in-law, "for whither thou goest, I will go; and where thou lodgest, I will lodge; thy people *shall be* my people, thy God my God" (I: 16). Although Ruth's words to Naomi are, ironically, used today at weddings—occasions that separate mothers and daughters—no more powerful words have been written of love and devotion between women.

The deaths of Naomi's husband and sons throw Naomi and Ruth into their narrative. Without these deaths, there would be no *Book of Ruth*. The deaths, in fact, allow for the subjectivity of Naomi and Ruth to take place; they find their voices. Similarly, the deaths of Marion's sons and Ruth's brothers throw them into their narratives as well: Each woman becomes a subject; each finds her "voice" for her own narrative that, at the same time, remains suffused with longing for the other. *The Book of Ruth* ends with Ruth's marriage to Boaz, who buys her and her inheritance. Naomi and Ruth's narratives become absorbed, literally, into the patrilineal plot of Boaz's descendants.

If death causes the disruption that begins the mother/daughter narrative in *The Book of Ruth*, rape and abduction provide the impetus for the narrative of Demeter and her daughter Persephone. This story of intense mother/daughter attachment and separation revolves around the abduction of Persephone by Hades, the father/husband figure, who takes her into the underworld for half the year. In this story, marriage and death seem to be the same thing.

The Demeter/Persephone narrative begins only through male intrusion, that of violent abduction and rape. Hades, the father/husband, not only forces the mother/daughter separation but also enforces the narrative. The classic story plays itself out over and over each year. As Demeter mourns her daughter's loss, she denies fruition in nature, causing destruction and grief. Thus this abduction has broad social consequences affecting the total community. The abduction of Persephone is not the whole story, however, since Persephone returns to her mother for one half of the year, for spring and summer, before returning to Hades for the remainder of the year. Unlike the Naomi/Ruth narrative, with its decidedly lineal ending, Demeter/Persephone's resolution is cyclical. Moreover, the daughter has a dual subject position: she is both a daughter, loving her mother, and a wife, loving (or at least loyal to) her husband.

Irving uses portions of these mother/daughter narratives, manipulating and transforming them, in opposition to the paternal—and Oedipal—plot in *A Widow for One Year*. Ted Cole's attempt to dominate the story is evident from the start. His irresponsibility places his sons in harm's way and causes their deaths. It is Ted's idea to have a replacement child, Ruth. Ted maneuvers sixteen-year-old Eddie O'Hare into the Cole household, setting up the situation that causes Marion to leave. Thus, Ted forces the separation of Marion and Ruth, which results in their subsequent narratives. Even though Ted takes over bringing up Ruth, she eventually beats him at his own game. Her victory over her father leads to their separation and his death but not the end of Ruth's story.

Ted replicates the narrative of his own life by the use of patrilineal plots in all of his children's stories, most significantly in the narrative of the moleman in *A Sound Like Someone Trying Not to Make a Sound*. In this tale, a revision of the Demeter/Persephone story, the moleman hunts little girls, abducts them, and takes them underground for several weeks. Ted writes and rewrites this story over the summer of 1958, when Eddie and Marion have their affair, shortly before Marion leaves the Cole home for Toronto. Irving makes clear the ambivalent connections between "Daddy" and the moleman. The little girl, left alone by her father who has gone for ice cream, puts Daddy's shaving cream on her face to save herself from abduction by the moleman who enters her house. But she also has dirt on her, making her both attractive and repellent to the moleman intruder. Daddy arrives home just in time to "save" his little girl—for himself—while the moleman remains curled up on the ledge of her window, just outside her bedroom.

This Freudian narrative, which Ruth accepts as "her" story, is repeated in the Scott Saunders rape narrative and later in the narrative of the moleman's murder of the prostitute Rooie, a murder that Ruth, immobilized by fear, witnesses. In this murder narrative, the plot is fully linear (for Rooie, at any rate). The father figure, whose very blandness—he could be any man—makes him frightening, conducts an "abduction" that is fully permanent and nearly perfect in its paternal power (although he is eventually caught).

Arguably, Ted's story is more than a children's book or Ruth's story; it is a Daddy's book. (Ironically, in Rooie's room at the time of her murder is a copy of Ruth's novel, *Not for Children*.) Daddy's book "saves" his daughter, through her silence, from being the moleman's victim. Thus, it seems Ruth can only be saved through her complicity with the father by not having a voice. The linkage between the murderous moleman and Ted is made strikingly clear in the Polaroid camera the killer uses; Ruth recognizes it as the same type camera her father used for taking pictures of his models.

Even though Ruth makes no sound in Rooie's room, her silence ends there. She writes down what she saw, has it translated into Dutch, and sends it to Detective Sergeant Harry Hoekstra. Ruth's decision to break her silence makes possible the capture of the moleman-killer. Ruth finds her voice.

Both the plot of Ruth's novel, *My Last Bad Boyfriend*, and all of Marion's Margaret McDirmid plots are narratives of abduction and violence committed by males. In these narratives the male presence is a horrific intrusion that, at the same time, acts as the force that sets the narratives in motion. No excuses or sympathy are wasted on the careless or intended murderousness of males, beginning with Ted, Scott Saunders, and the moleman. Not coincidentally, all of these men are themselves fathers. They comprise a not-so-pretty picture, a dark secret of the Oedipal family where the father exercises power by brute sexual force. In *A Widow*, the coercive paternal order of passing years—Father('s) Time—and the linearity of textual divisions nearly seduce us. We discover, if we are astute readers like Harry Hoekstra, that the so-called order is false, improbable, no matter how terrifying; in the end, only fragments of time, certain rich and revealing moments, are crucial.

The photos of Marion's dead sons represent such moments; they are images in crisis, relating to disaster, a catastrophe of one incredible instant when everything collapsed for Marion. Until she understands loss as not only an inevitable part of life, but also as only one segment of life's narrative—not the whole story—she cannot be a mother to her daughter. Similarly, Ruth must see the death of her first husband, Allan Albright, as only a part of her life story before she can risk loving, and thus possibly losing, Harry Hoekstra.

The ending of *A Widow for One Year* is nothing short of perfect in its completeness. The novel ends in the fall, around Thanksgiving, a holiday devoted to family. Indeed, Ruth and Harry marry on Thanksgiving morning. On the Sunday evening after Thanksgiving, Marion Cole, now seventy-six, returns to Eddie O'Hare, who is now fifty-three. Sometimes there is luck in life as well as loss. Marion's reunion with Ruth restores the bond between them. In the reconciliation scene, Ruth finds she cannot move, as she stands with her son, Graham, who is four, the exact age of Ruth when her mother left her. Harry Hoekstra and Eddie O'Hare, husband and lover, respectively, have the good sense to stand out of the way. At the instant of recognition between mother and daughter, time stops.

Eddie understands that these moments are the ones we "must be alert enough to notice" (537). The narrative of Demeter and Persephone has both a wonderful and strange never-ending end: Persephone continues to return to her mother, continues to leave her. She is both alive and not alive, both above and under ground. She is united with her mother, yet she is also united with her husband. So too it is in Irving's *A Widow for One Year*. The last line in the novel is given to Marion: " 'Don't cry, honey,' Marion told her only daughter. 'It's just Eddie and me' " (537), a line that echoes Marion's comment to Ruth when she was four and discovered Eddie in her mother's room.

Irving's novel, then, comes full circle, forcing us to rethink the impetus of narrative as well as its resolution. The powerful story of mother and daughter does not end in either separation or in reunion; the story is large enough to contain both. The ending of *A Widow for One Year* was always in the beginning; indeed, the ending itself *is* a beginning. In Irving's fictive world—as in life—there is always more to the narrative.

Bibliography

WORKS BY JOHN IRVING

Novels

Setting Free the Bears. New York: Random House, 1968.
The Water-Method Man. New York: Random House, 1972.
The 158-Pound Marriage. New York: Random House, 1973.
The World According to Garp. New York: E. P. Dutton, 1976.
Three by Irving. New York: Random House, 1980.
The Hotel New Hampshire. New York: E. P. Dutton, 1981.
The Cider House Rules. New York: William Morrow, 1985.
A Prayer for Owen Meany. New York: William Morrow, 1989.
A Son of the Circus. New York: Random House, 1994.
A Widow for One Year. New York: Random House, 1998.

Collection: Short Fiction and Memoir

Trying to Save Piggy Sneed. New York: Arcade, 1993.

Other Short Fiction

"A Winter Branch." *Redbook* Nov. 1965: 56–57, 143–146.
"Lost in New York." *Esquire* Mar. 1973: 116–117, 152.
"Students: These Are Your Teachers." *Esquire* Sept. 1975: 68, 156–159.

"Vigilance." *Ploughshares* 4 (1977): 103–114.
"Dog in the Alley, Child in the Sky." *Esquire* June 1977: 108–109, 158–162.
"A Bear Called State O'Maine." *Rolling Stone* 20 Aug. 1981: 22–27, 50–55.
"The Foul Ball." *New Yorker* 30 Jan. 1988: 28–56.
"The Courier." *New Yorker* 1 Aug. 1994: 60–69.

Selected Nonfiction

"Neglected Books of the Twentieth Century." *Antaeus* 27 (Autumn 1977): 131–
    132.
"Life After Graduation According to Garp." *Esquire* 27 Mar. 1979: 53.
"Works in Progress." *New York Times Book Review* 15 July 1979: 1, 14.
"Kurt Vonnegut and His Critics: The Aesthetics of Accessibility." *New Republic*
    22 Sept. 1979: 41–42.
"In Defense of Sentimentality." *New York Times Book Review* 25 Nov. 1979: 3, 96.
"The Narrative Voice." In *Voicelust: Eight Contemporary Fiction Writers on Style*,
    ed. Allen Wier and Don Hendrie, Jr. Lincoln: University of Nebraska
    Press, 1985, pp. 87–92.
"Getting Started: A Novelist Beginning a New Book Must Plan to Get the Reader
    Hooked—and Himself Involved." *Publishers Weekly* 24 Jan. 1991: 2.
"Pornography and the New Puritans." *New York Times Book Review* 29 Mar. 1992:
    1, 24–25, 27.
"Slipped Away." *New Yorker* 11 Dec. 1995: 70–76.

Reading/Q&A

Boston Center for Adult Education. Arlington Street Church, Boston. 18 Oct.
    1996.

WORKS ABOUT JOHN IRVING

Harter, Carol C., and James R. Thompson. *John Irving*. Boston: Twayne, 1986.
Miller, Gabriel. *John Irving*. New York: Frederick Ungar, 1982.
Reilly, Edward C. *Understanding John Irving*. Columbia: University of South Car-
    olina Press, 1991.

INTERVIEWS WITH JOHN IRVING

Anderson, Michael. "Casting Doubts on Atheism." *New York Times Book Review*
    12 Mar. 1989: 30.
Bernstein, Richard. "John Irving: 19th Century Novelist for These Times." *New
    York Times* 25 Apr. 1989: C13, C17.
De Coppet, Laura. "An Interview with John Irving." *Interview* 11 Oct. 1981: 42–
    44.

Feron, James. "All About Writing, According to Irving." *New York Times* 29 Nov.
    1981: Sec. 2: 4.
Hansen, Ron. "The Art of Fiction XCIII: John Irving." *Paris Review* 28 (1986): 74–
    103.
Herel, Suzanne. "John Irving." *Mother Jones* 1 May 1997: 64.
Kummer, Corby. "John Irving: Fascinated by Orphans." *Book-of-the-Month Club
    News* Summer 1985: 5.
McCaffery, Larry. "An Interview with John Irving." *Contemporary Literature* 23
    (Winter 1982): 1–18.
Neubauer, Alexander. "John Irving." In *Conversations on Writing Fiction: Inter-
    views with 13 Distinguished Teachers of Fiction Writing in America.* New York:
    HarperCollins, 1994, pp. 141–152.
Priestly, Michael. "An Interview with John Irving." *New England Review* (Summer
    1979): 489–504.
Renwick, Joyce. "John Irving: An Interview." *Fiction International* 14 (1982): 5–18.
Robinson, Phyllis. "A Talk with John Irving." *Book-of-the-Month Club News* Apr.
    1989: 3.
Sanoff, Alvin P. "A Conversation with John Irving: Humans Are a Violent Spe-
    cies—We Always Have Been." *U.S. News and World Report* 26 Oct. 1981:
    70–71.
West, Richard. "John Irving's World After Garp." *New York* 17 Aug. 1981: 29–
    32.
Williams, Thomas. "Talk with John Irving." *New York Times Book Review* 23 Apr.
    1978: 6.

REVIEWS AND CRITICISM

Setting Free the Bears

Levin, Martin. "Reader's Report." *New York Times Book Review* 9 Feb. 1969: 42.
Pfronger, Barbara. *"Setting Free the Bears." Library Journal* 1 Jan. 1969: 96–97.
Resnik, Henry S. "At Loose Ends in the Vienna Woods." *Saturday Review* 8 Feb.
    1969: 26.
Rubin, Stephen E. " 'Garp': Setting Free a Best Seller." *Chicago Tribune Book World*
    11 May 1980, Sec. 7: 2.
Ryan, Frank L. *"Setting Free the Bears." Best Sellers* 15 Apr. 1969: 27.
"Setting Free the Bears." Publishers Weekly 24 Nov. 1969: 43.
"Wednesday's Children." *Time* 14 Feb. 1969: 100.

The Water-Method Man

"Books Briefly Noted." *New Yorker* 22 July 1972: 78.
Carew, Jan. *"The Water-Method Man." New York Times Book Review* 10 Sept. 1972:
    46.

Dickerson, George. *"The Water-Method Man."* *Time* 24 July 1972: 82.
Majkut, Paul. *"The Water-Method Man."* *Best Sellers* 1 July 1972: 156–157.
Smally, Topsy. *"The Water-Method Man."* *Library Journal* 15 June 1972: 2200.

The 158-Pound Marriage

Felsenthal, C. J. *"The 158-Pound Marriage."* *Library Journal* 1 Sept. 1974: 2090.
Levin, Martin. "New and Novel." *New York Times Book Review* 3 Nov. 1974: 72.
Murray, J. J. *"The 158-Pound Marriage."* *Best Sellers* Dec. 15, 1974: 422.
Nicol, Charles. "Wrestling." *National Review* 24 Oct. 1975: 187–188.
Rocard, Marcienne. "Le Difficile Mariage de l'histoire et de la fiction dans *The 158-Pound Marriage* de John Irving." *Caliban* (Toulouse, France) 28 (1991): 49–59.

The World According to Garp

Bawer, Bruce. *"The World According to Garp*: Novel to Film." In *Take Two: Adapting the Contemporary American Novel to Film*, ed. Barbara Tepa Lepack. Bowling Green, OH: Bowling Green State University Popular Press, 1994, pp. 77–90.
Cosgrove, William. *"The World According to Garp* as Fabulation." *South Carolina Review* 19 (Spring 1987): 52–58.
Doane, Janice, and Devon Hodges. "Women and the World According to Garp." In *Nostalgia and Sexual Difference*. New York: Methuen, 1987, pp. 65–76.
Drabble, Margaret. "Musk, Memory, and Imagination." *Harper's* July 1978: 82–84.
French, Marilyn. "The *'Garp'* Phenomenon." *Ms* Sept. 1982: 14–16.
Lounsberry, Barbara. "The Terrible Under Toad: Violence as Excessive Imagination in *The World According to Garp.*" *Thalia* 5 (Fall–Winter 1982–1983): 30–35.
Marcus, Greil. "John Irving: The World of *The World According to Garp.*" *Rolling Stone* 13 Apr. 1979: 68–75.
Moynahan, Julian. "Truths by Exaggeration." *New York Times Book Review* 23 Apr. 1978: 1, 27–29.
Reilly, Edward C. "The *Anschluss* and the World According to Irving." *Research Studies* 51 (June 1983): 98–110.
Wilson, Raymond III. "The Postmodern Novel: The Example of John Irving's *The World According to Garp.*" *Critique* 34 (Fall 1992): 49–62.
Wood, Michael. "Nothing Sacred." *New York Review of Books* 20 Apr. 1978: 9–10.

The Hotel New Hampshire

Atlas, James. "John Irving's World." *New York Times Book Review* 13 Sept. 1981: 36.

Beatty, Jack. "A Family Fable." *New Republic* (Sept. 1981): 37–38.

DeMott, Benjamin. "Domesticated Madness." *Atlantic Monthly* (Oct. 1981): 101–106.

Jones, Edward T. "Checking into While Others Check out of Tony Richardson's *The Hotel New Hampshire.*" *Literary/Film Quarterly* 13.1 (1985): 66–69.

Kellerman, Steven G. "T. S. Garp Meets Franny and Zooey." *Commonweal* 6 Nov. 1981: 630–631.

Korn, Eric. "Trying to Grow the Freudian Way." *Times Literary Supplement* 6 Nov. 1981: 1302.

Nicol, Charles. "Happy Endings." *National Review* 23 Nov. 1981: 1428–1429.

Reilly, Edward C. "John Irving's *The Hotel New Hampshire* and the Allegory of Sorrow." *Publications of the Arkansas Philological Association* 6 (Spring 1983): 78–83.

Towers, Robert. "Reservations." *New York Review of Books*, 5 Nov. 1981: 13–15.

The Cider House Rules

Berson, Misha. "I Can't Believe We Staged the Whole Thing." *American Theatre* Mar. 1996: 2.

Blaustein, Arthur I. *"The Cider House Rules."* *Tikkun* 5 (Jan.–Feb. 1990): 67.

Burgess, Anthony. *"The Cider House Rules."* *Atlantic* July 1985: 98.

"The Cider House Rules." *New Yorker* 8 July 1985: 73.

Clemons, Walter. *"The Cider House Rules."* *Newsweek* 27 May 1985: 80.

DeMott, Benjamin. "Guilt and Compassion." *New York Times Book Review* 26 May 1985: 1, 25.

Fein, Esther B. "Costly Pleasures." *New York Times Book Review* 26 May 1985: 25.

Gray, Paul. *"The Cider House Rules."* *Time* 3 June 1985: 81.

Hawley, John C. *"The Cider House Rules."* *America* 12 Oct. 1985: 226–228.

Lehmann-Haupt, Christopher. *"The Cider House Rules."* *New York Times* 20 May 1985: C20.

Lewis, Roger. "Larger Than Life." *New Statesman* 28 (June 1985): 29.

Rockwood, Bruce L., and Roberta Kevelson, eds. "Abortion Stories and Uncivil Discourse." In *Law and Literature Perspectives*. New York: Peter Lang, 1996, pp. 289–340.

A Prayer for Owen Meany

Koenig, Rhoda. *"A Prayer for Owen Meany."* *New York* 20 Mar. 1989: 82–84.

Page, Philip. "Hero Worship and Hermeneutic Dialectics: John Irving's *A Prayer for Owen Meany.*" *Mosaic* 28 (Sept. 1995): 137–156.

Peterson, Eugene H. "Writers and Angels: Witnesses to Transcendence." *Theology Today* Oct. 1994: 394–405.

Prescott, Peter S. *"A Prayer for Owen Meany."* *Newsweek* 10 Apr. 1989: 14.

Pritchard, William. *"A Prayer for Owen Meany."* New Republic 22 May 1989: 36–39.

Sheppard, R. Z. "The Message Is the Message." *Time* 3 Apr. 1989: 80.

Steiner, Wendy. *"A Prayer for Owen Meany."* Times Literary Supplement 19 May 1989: 535.

Towers, Robert. *"A Prayer for Owen Meany."* New York Review of Books 20 July 1989: 394–405.

Walls, James M. "Owen Meany and the Presence of God." *Christian Century* 22 Mar. 1989: 299–301.

A Son of the Circus

Gabbard, Glen O. *"A Son of the Circus."* American Journal of Psychiatry 152 (Dec. 1995): 1821.

Graeber, Laurel. "Truth, Fiction, and Achondroplasia." *New York Times Book Review* 4 Sept. 1994: 22.

Gray, Paul. *"A Son of the Circus."* Time 12 Sept. 1994: 82.

Johnson, Webster. *"A Son of the Circus."* Times Literary Supplement 2 Sept. 1994: 11.

Kayton, Deborah. "Indian Circus." *Aperture* 134 (Winter 1994): 76–78.

Kirn, Walter. *"A Son of the Circus."* New York 29 Aug. 1994: 113.

Locy, Sharon. *"A Son of the Circus."* America 31 Dec. 1994: 27–30.

"A Son of the Circus." Publishers Weekly 4 July 1994: 51.

"A Son of the Circus." Economist 15 Oct. 1994: 121.

Tonkin, Boyd. *"A Son of the Circus."* New Statesman & Society 23 Sept. 1994: 40.

Towers, Robert. *"A Son of the Circus."* New York Times Book Review 4 Sept. 1994: 1, 22.

A Widow for One Year

Gray, Paul. *"A Widow for One Year."* Time 4 May 1998: 83.

Gussow, Mel. "John Irving: A Novelist Builds Out from Fact to Reach the Truth." *New York Times* 28 April 1998: B1, E1.

Kakutani, Michiko. "Randomness, Luck and Fate, But Whew, No Bears." *New York Times* 1 May 1998: B51.

Klepp, L. S. "Irving's Not Dickens, But He Tries." *Providence Journal-Bulletin* 10 May 1998: K8.

Koenig, Rhoda. *"A Widow for One Year."* Vogue May 1998: 166.

Pritchard, William H. *"A Widow for One Year."* New York Times Book Review 24 May 1998: 7.

OTHER SECONDARY SOURCES

Barry, Peter. *Beginning Theory: An Introduction to Literary and Cultural Theory*. Manchester: Manchester University Press, 1995.

Barthes, Roland. *Mythologies*, trans. Annette Lavers. New York: Hill and Wang, 1985.

———. *S/Z*, trans. Richard Miller. New York: Hill, 1974.

Brooks, Peter. *Reading for the Plot: Design and Intention in Narrative*. New York: Alfred A. Knopf, 1984.

Brook-Shepherd, Gordon. *Anschluss*. London: Macmillan, 1963.

Campbell, Joseph. *The Hero with a Thousand Faces*. The Bollingen Series 14. Princeton: Princeton University Press, 1973.

Cawelti, John G. *Adventure, Mystery, and Romance*. Chicago: University of Chicago Press, 1976.

Cawelti, John G., and Bruce A. Rosenberg. *The Spy Story*. Chicago: University of Chicago Press, 1987.

Cirlot, J. E. *A Dictionary of Symbols*, trans. Jack Sage. New York: Philosophical Library, 1962.

Cornford, Francis. *The Origin of Attic Comedy*. London: Cambridge University Press, 1914.

Dickens, Charles. *A Christmas Carol*. Philadelphia: J. B. Lippincott; London: W. Heinemann, 1934.

Dollimore, Jonathan, and Alan Sinfield, eds. *Political Shakespeare: New Essays in Cultural Materialism*. Manchester: Manchester University Press, 1985.

Ehrmann, Jacques. "*Homo Ludens* Revisited." In *Game, Play, Literature*, ed. Jacques Ehrmann. Yale French Studies 41. New Haven: Yale University Press, 1968, p. 34.

Eliot, George. *Adam Bede*. New York: Holt, Rinehart, and Winston, 1967.

Fiedler, Leslie. *Love and Death in the American Novel*, rev. ed. New York: Dell, 1966.

Fitzgerald, F. Scott. *The Great Gatsby*. New York: Scribners, 1953.

Freud, Sigmund. "Jokes and the Comic." In *Jokes and Their Relation to the Unconscious*, ed. and trans. James Strachey. New York: W. W. Norton, 1960, pp. 188–221.

Greene, Graham. *The Heart of the Matter*. In *The Portable Graham Greene*, ed. Philip Stratford. New York: Viking Press, 1973, pp. 92–367.

———. *The Lost Child and Other Essays*. New York: Viking Press, 1962, p. 189.

———. *The Power and the Glory*. New York: Viking Press, 1954.

Grotjahn, Martin. "Beyond Laughter: A Summing Up." In *Beyond Laughter*. New York: McGraw Hill, 1957, pp. 255–264.

Hawthorn, Jeremy. *A Concise Glossary of Contemporary Literary Theory*. London: E. Arnold; New York: Routledge, Chapman and Hall, 1993.

Hemingway, Ernest. *A Moveable Feast*. New York: Scribners, 1964.

Hill, Jane Bowers. "John Irving's Aesthetics of Accessibility: Setting Free the Novel." *South Carolina Review* 16 (Fall 1983): 38–44.

Hirsch, E. D. *Validity in Interpretation*. New Haven: Yale University Press, 1967.

Hopkins, Gerard Manley. *Poems*, ed. W. H. Gardner. Oxford: Oxford University Press, 1956.

Huizinga, Johan. *Homo Ludens*. Boston: Beacon, 1955.

Jordan, June. "Ruth and Naomi, David and Jonathon: One Love," in *Out of the Garden: Women Writers on the Bible*, ed. Christina Buchmann and Celina Spiegel. New York: Fawcett Columbine, 1944, pp. 82–83.

King James Version of The Holy Bible Containing the Old and the New Testaments Together with the Apocrypha, translated out of the Original Tongues in the Year 1611. New York: Limited Editions Club, 1935–1936.

Lévi-Strauss, Claude. *Structural Anthropology*. New York: Doubleday, 1967.

Lodge, David. *After Bakhtin. Essays on Fiction and Criticism*. London: Routledge, 1990.

Mitchell, Juliet. "The Making of a Lady." In *Psychoanalysis and Feminism: Freud, Reich, Laing, and Women*. New York: Random House/Pantheon Books, 1974, pp. 5–91.

Moi, Toril, ed. *The Kristeva Reader*. New York: Columbia University Press, 1986.

Ovid. *Metamorphoses*, trans. Rolfe Humphries. Bloomington: Indiana University Press, 1969.

Priestly, Michael. "Structure in the Worlds of John Irving." *Critique* 23 (1981): 82–96.

Propp, Vladimir. *Morphology of the Folktale*, trans. Laurence Scott. Austin: University of Texas Press, 1968.

Schell, Jonathan. "Plot as Repetition." *Critique: Studies in Contemporary Fiction* 37 (Fall 1995): 51–70.

———. *The Real War: The Classic Reporting on the Vietnam War with a New Essay*. New York: Pantheon, 1988.

Sherry, Norman. *The Life of Graham Greene*. New York: Viking, 1989.

Sypher, Wylie. "The Meanings of Comedy." In *Comedy*, ed. Wylie Sypher. New York: Doubleday & Company, 1956, pp. 193–258.

Todorov, Tzvetan. *Mikhail Bakhtin: The Dialogical Principle*, trans. Wlad Godzich. Theory and History of Literature 13. Minneapolis: University of Minnesota Press, 1984.

Turner, Victor. "Social Dramas and Stories About Them." *Critical Inquiry* 7 (Autumn 1980): 141–168.

Van Gennep, Arnold. *The Rites of Passage*. Chicago: University of Chicago Press, 1960.

Von Franz, Marie-Luise. *Interpretation of Fairytales*. Dallas: Spring Publications, 1982.

Von Schuschnigg, Kurt. *Austrian Requiem*. New York: G. P. Putnam's Sons, 1946.

Yanarella, Ernest J., and Lee Sigelman, eds. *Political Mythology and Popular Fiction*. Westport, CT: Greenwood Press, 1988.

Index

About the Author

JOSIE P. CAMPBELL is Professor of English and Women's Studies at the University of Rhode Island. She is the author of *Popular Culture in the Middle Ages* (1986), as well as numerous articles on medieval and Renaissance drama, Canadian women's writing, and American literature. She is also the editor of *ATQ: A Journal of 19th-Century American Literature and Culture.*

Critical Companions to Popular Contemporary Writers
Kathleen Gregory Klein, Series Editor

V. C. Andrews
  by E. D. Huntley

Tom Clancy
  by Helen S. Garson

Mary Higgins Clark
  by Linda C. Pelzer

Arthur C. Clarke
  by Robin Anne Reid

James Clavell
  by Gina Macdonald

Pat Conroy
  by Landon C. Burns

Robin Cook
  by Lorena Laura Stookey

Michael Crichton
  by Elizabeth A. Trembley

Howard Fast
  by Andrew Macdonald

Ken Follett
  by Richard C. Turner

Ernest J. Gaines
  by Karen Carmean

John Grisham
  by Mary Beth Pringle

James Herriot
  by Michael J. Rossi

Tony Hillerman
  by John M. Reilly

John Irving
  by Josie P. Campbell

John Jakes
  by Mary Ellen Jones

Stephen King
  by Sharon A. Russell

Dean Koontz
  by Joan G. Kotker

Robert Ludlum
  by Gina Macdonald

Anne McCaffrey
  by Robin Roberts

Colleen McCullough
  by Mary Jean DeMarr

James A. Michener
  by Marilyn S. Severson

Anne Rice
  by Jennifer Smith

Tom Robbins
  *by Catherine E. Hoyser and
  Lorena Laura Stookey*

John Saul
  by Paul Bail

Erich Segal
  by Linda C. Pelzer

Amy Tan
  by E. D. Huntley

Leon Uris
  by Kathleen Shine Cain

Gore Vidal
  by Susan Baker and Curtis S. Gibson

DATE			

4 - 11   1   3 - 11

8/18   3   4/17